P9-APS-085

Contents

262 Loh   211901
Lohfink.
Jesus and community.

The Lorette Wilmot Library
Nazareth College of Rochester

Jesus and Community

Jesus and Community

THE SOCIAL DIMENSION OF CHRISTIAN FAITH

GERHARD LOHFINK

Translated by JOHN P. GALVIN

FORTRESS PRESS
Philadelphia

PAULIST PRESS
New York/Ramsey

211901

This book is a translation of *Wie hat Jesus Gemeinde gewollt?* by Gerhard Lohfink. Copyright © 1982 by Herder Verlag, Freiburg/Basel/Vienna.

Biblical quotations, unless otherwise noted, are from the Revised Standard Version of the Bible, copyrighted 1946, 1952, © 1971, 1973 by the Division of Christian Education of the National Council of the Churches of Christ in the U.S.A., and are used by permission. (An asterisked biblical reference indicates that the translator has preserved the nuances of the German rendering of biblical texts.)

English translation copyright © 1984 by Fortress Press

All rights reserved. No part of this publication may be reproduced, stored in a retrieval system, or transmitted in any form or by any means, electronic, mechanical, photocopying, recording, or otherwise, without the prior permission of Fortress Press.

Library of Congress Cataloging in Publication Data

Lohfink, Gerhard, 1934–
  Jesus and community.

  Translation of: Wie hat Jesus Gemeinde gewollt?
  Bibliography: p.
  Includes index.
  1. Jesus Christ—Teachings.   2. Church—Biblical
teaching.   3. People of God—Biblical teaching.
4. Israel (Christian theology)—Biblical teaching.
I. Title.
BS2417.C53L6413   1984   262   84–47928
ISBN 0–8006–1802–5 (pbk.) (Fortress)
ISBN 0–8091–2661–3 (Paulist)

K970D84   Printed in the United States of America   1–1802

DISCARDED

TO

*Anne, Barbara, Dorothea, Fritz, Georg,
Christina, Gudrun, Heinz, Michael,
Erika, Christine, Johannes, Josef,
Susanne, Wilma, Birgitta, Felicitas,
Helmut, Renate, Stephanie, Brigitte,
Nicola, Rupert, Sibylle, Gabriele,
Bernadette, Hans-Konrad, Albert,
Andreas, Franziska, Georg, Judit,
Angela, Anja, Claudia, Wolfgang, David,
Hanna, Hans, Katja, Marianne, Teresa,
Etienne, Isabelle, Peter, Philipp.*

DISCARDED

Translator's Preface

This book is a translation of Gerhard Lohfink, *Wie hat Jesus Gemeinde gewollt? Zur gesellschaftlichen Dimension des christlichen Glaubens* (Freiburg: Herder, 1982). The English title, *Jesus and Community: The Social Dimension of Christian Faith*, seeks to reflect the author's interest in Jesus' public aims with regard to Israel and the basic intentions which he had for his community of followers.

Unless otherwise noted, biblical quotations are from the Revised Standard Version. An asterisked biblical reference indicates that I have altered the translation in order to preserve the nuances of Prof. Lohfink's German rendering of the text.

For suggestions concerning the translation and assistance in proofreading the manuscript I am indebted to Mr. Timothy A. Butler, Mr. David G. Caron, Mr. Kevin C. Koczela, Mr. Timothy J. MacGeorge, Rev. Frank J. Matera, and Rev. Laurence W. McGrath, Jr.

The translation is dedicated to Christopher Edmund O'Rourke, Amy Galvin O'Rourke, Elizabeth Donohoe, and Jeanne Donohoe.

John P. Galvin
Boston, Mass.
March 8, 1984

Preface

Critical theology has long asked emphatically if the historical Jesus really founded a church. Yet it has become increasingly clear that this question is posed in the wrong way. It is not much of an exaggeration to say that Jesus could not have founded a church since there had long been one — God's people, Israel. Jesus directed his efforts to Israel. He sought to gather it in view of the coming reign of God and to make it into the true people of God. What we now call church is nothing other than the community of those ready to live in the people of God, gathered by Jesus and sanctified by his death. From this perspective, it is foolish to look to the historical Jesus for a formal act of founding the church. But it is very meaningful to ask how Jesus gathered Israel and how he envisioned the community of the true Israel, because right here we reach the ultimately decisive question of *what the church should look like today.* All that follows seeks to pave the way for answering this question in the light of the New Testament.

In writing this book, I have drawn on lectures which I delivered in 1981 to the clergy of the dioceses of Limburg and Rottenburg-Stuttgart. These lectures were entitled "The Idea of Community in Jesus and in the Early Church." At the same time I have attempted to carry forward into the New Testament field what my brother Norbert has developed from the perspective of the Old Testament in his books: *Die messianische Alternative* and *Kirchenträume.* I am greatly indebted to these two works and to conversations with my brother. Through him and through Rudolf Pesch some of the experiences and some of the theology of the "Integrierte Gemeinde" have flowed into this work. For me this has opened up a new dimension of Scripture.

My greatest thanks, however, are due to all those whose names are mentioned in the dedication. We began as a circle of families in Rottenburg, and in the meantime have long since developed into much more than this. Without the joyful experience of our commonly lived faith this book could never have been written.

Finally, I thank my coworkers Thomas Kaut, Marius Reiser, and Agatha Ströbele for their tireless assistance in preparing and proofreading the manuscript.

Gerhard Lohfink
Tübingen, West Germany
All Saints' Day 1982

Introduction
The Heritage of
Individualism

In the winter semester of 1899–1900, Adolf von Harnack delivered sixteen lectures to students of all faculties at the University of Berlin, under the title "The Essence of Christianity." Approximately six hundred students attended these lectures. The book which Harnack published a few months later on the basis of class notes became a public event; it provoked a storm of theological discussion which was not to subside quickly.

Even today it is worthwhile to read Harnack's work.[1] Not only to savor his admirable prose. Not only to hear the voice of one of the most important and most influential Protestant theologians of the beginning of this century. No, it is worthwhile above all to sense the power of an influential theological movement of the late nineteenth century, one which Harnack himself described as *religious individualism* and *subjectivism*.[2]

Harnack was able to use both terms without a trace of criticism. He was convinced that both concepts also described Jesus' preaching rightly and appropriately. The third lecture concludes with a famous, often cited text:

> Anyone who wants to know what the kingdom of God and the coming of this kingdom mean in Jesus' preaching must read and meditate on the parables. There he will learn what the kingdom is all about. The kingdom of God comes by coming to *individuals*, making entrance into their *souls*, and being grasped by them. The kingdom of God is indeed God's *rule* — but it is the rule of a holy God in individual hearts. *It is God himself in his power.* Everything

1

externally dramatic, all public historical meaning vanish here; all external hope for the future fades also. Take any parable you wish—the sower, the pearl, the treasure in the field. In each case, the word of God, God himself is the kingdom. It is not a matter of angels and devils, nor of principalities and powers, but of God and the soul, of the soul and its God.[3]

According to Harnack, the reign of God does not come to a community; it comes to an *individual.* "The individual is to hear the good news of mercy and adoption, and to decide if he wishes to stand on the side of God and eternity or on the side of the world and time."[4] "Now for the first time everything external and everything merely future is cast off; it is the individual who is redeemed, not the people or the state."[5] Just as the reign of God occurs only in the individual, not in a community, so too it affects only the internal, not externals, only the inner man, the soul. "The gospel lies above questions of earthly developments; it is not concerned with things, but with human souls."[6] "The individual" and "the internal" are in fact key terms which occur frequently in Harnack. The expression "God and the soul, the soul and its God" is repeated by him frequently, almost like a refrain.[7]

Now Harnack was far too familiar with the New Testament to have overlooked the *notion of community* which accompanies the gospel of the reign of God. He knew that since its break with the Jewish national community the Christian movement had considered itself "church" and thus *the true Israel.*[8] He knew that the infant church understood itself as a *new people* composed of Jews and Gentiles, Greeks and barbarians.[9] And he also knew that the early church thought its chief task was to fulfill completely the will of God and in this way "present itself as a holy community."[10] So Harnack is in no way on the side of those for whom the church must essentially be purely internal and therefore *invisible.*[11]

But, in the end, the extreme individualism of his theology overwhelmed and absorbed all these valid insights. The "better justice" of the Sermon on the Mount is merely *the right intention of the individual,*[12] and the church is ultimately only a "fraternity" of all well-meaning people throughout the entire world.[13] More precisely, it is the fraternal union of the many individuals who are already saved *as individuals* through their faith in the gospel — the gospel of their immediacy to God the Father. Despite Harnack's knowledge that the church is visible inasmuch as it must continually become concrete in socially tangible associations, the church still remained for him a spiritual community, a society within human hearts (*societas in cordibus*), which could not be identified with any of the concrete churches of his day.

At the time, Harnack was in no sense isolated with his individualistic picture of church and salvation. He is rather representative of a broad tendency of liberal theology at the end of the nineteenth century and at the beginning of the twentieth. The idea that the reign of God could come only to each individual, that it is something profoundly internal and that the church therefore had to be a primarily spiritual community was widespread in Protestant theology at that time.

Is that true only of the past? Despite all opposing tendencies, the individualistic position of liberal theology, evident in Harnack, is even today influential in many forms and metamorphoses. Only a few years ago, for example, E. Grässer, whose ecclesiological position in other respects cannot be identified with Harnack's, wrote as follows:

> Jesus' message of salvation brings about a complete shift from the collective to the individual. The individualizing tendency is tangible everywhere. The prefiguration of the Old Testament-Jewish relationship to God, constituted through the relation of Yahweh to the people, through covenant, cult and Torah, loses its normative power. Jesus penetrates critically through and behind this to the sole decisive situation and relation, "God-individual," "Father-Son of Man (=man)."[14]

Positions of this sort cannot be dismissed as irrelevant. We ought not, for example, decide that it is simply a species of individualism, once typical of certain types of Protestant theology, but now largely overcome even within Protestantism and in any case never present in the Catholic church. It could well be that although the Catholic church retained concepts, formulas, and institutions which were originally marked with an intense sense of community, these concepts, formulas, and institutions were gradually (and unconsciously) interpreted and lived in a much more individualistic way than they were once conceived. Much suggests that Catholic theology and spirituality participated far more intensively than they realized in the individualism of Protestant theology. And it could well be that late nineteenth century theology's individualistic conceptions of redemption are far from overcome, that they determine our conceptions of pastoral ministry, our images of church, and the concrete appearance of our parishes far more strongly than we like to think.

Not long ago there was a report in the newspapers that church agencies in Berlin had established a mobile unit, an automobile equipped with short-wave radio, in which a priest, a physician and a psychologist could be summoned immediately at any hour of the day or night. That sounds very up to date: the church, in a sense, at the front, modern technology in service of the reign of God. But in reality this ecclesiastical mobile unit is a highly questionable symbol of what the church has largely become in our society: a church which takes care of the individual, an institution which offers its wares to a group of individuals.

This conception corresponds exactly to the situation of our consumer society, which Gisbert Greshake recently compared to a large supermarket. Everyone moves around with a cart and picks out what he likes and needs.[15] In the giant "Supermarket West Germany" there is among many other things a section which offers *religious* products to individuals. Responsibility for this section lies with the churches. Society is very anxious that this corner remain occupied; the stock should be complete. It seems to me that the mobile religious unit in Berlin is a perfect symbol of this *supermarket-church*, which takes care of individuals, provides for them, and leaves them in their anonymity.

Pastoral structures of this sort are not only a faithful mirror-image of the structures of contemporary society; they are also a hardy heritage of the religious individualism which we have illustrated with the example of Adolf von Harnack. We should not take for granted the way in which the average parishes of the major European churches conduct ministry. And Catholics should not be too sure that the issue of community is no problem for them, since

their church has always insisted on the principle of community—
the idea of visible, tangible community. It is of course true that
until the end of the Middle Ages "church" meant *concrete, identifiable, salvific community.*[16] The Catholic church has never
denied that and never really forgotten it. The question is if the
church has not brushed aside, ignored, and lost from view its own
traditions on this point to a far greater extent than it realizes.

What is needed is greater awareness of our own tradition. But
where is this tradition better and more originally available than in
Scripture? And where could it shine forth more clearly and more
normatively than in the praxis of Jesus himself? This leads us to ask
some questions. What did Jesus think of community? Did he in
fact abandon the Old Testament's basic relation, God—People of
God? Did he in fact address only the individual? Was he really
only concerned with God and the soul, with the soul and its God?

Here a number of very difficult questions arise. Their treatment
in New Testament scholarship has led nowhere near a consensus.
Yet answers to them would shed light on our contemporary situation and could illuminate the road which lies ahead. They would
also clarify what Jesus' preaching of the reign of God has to do
with the church. So let us venture an answer to them. What did
Jesus think of community? How did Jesus will community?

I

Jesus and Israel

1
THE PREACHING OF THE BAPTIST

The ground was already prepared for Jesus before he began his preaching. Preceding him was John the Baptist's preaching of repentance, which had awakened extraordinary attention in Israel and had unsettled many. Now Jesus differed from the Baptist on important points. Unlike him, Jesus preached the nearness of salvation, not a coming judgment of fire. Still, Jesus did have much in common with John. Above all, he considered the Baptist authorized by God (cf. Mark 11:30) and called him the "greatest of all men" (cf. Matt. 11:11‖Luke 7:28). Before he began preaching, Jesus, like John, probably even baptized for a time in the Jordan (cf. John 3:22, 26; 4:1). All of this—what Jesus had in common with the Baptist, his extraordinarily high estimation of John, and his own baptismal activity—can really only be explained if Jesus was himself for a time a disciple of the Baptist or if he was at least, inwardly and outwardly, bound very tightly to the Baptist's movement.[17]

It was precisely Israel that the Baptist addressed. He sought to gather Israel and to prepare it for the coming end. As J. Becker, who of all recent scholars has studied the figure of John the Baptist in the most detail, rightly states:

> John does not simply address humanity, or all sinners in the world, but rather the descendants of Abraham, Israel as a whole (Luke

7

3:8‖). He predicts judgment for the people of God. While his message contains no political, national statements, he does remind the people of salvation, a people upon whom God will now rigorously pass judgment, of its wasted relationship to God.[18]

Even the fact that the Baptist chose the *desert* as the site of his preaching (Mark 1:4), so that the people had to *go out* to him (Mark 1:5), is properly understood only against the background of Israel's exodus traditions. These traditions are always concerned with the new beginning, the repentance, or the final gathering of God's people in the desert. An example is provided by Hosea (2:14) in a divine oracle about the harlot Israel:[19]

> "Therefore, behold, I will allure her
> and bring her into the wilderness
> and speak tenderly to her."

In the desert situation, in other words, all false lovers remain far from Israel. There the people is alone with its God. There Israel can recognize its God as in the past (cf. Hos. 2:22, 25).

Even the threatening reference to the ax already laid at the roots of the trees (Mark 3:10‖Luke 3:9) speaks about Israel. Once again an established Old Testament tradition stands in the background: Israel as the *farm of God*, firmly rooted in the land.[20] In intertestamental Judaism this strand of tradition was extended further. In that period, Israel appeared as a plant of God which would not be eradicated *in all eternity*.[21] The Baptist very sharply opposed this collective security about salvation. Judgment comes precisely for the people of God. The ax is already laid to the roots of the trees which God himself planted. God will purify Israel, his farm. Every tree which bears no fruit will be chopped down and thrown into the fire.

The reference of the Baptist's preaching to Israel becomes even more clear in Luke 3:8 (‖Mark 3:9):

Do not begin to say to yourselves, "We have Abraham as our father"; for I tell you, God is able from these stones to raise up children to Abraham.

Here it is cuttingly said that descent from Abraham, that is, belonging to the nation of Israel, cannot save from the approaching judgment. But precisely this remark shows that Israel is the issue. Israel is so much the issue that John can threaten that if necessary, God will create for Abraham a new Israel from the stones of the desert.

Thus it is clear that John the Baptist addressed neither humanity in general nor the individual as such, but rather the members of the people of God. He was concerned with Israel's existence, just as the Pharisees, the Essenes, and the Zealots were concerned with Israel's existence. All of these groups and movements ultimately sought the renewal of Israel, the gathering of the true Israel, an Israel which did the will of God. In contemporary language we could say that there were at that time in Israel all sorts of groups and movements in quest of the true identity of God's people.[22]

It is precisely in this historical constellation that Jesus, his message and his praxis, must be located. In doing this we in no way detract from the uniqueness and divinity of his mission. Jesus too wanted to gather the people of God.[23] Jesus too wanted to prepare Israel for God. Jesus too wanted to answer Israel's profound identity crisis. But his was an answer which reached infinitely deeper than all the other answers ventured at that time.

This connection of Jesus with the Baptist sheds initial light on the relationship of Jesus' public life to *community*, more precisely to *Israel*.

2
THE INSTITUTION OF THE TWELVE

A second phenomenon speaks even more clearly. Jesus chose twelve disciples—surely from a larger circle of disciples—and sent them out in pairs (Mark 3:13–19; 6:7–13). The key text is Mark 3:14–16*:

> He named twelve as his companions whom he would send to preach the good news; they were likewise to have authority to expel demons. He created the Twelve.

The verb "he created" refers to a unique event at a particular time and in a particular place. At that time, Mark intends to say, Jesus instituted twelve of the disciples as *the Twelve*. They were to do what he himself did: preach the kingdom of God and expel demons as a sign of the power of the inbreaking kingdom.

Thus Jesus did not simply institute disciples in an *eschatological office of witness*; he instituted *twelve* disciples. And he evidently did this in a demonstrative manner which people discussed and remembered. Why this gesture, and why precisely twelve disciples?

The meaning of an action of this sort must at that time have been so evident that the early Christian witnesses did not find it necessary to explain: the twelve disciples could refer only to the twelve tribes of Israel. But reference to the twelve tribes evoked a central point of Israel's eschatological hope. Although the system of twelve tribes had long since ceased to exist — according to contemporary views there remained only two and one-half tribes: Judah, Benjamin, and half of Levi[24] — the complete restoration of the twelve-tribe people was expected for the eschatological time of salvation. Texts as early as the end of the Book of Ezekiel describe a prophetic program according to which the twelve tribes, brought back to life in the last days, would receive their permanent share of the land (cf. Ezekiel 37; 39:23–29; 40–48).

Against the background of this very lively hope Jesus' constitution of twelve disciples could only be grasped as a *symbolic prophetic action*:[25] The Twelve exemplified the awakening of Israel and its gathering in the eschatological salvific community, something beginning then through Jesus. They exemplified this gathering simply through the fact that they were created as *Twelve*, but they also exemplified it through being sent out to all of Israel. Institution and mission were two aspects of one and the same symbolic prophetic action.

We would seriously underestimate the depth of such a symbolic action if we considered it merely an *exemplification* or *demonstration*. It was certainly both. But above and beyond this it was the initiation of something future, something which was already present in an anticipatory manner in the prophetically performed sign, and which in its incipient realization outlined what lay ahead. The existence of eschatological Israel began with the constitution of the Twelve and their preaching of the reign of God.

It was of course implicit in the symbolism of the number twelve that the disciples on mission turned only to the Israel which was tangible, empirical, at that time. Thus the ancient saying, preserved only in Matthew (10:5–6), belongs precisely in this context:

Go nowhere among the Gentiles and enter no town of the Samaritans, but go rather to the lost sheep of the house of Israel.

Whether or not the first part of this saying comes from Jesus himself need not be settled here. In any case, its second part ("go rather to the lost sheep of the house of Israel") fits exactly in the historical situation of the mission of the Twelve.[26] They were sent by Jesus to proclaim the message of the reign of God to *the whole house of Israel*. They exemplified Jesus' claim on Israel as a whole.

The lost sheep of Matt. 10:6 are not a reference to only a part of the people — such as the sinners or apostates — but to the *entire* people, which is compared to a scattered flock that has been led astray. Ezekiel in his shepherd chapter (chap. 34) had already described the situation of the deceived and corrupt people of God in such comprehensive terms. Thus there is reason to believe that Jesus alluded to Ezekiel in his reference to the lost sheep of the house of Israel. This would mean that Jesus was convinced that now, in this hour, the eschatological gathering of the sick and lost sheep of Israel, promised by the prophets, had begun. God himself now gathered his people, through Jesus, the messianic shepherd (cf. Ezek. 34:23–24).

On the whole, the institution of the Twelve is one of the clearest points of reference for Jesus' determined turning to Israel.[27] Jesus tried to gather the people of God; he sought the restoration of lost and scattered Israel. In all probability, the symbolic prophetic sign of creating the Twelve was at that time much more significant than it appears to us today. Some evidence suggests that Jesus deliberately chose the Twelve from different regions of the country and from different factions within the Judaism of the day in order to make obvious the gathering of *all* Israelites.[28] The Twelve must have been an odd mixture — from Matthew the tax collector (Matt. 10:3) to Simon the Zealot (Luke 6:15). Including both a tax collector and a Zealot in a single group united the most opposed forces that existed anywhere in Israel at the time, for the tax collectors collaborated with the Romans, while the Zealots emphatically rejected the Roman occupation as incompatible with the reign of God.

But Jesus sought to draw together an Israel fractured by struggling parties and groups; and so he went to tax collectors and to

Zealots, to the poor and to the rich, to the rural population of Galilee and to the capital city of Jerusalem.

3
THE SICK MEMBERS OF THE
PEOPLE OF GOD

We must now speak of Jesus' concern for the sick. The days in which Jesus' healing miracles have been minimized or even dismissed historically by biblical criticism are drawing to a close. It has now become clear that divine salvific action and natural, psychosomatic healings are theologically in no way mutually exclusive. The old axiom that grace presupposes and perfects nature applies here as well as elsewhere. There is no longer any reason to refrain from taking the New Testament healing miracles quite seriously. Jesus evidently healed the sick with extraordinary frequency and in a variety of situations. It was precisely his miracles of healing which made him known so quickly and permanently throughout the country.

We do not really grasp Jesus' cures, which include the healing of those then considered *possessed*, if we understand them solely as miracles performed for individuals out of sympathy for their illness. Since the eschatological horizon of Jesus' activity has reentered consciousness, it has been clear that Jesus' miracles of healing must be seen in connection with his preaching of the kingdom of God.

His mighty works were signs of the kingdom's proximity. This is, for example, the original[29] meaning of the parable of the blossoming fig tree (Mark 13:28–29). Palestinians know that summer is near when its branches bloom. In the same way, one who sees *all this* (Jesus' many mighty works) should know that the kingdom of God is near (cf. Luke 21:31).

But Jesus' mighty works on behalf of those who were ill and socially isolated were not only signals of the *proximity* of the approaching kingdom. As Luke 11:20‖Matt. 12:28* indicates, they showed over and above this that the reign of God was already *present*:

But if it is by the finger of God that I cast out demons, then the king-dom of God has (already) come upon you.

Miracles of healing, then, occupied an important place in Jesus' activity. They stood in close connection with his preaching of the kingdom of God. When the kingdom of God arrived, sickness simply had to disappear.

Up to this point there exists a certain consensus in contemporary New Testament exegesis. But the relationship of Jesus' healing miracles to the people of God, to the eschatological Israel, is still often overlooked. Precisely because the mighty works of Jesus were so closely connected with the inbreaking *reign of God*, they were also decisively concerned with the *people of God*. Inseparable from the eschatological horizon of Jesus' miracles is their relation-ship to community: they served the restoration of the people of God, among whom, in the eschatological age of salvation, no dis-ease is permitted.

The relationship of Jesus' mighty works to community is espe-cially evident in the jubilant exclamation of Luke 7:22 (‖Matt. 11:5):

The blind receive their sight, the lame walk, lepers are cleansed, and the deaf hear, the dead are raised up, the poor have good news preached to them.

There is no convincing reason to deny this text to Jesus. It alludes in a very free and sovereign manner to the salvific promises of the Book of Isaiah, which, along with Ezekiel, obviously represents the decisive biblical background with whose help Jesus interpreted his own message and praxis. The allusion is primarily to Isa. 35:5–6:

Then the eyes of the blind shall be opened,
    and the ears of the deaf unstopped;
then shall the lame man leap like a hart,
    and the tongue of the dumb sing for joy.

Now the decisive point is that in Isaiah the seeing of the blind, the hearing of the deaf, the leaping of the lame and the sing-ing of the dumb are an integral part of Israel's eschatological resto-ration. In the eschatological time of salvation which the Book of

Isaiah proclaims, God will heal and lead his people (57:18); he will bind up their wounds (30:26); no one in Israel in those days will any longer say, "I am sick" (33:24); the entire people will then see what the hands of God have wrought in their midst (29:23).

In considering the healing miracles which Jesus performed, we need not exclude deep compassion with the individual who was suffering (cf. Mark 1:41). But the miracles are not adequately understood if their Old Testament background is overlooked. Even Jesus' healing of the sick aimed directly at the gathering and restoration of Israel. In the eschatological people of God no one may be excluded from salvation: not outsiders, not sinners, not the sick.

And so we continually encounter in Jesus, often quite unexpectedly, the intention of *gathering Israel*. We find this even in the Our Father, which at first glance seems not to speak of Israel at all.

4
THE PRAYER FOR GATHERING
IN THE OUR FATHER

In Luke's version of the Our Father (Luke 11:2–4*), unlike Matthew's (Matt. 6:9–13), there are after the address only two petitions which use the second person singular:

> Father, hallowed be your name,
> your kingdom come.

These two petitions correspond to one another so exactly in their formal structure that they are clearly distinguished from the following petitions in the first person plural. First, both petitions are very brief. In the Greek text each consists of four words; if translated back into Aramaic, each has only two words. Second, in each instance the verb stands without connection (asyndetically) at the beginning of the sentence. Third, in Greek (the same was also true of the Aramaic) each of the two ends with the possessive pronoun "your." Fourth, it is above all striking in each case that God's action is described through an indirect construction, in which his *name*, of his *kingdom*, is the subject of the sentence; this is characteristic of Jewish spirituality. Still the logical subject of each sentence is *God*. We could quite legitimately translate into English:

>Sanctify your name,
>let your kingdom come!

These obvious *formal* similarities of the first two petitions of the Our Father are a verbal indication that the two petitions are also intimately connected in *content*. Neither petition is concerned with human activity; both speak of God's own work, his eschatological action. But the prayer is not for an act of God which lies in the far distant future. That would in no way correspond to Jesus' preaching of the kingdom. For him the kingdom is not merely very near, but already arriving. Anyone able to interpret Jesus' mighty works knows that the kingdom is already making its presence felt.

The second petition for the coming of the kingdom corresponds to the first. It concerns an event which ultimately coincides with the kingdom's arrival, but which illuminates its coming from a different perspective and which therefore can be mentioned in a distinct petition. The event in which God sanctifies his name stands in the same temporal tension between *already* and *not yet*, between the fulfilling *present* and the *future* that is still ahead, as does the coming of the kingdom. In the very near future, God will sanctify his name in powerful action—but this powerful action is starting right now. It has already begun, just as the coming of the kingdom has already begun.

What is really meant by the prayer, now so strange to us, *that God sanctify his name?* Once again the answer is given in the Old Testament, in Ezekiel 36. There it is said that the name of God has been desecrated by the dispersal of Israel among the nations. As a result of this, all the nations say: "So this is the people of God! This Yahweh must be a miserable God, if he is unable to preserve his own people from the loss of their land!" (cf. Ezek. 36:20). In this situation God speaks through Ezekiel (36:22–24):

>It is not for your sake, O house of Israel, that I am about to act, but for the sake of my holy name, which you have profaned among the nations to which you came. And *I will vindicate the holiness* of *my* great name, which has been profaned among the nations, and which you have profaned among them; and the nations will know that I am the Lord, says the Lord God, when through you I vindicate my holiness before their eyes. For I will take you from the nations, and *gather you* from all the countries, and bring you into your own land.

The text clearly shows that *God himself* will sanctify his name. He will sanctify it by gathering Israel in the last days from all over the world, renewing it, and making it again into a holy people. The statement that God sanctifies his name thus has a precise, exactly determined meaning. Its content is in no sense variable. This is above all true since in the Old Testament the formula is to be found practically only in the Book of Ezekiel (much less emphatically in Lev. 22:32; Isa. 42:8; 48:11). And in Ezekiel the connection of sanctifying the name with the restoration of the people of God is so close that Ezek. 20:41, 44 can say succinctly:

> As a pleasing odor I will accept you, when I bring you out from the peoples, and gather you out of the countries where you have been scattered; and I will manifest my holiness among you in the sight of the nations. . . . And you shall know that I am the Lord, when I deal with you *for my name's sake.*

Although the theme of gathering Israel out of exile could not have been an issue for Jesus, he was still in a position to adopt Ezekiel's language. For even in Ezekiel the gathering of Israel was not only a matter of the people's return from exile, but also of a return of the people to their God (36:25–32). At stake was the "new heart" and the "new spirit" which God will give Israel (36:26–27) in order that it may truly become the holy people of God (36:28).

"Sanctify your name"—this means, in other words, nothing other than "Gather and renew your people! Let it become anew the true people of God!" Jesus was obviously convinced that this eschatological gathering of the people by God had already begun *now*, just as the coming of the kingdom was *now* taking place. And Jesus was convinced that the gathering of the people and the coming of the kingdom were occurring *through him*. For when Jesus acted, God acted. Precisely this was Jesus' mystery.

Recognizing the precise content of "sanctify your name" sheds new light on the connection, previously noted, between the first and second petitions of the Our Father. God is to sanctify his name by acting on Israel and gathering it into the true people of God (first petition). But God is also to bring about his kingdom (second petition). Evidently there is a profound connection between the two. *It is precisely in God's re-creation of Israel, precisely in sanctifying his name in Israel, that the kingdom of God arrives. It shines forth in the people of God.*

5

THE PILGRIMAGE OF THE NATIONS

Binding the kingdom of God to the people of God in this fashion may seem strange at first glance. We are accustomed to thinking in universal terms. Behind our universalism stands ultimately a basic Christian experience which the church has had for ages: the experience of the gospel which transcends all boundaries. A universalism of salvation thus has its legitimacy and its truth. It was also present in Jesus. But it must be located in the proper place. *Jesus in no way excluded the Gentiles from salvation. But he himself directed his attention exclusively to Israel.* Each of these statements is to be taken seriously and to be explained in a manner which preserves the tension between them.

First of all, Jesus did not envision a mission to the Gentiles. He himself held to the rule which he gave the Twelve for their journey: "Go only to the lost sheep of the house of Israel" (Matt. 10:6*). For this reason Matthew quite appropriately has Jesus say: "I was sent only to the lost sheep of the house of Israel" (15:24). Jesus did often enter pagan territory, but not in order to preach the kingdom of God there. His encounters with Gentiles were sporadic, and they were not deliberately brought about by him. Precisely these encounters, when they did occur, show that despite all openness to the Gentiles he was concerned exclusively with Israel. The Syro-Phoenician woman, a pagan, who asked Jesus to heal her daughter was first turned down with the very significant reply, "Let the children first be fed" (Mark 7:27). Jesus was reserved with Gentiles, even in the use of his miraculous powers. His power to make the kingdom of God present in signs and wonders was for the sake of the *children of Israel.*

How then do the Gentiles achieve salvation? The answer is provided in the threat contained in Matt. 8:11–12* (‖Luke

13:28–29), which Jesus must have uttered at a time when the hardening of Israel as a whole was underway. In its original form, it must have run something like this:

> I say to you: Many will come from the east and the west and lie at table with Abraham, Isaac and Jacob in the kingdom of God. But you will be expelled to the outermost darkness.[30]

The saying looks ahead to the time when salvation will be complete. Abraham, Isaac and Jacob, the patriarchs of Israel, will have risen from the dead and been united with the eschatological people of God; more exactly, they are the core of eschatological Israel. These individuals are obviously mentioned only vicariously, as the most important representatives of God's people. With them all of Israel's just will have been raised. The kingdom of God will reach a perfection illustrated in the image of the eschatological meal, taken from Isa. 25:6–8. Here the meal is the image of fullness, of feast, of life without interruption.

Now the *many* from the rising and the setting of the sun, from the east and the west, come into this situation. In Jesus' threat the many form the opposite of his Jewish listeners. The reference must be to the Gentiles. "Many" is a Semitic expression and means a large, immense number. An immense number of Gentiles will participate in the meal of perfection which was prepared for Israel. They will lie at table with the sacred patriarchs of the people of God, whereas the Israel which rejects Jesus will be expelled into the outermost darkness.[31]

In this saying as well Jesus draws upon the Old Testament. Some of the prophets, especially the prophets of the Book of Isaiah, foresee a pilgrimage of the nations to Jerusalem, namely, in the last days, when Israel has become the true people of God. Important above all is Isa. 2:2–3:

> It shall come to pass in the latter days
>   that the mountain of the house of the Lord
> shall be established as the highest of the mountains,
>   and shall be raised above the hills;
> and all the nations shall flow to it,
>   and many peoples shall come, and say:
> "Come, let us go up to the mountain of the Lord,
>   to the house of the God of Jacob."[32]

A decisive element of the prophetic conception of the pilgrimage of the nations to Zion[33] is that the Gentiles, fascinated by the salvation visible in Israel, are driven of their own accord to the people of God. They do not become believers as a result of missionary activity; rather, the fascination emitted by the people of God draws them close. In this connection, the prophetic texts speak mostly of the radiant light which shines forth from Jerusalem. This light is God himself, who in the last days will become the "eternal light" (Isa. 60:19) of Israel. As Isa. 60:2–3 states:

> For behold, darkness shall cover the earth
>   and thick darkness the peoples;
> but the Lord will arise upon you,
>   and his glory will be seen upon you.
> And nations shall come to your light,
>   and kings to the brightness of your rising.

That the nations are drawn to the people of God is thus due to God alone. The pilgrimage of the nations is his eschatological work. If he did not let his light shine upon Israel, if he did not sanctify his name in Israel, the Gentiles would not be able to come. And yet the light of God cannot truly radiate unless the people of God itself shines as God's light. Thus the summons of Isa. 60:1: "Arise, shine; for your light has come," and the appeal of Isa. 2:5: "O house of Jacob, come, let us walk in the light of the Lord!" The salvation which God has prepared must shine in Israel itself if it is to entice others to life with God's people.

God wills the salvation of the nations. But this salvation is accessible only in Israel. The pagan peoples achieve participation in salvation by achieving participation in Israel. They will go to Jerusalem and lie at table with Abraham, Isaac and Jacob.

From this perspective, it becomes clear why Jesus, despite his openness to Gentiles, restricted himself to Israel, why he turned so automatically to Israel alone. Jesus in no way excluded the Gentiles from salvation. He could stand astonished before the faith of pagans, which was often greater than faith in Israel (cf. Matt. 8:5–10). But Jesus had to work in Israel, for only if the light of the reign of God shone in God's people would it be possible for the nations to undertake the eschatological pilgrimage.

This basic presupposition of Jesus' activity would stand out even more clearly if his provocative action in the temple (Mark 11:15–19) was directed positively toward the *eschatological opening of the temple to the nations,* who in the last days will come to Jerusalem to worship there, and not only negatively against the *misuse of the temple.*[34] This interpretation of the events in the temple has some points in its favor, since it is the court of the Gentiles that Jesus cleanses. The biblical text cited by Mark (Isa. 56:7‖Mark 11:17) also points in this direction:

> My house shall be called a house of prayer
> for all peoples.[35]

6

THE CRISIS OF ISRAEL

In the previous section, Matt. 8:11–12 was considered from the perspective of the universal pilgrimage of the nations. Yet we must not lose sight of the fact that this saying was a *threat* directed against Israel. Jesus wished to tell his listeners that if they rejected the message of God's kingdom, they would not, as they imagined, lie at table with Abraham, Isaac and Jacob. The nations would share in the light of God's kingdom, but those who actually ought to be the light of the nations would be ejected into the darkness.

There are several similar threats of Jesus, which, like Matt. 8:11–12, compare unfaithful Israel to the nations. For example, Matt. 12:41–42 (‖Luke 11:31–32):

> The men of Nineveh will arise at the judgment with this generation and condemn it; for they repented at the preaching of Jonah, and behold, something greater than Jonah is here. The queen of the South will arise at the judgment with this generation and condemn it; for she came from the ends of the earth to hear the wisdom of Solomon, and behold, something greater than Solomon is here.

"Here is more than Jonah! Here is more than Solomon!" The evangelists understand these exclamations as christological. But on the lips of Jesus they could have still referred primarily to the reign of God—in the following sense. The gospel of God's reign, now being preached by Jesus in Israel's midst and confirmed through many mighty works, means infinitely more than Jonah's call to repentance and Solomon's words of wisdom could express in their day. And yet at that time the pagans heard the call and responded to it. God's chosen people, however, was not accepting the gospel.

In even sharper words, Matt. 11:21–22 (∥Luke 10:13–14) contrasts two cities of Israel, in which Jesus had evidently worked a particularly large number of signs, with two pagan cities which the Old Testament considered profoundly godless:

> Woe to you, Chorazin! woe to you, Bethsaida! for if the mighty works done in you had been done in Tyre and Sidon, they would have repented long ago in sackcloth and ashes. But I tell you, it shall be more tolerable on the day of judgment for Tyre and Sidon than for you.

These threats, selected here from a much wider tradition, have two things in common. First, they refer to *Israel as a whole*. Chorazin and Bethsaida merely represent all the cities of the country. And Matt. 12:41–42 speaks of "this generation," a common expression in the Jesus tradition. This does not mean the human race as a whole, but the currently living generation of Israel which was confronted with Jesus' message. At stake was the fate of *Israel as a whole*. This is also clear, finally, from the contrast of the nations with the people of God in Matt. 8:11–12; 11:21–22 and 12:41–42.

Second, these threats address a *failure* on Israel's part. Jesus certainly did not utter them at the start of his public ministry; they presuppose a longer period of activity. They were spoken in a situation in which his violent death was already foreshadowed. But they also show that, according to Jesus, the people had entered the decisive crisis of their history. Contrary to the opinion of many scholars, it is certain that Israel's crisis is not depicted here from a post-Easter perspective due to the negative experience of the early Christian mission to Israel. This is established by the parable of the great banquet in Luke 14:16–24, which unmistakably stems from Jesus. The parable intends to say that while anyone who is invited and still does not come excludes himself from the meal, the banquet will still take place even without him. Luke 14:16–24 speaks of the crisis of Israel in a radical form similar to the threats cited above. Yet the decision of the people is not yet final. There still remains a last hope that Jesus' listeners will grasp the signs of the time and understand their own situation. This is what causes the extremely harsh tone of the address. The sharpness of the threat seeks to bring about repentance in the last minute.[36]

Here we must again consider the prophetic sign which Jesus created with the institution of the Twelve. We already saw that the Twelve illustrated the claim which Jesus made upon Israel as a whole. Above and beyond this, they were an efficacious sign of the awakening and gathering of the eschatological twelve-tribe people.

Now it is characteristic of prophetic words and symbolic actions that they can assume new dimensions of meaning. It is therefore to be presumed in advance that the notion of the Twelve could be *changed*, or, to put it more accurately, *expanded* — even by Jesus himself.

Toward the end of his public activity, as it became clear that, while the people itself remained undecided, the leaders of Israel wished to do away with Jesus, the Twelve received a new function, most likely from Jesus himself. From then on they were witnesses, not only to the salvation which was near, but also to the judgment which threatened a recalcitrant Israel. The saying of Matt. 19:28 (∥Luke 22:30) must be understood in this sense:

> Truly, I say to you, in the new world, when the Son of man shall sit on his glorious throne, you who have followed me will also sit on twelve thrones, judging the twelve tribes of Israel.

No one other than the circle of the Twelve is addressed by this saying. It therefore shows conclusively that the Twelve can only be understood as a sign *for the people of God*. But it also shows that they are not only a sign *promising salvation*, but also a sign of *judgment*. At the last judgment they will testify against Israel if Israel does not repent.

It would be foolish to play off the two functions of the Twelve, the positive and the negative, against one another. Prophetic words and signs are not mathematical definitions; they belong to a symbolic language which always admits of new (though not arbitrary) applications and interpretations. The full significance of a sign is revealed by the situation from which it comes and to which it is addressed.

Sometime toward the end of Jesus' public ministry, the Twelve became for him witnesses *against* Israel. Thus it is clear precisely from Matt. 19:28 that in Jesus' view the crisis of Israel was approaching its climax.

7

DEATH FOR THE MANY

When the crisis did reach its climax, Jesus, facing certain death, spoke at the Last Supper of giving his life "for many." This formulation is to be found in the Marcan tradition of the words interpreting the cup of blessing (Mark 14:24):

> This is my blood of the covenant,
> which is poured out for many.

Before we ask what "many" might mean, two comments must be made. First, the historicity of the words at the Last Supper is still disputed. Many New Testament scholars are of the opinion that the Last Supper tradition has been subjected to so much *liturgical* influence that it is impossible to search historically behind that influence with any prospects of success. But this skepticism is inappropriate. Liturgical tradition does not exclude careful preservation of verbal tradition; if anything, it tends to favor it. Nor is much proven by the argument that the notions of *covenant* and *atonement* are otherwise unattested for Jesus. It was surely not impossible for Jesus to say something new in a situation which he had never confronted before in his life. When faced with the necessity of interpreting his approaching death with reference to God, he appealed to categories of interpretation which, while new for him, were available in the Scriptures: the notion of covenant and the conception of vicarious atonement.

Second, there is a further difficulty. The words interpreting the cup of blessing are transmitted in a different form in Paul than they are in Mark. In 1 Cor. 11:25 Jesus says, "This cup is the new covenant in my blood."

The difference between the two versions of the word over the cup is less extensive than it may seem to be at first glance. In both versions the bloody death of Jesus is interpreted as *divine establishment of new salvation* (new covenant). Each form, however, has a different biblical text in its background: Exo. 24:8 in the Marcan tradition, Jer. 31:31 in the Pauline. Moreover, in each strand of tradition Jesus' death is *vicarious atonement*, though in Paul the pertinent expression is not in the word over the cup but in that over the bread, and it reads not "for many," but "for you" (1 Cor. 11:24). On at least this final point, the application of Jesus' death to the many, the Marcan tradition has preserved the original language more exactly. Jesus obviously interpreted his approaching death in the light of the servant theology of Isa. 52:13 – 53:12. In Isa. 53:11-12 it is said of the Servant of Yahweh:

> By his knowledge shall the righteous one, my servant
>   make *many* to be accounted righteous;
>   and he shall bear their iniquities.
> Therefore I will divide him a portion with the great,
>   and he shall divide the spoil with the strong;
> because he poured out his soul to death,
>   and was numbered with the transgressors;
> yet he bore the sin of *many*,
>   and made intercession for the transgressors.

But who are the "many" to whom the salvific power of Jesus' death is applied? The most common reply is that all humanity is envisioned. The text is said to show plainly the universal thinking of Jesus and the evangelists. It is claimed that Jesus' outlook, at the end of his life, broadened to include the salvation of the entire world.

There is need to distinguish carefully here. The universal interpretation certainly captures the meaning which Mark wanted to give his tradition. But as far as Jesus is concerned, it is necessary to examine matters more closely.[37]

If we presuppose that Jesus himself, with the help of the Scriptures, interpreted his approaching death as a *salvific death for others*, then it is completely excluded that he would have looked *away from Israel* only to those all over the world who would in the future find salvation through faith in his word and work. Was not the entire existence of Jesus first and foremost *existence for Israel*? How could he have forgotten his people, to whom his whole mission was directed, precisely in this hour? Both the linguistic usage then current and the contemporary Jewish interpretations of Isaiah 53 easily permit the *many* to refer first of all to Israel itself, just as the (new) covenant must first refer to Israel. Jesus would then have given his life quite consciously for the Israel which did not accept his message and which was taking steps to have him done away with.

Jesus would then have understood his death as a salvific act of God who heals what unbelieving Israel did to him. Israel's dreadful deed would be overcome, and the people's path to repentance would once again be open. Those who had ruined their lives through their hardening against Jesus receive from God, freely and without merit, the possibility of new life (in biblical terms, atonement). God transforms the murder of his emissary into a deed of his *faithfulness* to Israel (in biblical terms, covenant); he turns the death of his emissary, planned and brought about by men, into the establishment of *definitive and irrevocable* faithfulness to Israel (in biblical terms, new covenant) and thus preserves his claim on the chosen people of God.

Only when the full implications of the relationship of atoning death and renewal of the covenant with Israel are taken seriously is it possible to go a step further. According to its basic linguistic character, the formula "for many" is an *open formula*. Although it speaks primarily of guilty Israel, which is granted atonement, completely freely, through Jesus' death, it still does not exclude the many from the nations, mentioned in Matt. 8:11. If Israel accepts the offered atonement and repents, it will become a signal to the nations, who will then be able to participate in the salvation now established in Israel in an even deeper and more permanent way through Jesus' death.

If these reflections are correct, Jesus showed his concern for Israel even when confronted with death; in fact, he showed that concern more deeply and more radically at that time than ever before. His threatening words against "this generation" were extreme expressions intended as a last resort to win over his people.

When even these attempts failed, there remained only the way of the Servant of Yahweh, who takes on himself the guilt of the many.

8
THE REIGN OF GOD AND THE PEOPLE OF GOD

The two previous sections have surely once again made it clear how much Jesus was concerned with the gathering and restoration of the people of God. All the threats, all the denunciations, all the parables of crisis, all the sayings against "this generation," even Jesus' words at the Last Supper show plainly enough that Jesus' entire activity was related to Israel. Jesus' preaching of the reign of God cannot be isolated from his turning to the people of God. It led necessarily to the gathering of Israel.

The fact that the words of Jesus which have been passed on to us rarely have the "gathering" of Israel as their explicit theme (but cf. Matt. 23:37‖Luke 13:34; Matt. 12:30‖Luke 11:23) can be explained only by seeing that for Jesus the idea of the reign of God automatically implied the gathering of Israel. A people of God simply must belong to the kingdom of God. As Rudolf Schnackenburg rightly states, anyone who denies Jesus' intention of gathering a community "misunderstands the messianic-eschatological thought of Israel, in which eschatological salvation cannot be separated from the people of God and in which the community of God necessarily belongs to his reign."[38] For this reason, Jesus' expectation of an imminent end of the world in no way excluded efforts to form a holy people of God. "On the contrary!," as Joachim Jeremias has observed. "Precisely if Jesus thought the end was near, then he must have wanted to gather the people of God of the salvific age. For the people of God belong to the emissary of God, just as the crowd of disciples belong to the prophet. We must express this very pointedly: the *sole* meaning of the entire activity of Jesus is the gathering of God's eschatological people.[39] Jeremias' formulation is indeed pointed, but his comments are correct.

Exegetical discussions constantly emphasize that Jesus understood the notion of the reign of God in a thoroughly universal way and freed it of all *national Jewish* content. This is of course correct. There were in Jesus no restorative national tendencies of any sort. In the Our Father, Jesus had his disciples pray for the gathering of God's people, but not for the glorification of Jerusalem or for the liberation of the country from Roman rule. Jesus rejected the efforts of the Zealots (cf. Mark 12:13–17). Unlike the Essenes, he strictly avoided the metaphorical imagery of the holy war. In Jerusalem he fell into conflict with the restorative theology of the Sadduccees, a conflict which brought him to death.

Universality is indeed implicit in Jesus' concept of the reign of God.[40] This is shown by the conception of the pilgrimage of the nations in Matt. 8:11, and by the later mission to the Gentiles, which would not have been possible at all had Jesus not been *open* to Gentiles. But none of this changes the fact that Jesus' preaching of the reign of God had its *Sitz im Leben* in his turning to Israel. His goal was that the rule of God be fully established, that it come *visibly* into appearance. Where could this visibility, this tangibility of the rule of God be more appropriately realized than in the people of God?[41] The rule of God shone forth already in Jesus' salvific deeds for Israel, in his exorcism of demons, in his healing of the sick and in his acceptance of sinners. As K. Müller rightly notes, "God's eschatological rule is not to be present generally and absolutely in the world; it is to affect a concrete people, long since chosen and with clearly defined outlines."[42]

That Matthew is able to describe the Jews as the "sons of the kingdom" (Matt. 8:12; 13:38) is highly significant in this connection. For him, the members of the people of God stand in a firm relationship to the reign of God. Matthew can even say that the reign of God will be taken away from Israel and given to another people (Matt. 21:43*). What is striking in this formulation is the unambiguous binding of the reign of God first to Israel and later to *another* people (in the singular!). It is not said that it will be given "to other peoples." The rule of God evidently presupposes a people, a people of God, in whom it can become established and from whom it can shine forth. The texts of the New Testament must not be read through the lens of a theological individualism able to imagine the reign of God only as a universal, interior reality in the souls of individual believers scattered over the face of the earth.

Foundational to an important strand in the tradition of Old Testament theology is the idea that God has selected a single people out of all the nations of the world in order to make this people a sign of salvation. His interest in the other nations is no way impeded by this. When the people of God shines as a sign among the nations (cf. Isa. 2:1–4), the other nations will learn from God's people; they will come together in Israel in order to participate, in Israel and mediated through Israel, in God's glory. But all this can happen only when Israel really becomes recognizable as a *sign of salvation*, when God's salvation transforms his people recognizably, tangibly, even visibly.

Jesus did not envision the people of God which he sought to gather as a purely spiritual, purely religious community — as a society in human hearts (*societas in cordibus*). Theses of this sort, which are frequently defended either covertly or openly, fail to do justice to his intentions. The discipleship to which Jesus called was not invisible discipleship; his eating with sinners was not invisible eating; his cures of the sick were not invisible cures — no more than his bloody death on the cross was an invisible event.

Jesus' effort to gather Israel was very concrete and visible. That Jesus gave the movement no firmly established, institutionally fixed form has nothing to do with "invisible community;" it stems simply from the fact that he was concerned with Israel, which had *long since existed* as a community before God (though as a sick and fractured community).

It is time to summarize. God selected out of the many peoples of the world a single people, precisely in order to make this people a visible sign of salvation. According to biblical theology, God establishes his eschatological rule, which should in principle encompass the entire world, precisely by beginning very small: with a family (in biblical terms: with Abraham), a clan, a group, a small people. According to this divine pedagogy, the reign of God does not mean subjugation of the world but a call into freedom — a call, actually an alluring, according to the model of those called first.

Jesus must have appropriated personally this prophetic interpretation of God's history with the world, this understanding of Israel's history of election. For even when Israel as a whole refused his message, he did not abandon the idea of community, the idea that the reign of God must have a *people*; instead he concentrated on his circle of disciples. Without losing from sight the whole of Israel, he bound the reign of God to his community of disciples. As Luke 12:32 (cf. 22:29) puts it:

> Fear not, little flock, for it is your Father's good pleasure to give you the kingdom.

II

Jesus and His Disciples

How did Jesus will community? Our investigation up to now has already established some points that are important for answering this question. We have seen that Jesus' thinking was to an extraordinary degree *related to Israel*, though it was not *limited to Israel*. To him, Israel was a way to a greater goal, a sign of universal salvation. But precisely as a sign it could not be circumvented.

Nonetheless, what has been said so far is clearly not a complete answer to the question this book seeks to address. We must go on to ask *how Jesus envisioned, more exactly, the Israel which he sought to gather, the true people of God*. This question is answered decisively by Jesus' instruction of his disciples. But before pursuing this issue we must clarify what the circle of disciples is.

1
THE CIRCLE OF DISCIPLES

There were basically two groups in Israel which heard Jesus and believed in him.

On the one hand, there were those who accepted Jesus' message, but remained in their village or town to await the reign of God. "Wherever Jesus appears, he leaves behind followers who wait with the families for the kingdom and who accept him and his messengers; people like this are all over the country, especially in Galilee, but also in Judea, in Bethany for example, and in the Decapolis (Mark 5:19–20)."[43] It is said, for example, of Joseph of

Arimathea, a distinguished member of the Sanhedrin, that he awaited the reign of God (Mark 15:43). He surely did not do this uninfluenced by Jesus' message. As the burial story of Mark 15:42–47 shows, Joseph must have esteemed and respected Jesus. Zacchaeus, who was transformed by his encounter with Jesus in Jericho, should also be mentioned in this connection. Zacchaeus promised that in the future he would give half his belongings to the poor and repay fourfold any excess he had collected; Jesus spoke of the salvation which had come upon "this house," that is upon Zacchaeus and his family. The best example of a "sedentary" follower of Jesus is Lazarus, who lived in Bethany (John 11:1). He is called a friend of Jesus and his disciples (John 11:11).

On the other hand, there were "disciples" in the stricter sense who are to be distinguished from followers of the sort just described.[44] The pertinent Greek word (*mathētēs*) should really be translated as "student." This translation would make clear immediately that, at least as far as the terminology is concerned, the rabbinic teacher-student relationship stands in the background. The same is true of the word "follow." The frequent comment in the gospels that the disciples *followed* Jesus must be understood quite literally. When he travelled through the country they came along a few steps after him, just as students of the Torah always remained a respectful distance behind their rabbi.

The circle of disciples who followed Jesus was a firmly fixed group. When the disciples pulled off heads of grain on the sabbath, Jesus was called to task for their actions: "Look, why are they doing what is not lawful on the sabbath?" (Mark 2:24). In the eyes of the onlookers Jesus was responsible for his disciples, just as every teacher of the Law was responsible for his students.

Yet in many respects Jesus' students differed from the students of the rabbis. They came, not because they wished to learn the Torah, but because they had heard Jesus' message of the nearness of the reign of God. They did not seek out their own teacher, as rabbinical students were accustomed to do, but were instead *called* by Jesus (cf. Luke 9:59). He called them to a discipleship which required that they give up their prior occupations and leave their families (cf. Mark 1:16–20). The severity of such a demand is clear from a saying of Jesus (cf. Matt. 10:37 and Luke 14:26) which seems to have been worded originally like this:

> He who does not hate father and mother cannot be my disciple. He who does not hate son and daughter cannot be my disciple.

Thus Jesus required of his disciples a determined turning away from their own families — this is what is meant by *hate.* Common life with Jesus took the place of family and of all previous ties. This common life meant more than merely being with a teacher, listening to him and observing him, in order to learn the Torah from his statements and his manner of life. The disciples' community of life with Jesus was a *community of destiny.* It went so far that the disciples had to be prepared to suffer what Jesus suffered — if necessary, even persecution or execution. As Matt. 10:38 states:

> He who does not take his cross and follow me is not worthy of me.

Despite these radical demands, we must not imagine that Jesus' circle of disciples was small. It was certainly far larger than the Twelve. The identification of the disciples and the Twelve is a schematic element introduced by Matthew. We know by name at least three men who belonged to Jesus' group of disciples but not to the pre-Easter Twelve: Cleopas (Luke 24:18), Joseph Barsabbas and Matthias (Acts 1:23). Five women who followed Jesus and supported him with their possessions are also known by name: Mary Magdalene, Johanna the wife of Chuza, Susanna, Mary the mother of James, and Salome (Luke 8:1–3; Mark 15:40–41). It would be wise not to underestimate the size of Jesus' group of disciples.

Far more important than this is the question why Jesus called disciples (above and beyond the Twelve) at all. The best answer is given by Luke 10:2 (‖Matt. 9:37–38):

> The harvest is plentiful, but the laborers are few; pray therefore ask the Lord of the harvest to send out laborers into his harvest.

The "Lord of the harvest" is obviously God. The harvest is an ancient biblical image both for judgment and for the eschatological time of salvation. Reaping the harvest must mean gathering Israel into the people of God of the final age. There can never be enough workers, Jesus says, to help with this gathering, for time flies as it does during the harvest.

When Israel *as a whole* did not accept Jesus' message, the circle of disciples acquired a new function. It received the task of representing *symbolically* what really should have taken place in Israel as a whole: complete dedication to the gospel of the reign of God, radical conversion to a new way of life, and a gathering unto a community of brothers and sisters.[45] It was obviously not Jesus' intention that the circle of disciples close itself off from Israel, still less that it solidify against Israel; he wanted it to remain open for Israel and directed continually toward Israel as a whole.

Thus the circle of disciples did not form a new community outside the old people of God, one assembled by Jesus as a *surrogate* or *replacement* for Israel. A conception of this sort would be thoroughly unbiblical.

The most that would be biblical would be the notion of the "holy remnant" (cf. 1 Kings 19:18; Isa. 10:20–22). Did Jesus understand his community of disciples as the holy remnant of Israel?

We now know that this very conception was theologically current at the time of Jesus. The Essenes in Qumran used the idea of the remnant to interpret the existence of their community in the midst of Israel. They saw themselves as the sacred remnant of Israel, chosen by God. They considered all other Jews, those who did not belong to their community and who did not participate in their sanctification, as a condemned group. They saw themselves as *sons of light*, and everyone else as *sons of darkness*.

It is characteristic of Jesus that he did not draw upon Isaiah's notion of remnant in order to interpret his work with the people of God.[46] He persisted with his claim on Israel as a whole. The concepts of a holy remnant or of a special community within Israel are excluded as possible interpretations of the circle of disciples by the fact that Jesus never specified membership in the circle of disciples as a condition for entering the kingdom of God. *He never made discipleship a general prerequisite for salvation.* Jesus' community of disciples must therefore not be understood along the lines of Qumran. Jesus' community of disciples is intelligible only in its symbolic reference to the whole of Israel. It was intended to prefigure the eschatological people of God with whom Jesus was concerned. It was intended to depict symbolically what Israel was to become. It was intended to allow the eschatological existence of Israel to begin.

2
THE SERMON ON THE MOUNT

Those who study in detail Jesus' moral teaching frequently observe something which corresponds on the level of ethics to the relationship of the disciples to Israel as a whole. It is extremely difficult to distinguish between instructions Jesus intended *for the disciples alone* and those he intended *for the whole of Israel.* This difficulty in distinguishing must have a basis in the reality itself. The moral teaching of Jesus was to be practiced within the circle of disciples, but it was at the same time instruction for the entire people. The apparent ambiguity is connected with the fact that the circle of disciples symbolically depicted eschatological Israel.

In any case, the Sermon on the Mount—the term is used here to refer to the whole of Jesus' ethical teaching—was not addressed to isolated individuals or (what would amount to the same thing) to humanity as a whole. *The addressee of the Sermon on the Mount was Israel, or the circle of disciples which represented Israel.* Since both the basic thesis of this book and the contemporary discussion of the relevance of the Sermon on the Mount to political matters are extraordinarily dependent on this insight, we must consider in greater detail the framework of Matthew's Sermon on the Mount and Luke's Sermon on the Plain.

The core content of both the Sermon on the Mount and the Sermon on the Plain derives from the first programmatic speech of the so-called Q document.[47] Luke adhered more closely to this source; Matthew expanded it considerably through the use of other traditional material. Even in Q, then to a greater extent in Luke, and still more so in Matthew, we are dealing with secondary compositions of originally disparate sayings—sayings which in themselves are quite old and for the most part go back to Jesus. The frameworks of the Sermon on the Mount and the Sermon on the Plain are redactional; they do not simply reproduce a historical situation in the life of Jesus. Nonetheless, these frameworks are of great value for our topic. They show at least whom the authors of two major gospels viewed as the addressees of an important part of Jesus' ethical instruction.

What, then, are these frameworks? Matthew (4:23−5:2) begins the Sermon on the Mount as follows:

> And he [Jesus] went about all Galilee, teaching in their synagogues and preaching the gospel of the kingdom and healing every disease and infirmity among the people. So his fame spread throughout all Syria, and they brought him all the sick, those afflicted with various diseases and pains, demoniacs, epileptics, and paralytics, and he healed them. And great crowds followed him from Galilee and the Decapolis and Jerusalem and Judea and from beyond the Jordan. Seeing the crowds, he went up on the mountain, and when he sat down his disciples came to him. And he opened his mouth and taught them, saying: . . . .

Matthew quite deliberately places an extended summary before the Sermon on the Mount. He wants to make clear that the demands of the Sermon on the Mount *presuppose from the perspective of salvation history* that Jesus has announced the reign of God and made it present both in word and in mighty deeds on behalf of the afflicted members of God's people. In effect, the whole of Israel is assembled before Jesus. All sections of the country are carefully enumerated: Galilee, Judea, Jerusalem and the land beyond the Jordan. Jesus now proclaims the new social order of the people of God *before the whole of Israel*, just as the social order of the Old Covenant was once proclaimed on Mount Sinai. Still it is decisive that the disciples are mentioned specifically as Jesus' audience. Is it possible that the Sermon on the Mount is not meant for the people, but only for them? Are the people there in the long run merely as a backdrop, to make Jesus' speech more imposing? This interpretation is definitively excluded three chapters later, in the conclusion of the Sermon on the Mount (Matt. 7:28–29):

> And when Jesus finished these sayings, the crowds were astonished at his teaching, for he taught them as one who had authority and not as their scribes.

Here the disciples are no longer mentioned at all. The Sermon on the Mount is clearly addressed to the people, to the whole of Israel. Yet the mention of the disciples in Matt. 5:1 is no accident. The disciples are the inner core of Jesus' audience. *They*, at any rate, are to hear and do what is said to the entire people.

The situation in Luke is quite similar. After relating how Jesus, on the mountain, had called the Twelve from a larger group of disciples, Luke introduces the Sermon on the Plain as follows (6:17–20):

> And he came down with them and stood on a level place, with a great crowd of his disciples and a great multitude of people from all Judea and Jerusalem and the seacoast of Tyre and Sidon, who came to hear him and to be healed of their diseases; and those who were troubled with unclean spirits were cured. And all the crowd sought to touch him, for power came forth from him and healed them all. And he lifted up his eyes on his disciples, and said: . . . .

The theological scenery is similar to Matthew's. The Magna Charta of Jesus' ethical requirements presupposes that the salvation of God's reign has already been preached and concretized, even into the corporal dimension, through the many healings. But Luke arranges the audience for the Sermon on the Plain even more carefully than Matthew. First there is the circle of the Twelve, just established, then a large number of the other disciples, and finally in a wider circle the whole crowd of people. In contrast to Matthew, Luke even uses the term *laos* for the people. The word *laos* acquires a solemn tone from the Septuagint, the Greek translation of the Old Testament; it refers to the people of Israel, chosen and led by God.

But is not, at least in Luke, Jesus' major speech addressed exclusively to the disciples? Luke 6:20 does read, "And he lifted up his eyes on his disciples, and said . . ." This comment establishes in any case that the disciples are the most important listeners to the Sermon on the Plain. Yet even in Luke, just as in Matthew, at the end of the address the people of God are clearly designated as the audience. The Sermon on the Plain concludes with these words (Luke 7:1*):

> When he had finished this discourse
> in the ears of the people . . .

"To speak into someone's ears" is once again language from the Septuagint. In the Old Testament, this expression shows the presence of a legally binding address which is proclaimed publicly.[48] Thus Luke too makes clear that Jesus' great programmatic address is intended not only for the circle of disciples, but for the entire people of God.

The twofold address of the Sermon on the Mount, the oscillating between disciples and people, is surely no coincidence. Both evangelists evidently place great weight on making clear that the Sermon on the Mount is directed primarily and most forcefully to the disciples, but that it applies above and beyond this to the whole people of Israel, which has heard the good news of the reign of God, and whose afflicted members have been healed by the preacher of this message.

As mentioned earlier, all of this is immediately the theology of the two evangelists. On the whole, however, this theology must correspond pretty exactly to the historical facts. Certainly Jesus both proclaimed the reign of God and preached to the people on the one hand, and offered specific instruction to his disciples on the other. The sayings incorporated into the Sermon on the Mount derive from both of these sources. It is often hardly possible now to establish the original situation of individual sayings in Jesus' life. Ultimately the question whether an individual saying of Jesus comes from instruction of the disciples or from preaching to the people is not very important. Even if the addressee of a particular instruction was originally only the circle of disciples, it still remains true that the disciples represented Israel as a whole, and so everything said to them was ultimately intended for the entire people of God.

This consideration shows the objective legitimacy of the framework with which Matthew and Luke surround the Sermon. It also shows the legitimacy of the evangelists' procedure of gradually relating the concept of "Jesus' disciples," originally a strict and unambiguous term, to all believers, and of increasingly expanding the notion of "following" to embrace the entire people of God.

Taken as a whole, the framework of the Sermon on the Mount confirms our thesis that the addressee of Jesus' ethical instruction was neither the individual as such nor humanity in general. The addressee of his teaching was Israel, or the circle of disciples which represented Israel.

3
THE NEW FAMILY

The last two sections leave a difficulty which must not be concealed. As we have already seen, Jesus made particularly radical demands on the circle of disciples that followed him — above all, that of sacrificing their previous vocation and leaving their own family. More could be added to this list, such as abandoning possessions (cf. Luke 14:33) and renouncing preparation for the future (cf. Luke 12:22–32). It is simply impossible to equate these demands which Jesus placed on the limited circle of his followers with his instructions for the entire people of God. A concrete example will illustrate the problem.

Jesus himself remained unmarried for the sake of the reign of God (cf. Matt. 19:12), and he required that his disciples leave their families. In the Middle East, that action had in some cases major repercussions. "If the father of a household decided to join the company of Jesus, his wife would have had no choice but to return with the children to her parents' home, even though this was considered a blemish."[49] However problems of that sort may have been resolved in those days, it is clear that leaving one's family was a very radical and severe demand. For this reason, Jesus placed this demand only on those who literally followed him, not on the entire people, not even on his "sedentary" adherents. To this extent it is impossible to avoid distinguishing in Jesus between *an ethic of discipleship* and *an ethic of the entire people of God*.

Does this not call into question the conclusion we have drawn up to now? Moreover, does it not immediately give rise to the well-known problem of a *two-level ethic*, one for those who are "better," one for the "average person," with all the consequences which such a conception has had in the Catholic Church — even to the point of dividing the people of God into two states of life?

If we look more closely, we find that although there is in Jesus' teaching a specific ethic of discipleship, there is no two-level ethic. In order to clarify this, let us remain with our example of leaving one's family. This action produces no state of the perfect, in comparison to a state of the less perfect, because Jesus places on those who remain at home with their family demands just as radical as those placed on those who follow him. The Sermon on the Mount contains a text which—in contrast to the practice which prevailed in Israel at that time—sharply forbids a man to dismiss his wife (Matt. 5:31–32). It also contains a passage in which the lustful glance of a man at a woman is equated with the act of adultery (Matt. 5:27–28). All this is fundamentally just as severe and demanding as the requirement that the disciples leave their families. Jesus requires of some absolute and indissoluble faithfulness to their spouses, and he requires of others absolute and indissoluble faithfulness to their mission of preaching. In other words, the concrete form of life, whether it be marriage or the service of preaching, is taken by Jesus in each case with radical seriousness. Both ways of life are possible in this radical form only in view of the reign of God. The inner freedom to live either marital fidelity or discipleship to such a radical degree is given only by a fascination with a reign of God which is already present.

What has been shown here paradigmatically with reference to marriage and celibacy could also be exemplified with reference to other elements of the ethic of discipleship. There is in Jesus an ethic of discipleship which is at least in theory distinguishable. However, in comparison with the ethic of the entire people of God it is not a higher form of morality; it is rather determined—quite functionally—by the concrete form of life of those who are underway with Jesus.

These considerations suffice to establish that Jesus did not teach a two-level ethic. But above and beyond this, it is necessary to see the inner connection of the ethic of discipleship with the ethic of the entire people of God. In order to recognize this connection, let us look first at a text which was certainly originally directed to the literal followers of Jesus. In Mark (10:29–30) it runs as follows:

> Truly, I say to you, there is no one who has left house or brothers or sisters or mother or father or children or lands, for my sake and

for the gospel, who will not receive a hundredfold now in this time, houses and brothers and sisters and mothers and children and lands, with persecutions, and in the age to come eternal life.

In the form presented here, the saying has already been revised from the perspective of early Christianity. The notion of the gospel has been inserted. The words "with persecutions" have been added. Above all, the idea of the two ages has been introduced. The original saying must have been an even more radical promise with *reference to the present*:

Amen, I say to you, no one leaves house, brothers, sisters, mother, father, children or *fields* for my sake without receiving in return a hundredfold — even now, in this hour, houses, brothers, sisters, mothers, children and fields.

It is essential to sense the enormity of Jesus' words. *Brothers and sisters* are blood relatives, the clan to which a Semite belongs and to which he is accountable; they are also a source of protection. Behind *father and mother* stands the ancient patriarchal family, whose sacred structure is confirmed by Scripture. *Children* are both the Semite's greatest joy and his social security, in a sense insurance for old age. *Fields* are the Israelite's portion of the sacred heritage promised by God. An example is provided by the Acts of the Apostles (4:36–37) which tells of a man named Barnabas who came from Cyprus but possessed a farm in Jerusalem. Like many other Jews from the Diaspora, he had presumably purchased a lot in the Holy Land to establish his union with Israel and participate in the blessing of the messianic age. We must recognize the concept of "land," so highly significant for every devout Jew, behind the reference to "fields" in Mark 10:29–30.

Jesus relativized all of this: clan, parents, children, land. It is possible, in some circumstances even necessary, to leave all this behind. This is not done for the sake of renunciation, as if renunciation were something positive in itself, but rather because something new is appearing, the reign of God is arriving. Its arrival changes everything. Those who follow Jesus, who for the sake of the reign of God leave behind everything they have had, become a *new family*, a family in which, paradoxically, there are again brothers, sisters, mothers and children.

Even *now, in this hour*, the disciples will receive a hundred times what they have left. Jesus spoke here from personal experience, which gradually also became the experience of his disciples. They left their families, but then found new brothers and sisters among the disciples. They left their parental home, but found new mothers throughout the country where they had been received hospitably. They left their children, but new people whom they had not previously known, all filled with something new, constantly stream to them. They left their fields, but found a firm and supportive community as a "new land."

In addition to all these experiences, we should think particularly of the table community in which the disciples continually shared.[50] Here Jesus was the head of the house, who gathered the new family around himself and pronounced the prayer of blessing (Mark 8:6–7). Later on the disciples would recognize him in the breaking of the bread (Luke 24:30–31, 34). Their community at table with the earthly Jesus must have impressed itself unforgettably upon them.

Jesus did indeed demand of his disciples that they leave everything, but he did not call them into solitude and isolation. That is not the point of discipleship. He called them into a new family of brothers and sisters, itself a sign of the arriving kingdom.

The decisive question is whether what we, on the basis of Mark 10:29–30, have described as the reality of the new family can be brought into connection with the whole of the people of God. The promise of Mark 10:29–30 is made only to the disciples; it presupposes the ethic of discipleship. There is another text which brings us further here, Mark 3:20–21, 31–35.

Jesus is in a house, surrounded by so many people that he and his disciples cannot even eat (Mark 3:20). At this point his relatives come to bring him home by force. Jesus' family, in other words, is upset at his public activity. Those influential in the family are convinced that he has gone mad (3:21). When Jesus is told, "Your mother and your brothers, (and your sisters) are outside, asking for you" (3:32), he replies (3:33–35):

> "Who are my mother and my brothers?" And looking around on those who sat about him, he said, "Here are my mother and my

brothers! Whoever does the will of God is my brother, and sister, and mother."

The theme of the new family appears again here. Jesus dissociates himself from his family "in highly rhetorical, but also highly juridical ancient language"[51] and inserts himself into another family. In fact, he establishes this other family: "These are my brothers!"

Who is this new family? Only the disciples? The reference in Mark 3:32 to a "crowd seated around him" argues against this. But we do not wish to make too much of this narrative comment. The word of Jesus himself is more important:

Whoever does the will of God is my brother, and sister, and mother.

What does it mean in this context *to do the will of God*? In a rabbinic context it would mean to fulfill the Torah, the law from Sinai. But that cannot possibly be meant here, for Jesus' family surely fulfills the law and yet in this situation clearly has no relationship to God's will. Here, as in many other places in the New Testament (cf. especially Eph. 1:3–14), the will of God can only be the salvific plan which God is now carrying out and which one is called upon to join in an ultimate willingness to God to transform one's life. Put in even more concrete terms, the will of God is the coming of the kingdom and the gathering of the true Israel (cf. Matt. 6:9–10). The ones who do the will of God are those who believe Jesus' message of the nearby reign of God and let themselves be gathered into God's eschatological people. In Mark 3:35 Jesus speaks not only of his disciples, but of all who recognize the initiative God is taking in Israel and rush toward his reign.

This makes it clear that the new family of Jesus' brothers and sisters extends far beyond the circle of actual disciples. Something new is happening everywhere in Israel that the gospel of the reign of God is believed, not only in the circle of those literally following Jesus. The reign of God breaks its own trail with force (Matt. 11:12). Jesus casts his message like fire on the earth and seeks to set everything ablaze (Luke 12:49). The message of the reign of God causes division and discord in Israel (Luke 12:52–53):

Henceforth in one house there will be five divided, three against two and two against three; they will be divided, father against son and son against father, mother against daughter and daughter against her mother, mother-in-law against her daughter-in-law, daughter-in-law against her mother-in-law.

It is *because of the gospel* that this division cuts through the families of Israel. There are people everywhere who commit themselves to the reign of God and are forced to accept conflict with their own family, with their own clan, as part of the package. They form, in the midst of Israel and in the midst of the old families and clans, the new family of Jesus.

In conclusion, it is necessary to recognize that Jesus taught a specific ethic of discipleship which has its authentic location in the circle of disciples (and later in the circle of early Christian prophets and itinerant missionaries). But it is also necessary to recognize that this ethic is tied in many ways to the ethic of the rest of the people of God (concretely, the "sedentary" adherents of Jesus). There are constant mutual influences and overlappings.

With regard to the concrete example which we chose, this means that only relatively few of those in Israel who accepted Jesus' message left their home and joined Jesus' nomadic life of wandering through Palestine. The majority remained with their families. But the families of those who remained home were transformed. They became more disposable, more open. They no longer revolved merely around themselves. They offered hospitality to Jesus and his messengers. They entered relationships with one another. Or, in contrast to this, just the opposite happened. Families divided within themselves. Jesus and his movement became a sign of contradiction (Luke 2:34). Many individuals separated themselves from the old structures (Mark 2:21–22) and joined the new family of which Jesus spoke (Mark 2:21–22). Thus there arose in the midst of ancient Israel — unobtrusively at first and yet irreversibly — the new society planned by God.

4
THE END OF THE FATHERS

Jesus promised those who followed him that they would at once find again what they had left behind: homes, brothers, sisters, mothers, children and fields. But not fathers. Fathers are not included in the second half of the carefully constructed parallelism of Mark 10:29–30. Is this fortuitous? The question would have to be left unanswered if other texts did not show that the absence of any reference to fathers is anything but coincidence or forgetfulness.

Fathers are deliberately not mentioned in the second part of the saying because in the new family there are to be no "fathers." They are too symbolic of patriarchal domination. Jesus' community of disciples and together with it the true Israel are to have only a single father, the One in heaven. This is shown by Matt. 23:9.

Matthew incorporates into his major address against the scribes and Pharisees (23:1–36) a section which represents a sort of catechesis for leaders of the Christian community. This section is attached to the observation that the scribes are fond of being addressed with the title "*rabbi*"(= my Lord); in deliberate contrast Matt. 23:8–12 says:

> But you are not to be called rabbi, for you have one teacher, and you are all brethren. And call no man your father on earth, for you have one Father, who is in heaven. Neither be called masters, for you have one master, the Christ. He who is greatest among you shall be your servant; whoever exalts himself will be humbled, and whoever humbles himself will be exalted.

Part of this passage is clearly the formulation of either Matthew or the pre-Matthean tradition; the presence of the christological title in the third saying is sufficient by itself to show this. The passage also clearly discusses problems of the early church quite directly. The temptation to enjoy ecclesiastical prestige in the form of honorific titles must have beckoned as early as the first century. Matthew takes a stance against this with extraordinary sharpness. He prohibits ecclesial officeholders from using not only honorific titles like "father" or "rabbi" — at that time in Israel any distinguished man could be addressed as *rabbi*, which literally means "my great one," — but even functional titles such as "master" ("teacher").

Why did Matthew have such great sensitivity on a subject to which the later church, unfortunately, has never been sensitive? The later church has not only created a multiplicity of official designations and honorary titles, but even introduced the address "Holy Father" for the pope, in direct disobedience to Matt. 23:9. Where did Matthew acquire his sensitivity, which cannot simply be taken for granted, on this matter? He can only have taken it from Jesus. Although the catechesis of Matt. 23:8–12 is in part formed redactionally (especially in the first and third sayings), each line of it breathes the spirit of Jesus. Let us examine the passage in detail.

First there is the question of honorific titles (the first three sayings). Jesus was in general addressed as *rabbi*, even by his disciples (cf. Mark 11:21; Matt. 26:25, 49; John 1:38). But that was simply a matter of courtesy, which Jesus permitted. When this respectful language, customary at the time, was intensified even slightly, Jesus could immediately overcome his reticence. Once, when addressed as "good rabbi" (roughly equivalent to "honorable master"), he commented on the language and corrected the one who used it so sharply that he was almost impolite: "Why do you call me good? No one is good but God alone" (Mark 10:17–18). This saying, which Matthew reinterprets for christological reasons and dilutes in the process (cf. Matt. 19:16–17), is sufficient to establish that Jesus put a stop to things as soon as those speaking to him exceeded the customary norms of courtesy.

In addition to the prohibition of Christian honorific titles, the question of proper official conduct plays an important role in the catechesis of Matt. 23:8–12. The one who is greatest in the community is to be the servant of all (fourth saying). Here too the conduct of Jesus unmistakably forms the background. Though Jesus did in general tolerate being addressed as "rabbi," he called into question the rabbis' customary practice of being served by their students. In principle, a fine idea stood behind this practice; the rabbis' students were to learn the Torah, not only from the *teaching* of their master, but also from daily contact with him. Concretely, daily contact meant that they waited on their master as his personal servants. The rule was that knowledge of the Torah could not be gained without service of the experts. At a later date, Rabbi Jochanan was to express matters by saying, "Anyone who prevents his students from serving him is like one who denies them love."[52] But this is precisely what Jesus did at the Last Supper. He prevented his students from serving him. He did not allow his disciples to wash his feet, but performed for them this service which was part of the meal (John 13:1–20). He was in their midst as one who served (Luke 22:27). He did not come to let himself be served, but to serve (Mark 10:45).

Jesus' words about *service* are part of the most widely attested tradition which stems from him. All of this establishes a second point in which Matt. 23:8–12 has preserved the spirit of Jesus with great sensitivity. "He who is greatest among you shall be your servant" (23:11). That Jesus did not let himself be served but rather himself served others — presumably not only at the Last Supper — must have impressed his community of disciples so deeply that they later termed their own offices *diakonia*, services.

The part of the catechesis for community leaders which is most important for our topic is the second saying:

And call no man your father on earth, for you have one father, who is in heaven.

Here we not only find the spirit of Jesus, but hear the historical Jesus himself speaking. The context proves that Matthew understood the word "father" as an honorific title, and held that in the Christian community no one should allow himself to be honored in that way. In doing this, Matthew applied the original words of Jesus to his own situation in a thoroughly appropriate manner. But Jesus himself addressed a deeper issue.

In this saying Jesus in all probability used the word *abba*, which at that time in Palestinian Aramaic was the normal way for children to address their father, but which was also still used by adults: You shall call no one on earth *abba*, "dear father." Did Jesus then in general forbid the families of Israel to use the tender and loving word "father?" This seems so absurd that many exegetes do not even consider the possibility that Matt. 23:8 might be an authentic word of Jesus. Others propose that behind this saying stands a warning of Jesus against reliance on Israel's patriarchs — roughly along the lines of John the Baptist's word, "Do not presume to say to yourselves, "we have Abraham as our father" (Matt. 3:9).[53] At first glance an astonishing, imaginative interpretation!

But it is not at all necessary to go to these lengths to interpret the passage.

If we wish to understand Matt. 23:9, we must take seriously the fact that it was originally a part of the radical ethic of discipleship, initially directed only to the circle of disciples. Jesus' disciples had left everything, occupation and family. Now the father was part of the family (cf. Mark 1:20), a family which must not be equated with the reduced modern nuclear family. Jesus' disciples were far from their fathers, whom they had until then trustingly and lovingly addressed as *abba*. In this situation, Jesus told them that they would not, and must not, henceforth address anyone on earth *abba*. Whoever does not separate himself radically from his family cannot be my disciple (Luke 14:26). But you need not call anyone on earth father, for you now have another *abba*, the One who is in heaven.

If this interpretation is correct, Jesus was convinced that his disciples had entered a new relationship to God through their discipleship. God had now become their father, in place of their earthly fathers; they were allowed to address him as Jesus himself did, with the familiar *abba*, in departure from the customary religious language of the day. It was here, in this new situation of Jesus' disciples, that Jesus' expression "your father," always addressed to the disciples and never to outsiders, had its *Sitz im Leben* (cf. Matt. 5:48; 6:32; Mark 11:25; Luke 6:36; 12:32). Jesus wanted to make clear with this saying that in leaving their families his disciples had received God as their father in a new and radical sense. They no longer had their earthly father, who could plan and prepare for the future with the wisdom of experience, but instead had God himself. As Jesus says in Matt. 6:31–33 (∥Luke 12:29–31):

> Therefore do not be anxious, saying "What shall we eat?" or "What shall we drink?" or "What shall we wear?" For the Gentiles seek all these things; and your heavenly Father knows that you need them all. But seek first his kingdom and his righteousness, and all these things shall be yours as well.

It is right here, in this special situation of the circle of disciples, that the Our Father has its oldest *Sitz im Leben*. It was originally a prayer for disciples who had left everything behind. In this prayer they addressed God as their *abba*, their beloved father, from whom they requested each day's bread.

In this way Matt. 23:9 receives its precise meaning. The disciples may not and need not address anyone other than God alone as *abba*. In God they have received a caring and kind father, in whom they can place unconditional trust.

But the saying also has a reverse side. Power and rule belong only to the God whom the disciples may address as *abba*. If there no longer exist for them the kind and caring fathers of the past, but only the one Father in heaven, then it is all the more true that authoritarian fathers exercising power have gone out of existence. It would be paradoxical to leave tender fathers behind and then find authoritarian fathers in the circle of disciples. It was precisely for this reason that Jesus mentioned no fathers in Mark 10:30. The disciples will find everything again in the new family of God, brothers and sisters, mothers and children; but they will find fathers no longer. Patriarchal domination is no longer permissible in the new family, but only motherliness, fraternity and childlikeness before God the Father.

The pericope Mark 10:35–45, which tells the story of the request of the sons of Zebedee, suggests how seriously Jesus took this point. In Mark (10:42–45), the pericope ends with a brief address which has programmatic character:

> You know that those who are supposed to rule over the Gentiles lord it over them, and their great men exercise authority over them. But it shall not be so among you; but whoever would be great among you must be your servant, and whoever would be first among you must be slave of all. For the Son of man also came not to be served but to serve, and to give his life as a ransom for many.

This text, every line of which reflects the thought and conduct of Jesus, addresses precisely what we would today call *structures of domination*. Such structures are standard in the societies of this world. In the community of disciples, however, relationships of domination are not permitted. Whoever wishes to be first there must be the slave of all. The greatest shall become like the smallest (cf. Luke 22:26). Jesus, in other words, demanded of his disciples a completely new type of relationship with each other, something otherwise not typical of society. But this means that he required a *contrast-society*. What that implies will be made clear in the following section by reference to a particular complex of issues which has been discussed increasingly in recent years: Jesus' insistence on renouncing violence.

5
THE RENUNCIATION OF VIOLENCE

Jesus' insistence on renouncing violence is expressed most clearly in Matt. 5:39–42 (‖Luke 6:29–30). It is lacking in Mark. This in itself indicates that the text goes back to Q. In this particular case it is evident that Matthew has preserved the original wording better than Luke. The section of Q on the renunciation of violence can be reconstructed as follows on the basis of a synoptic comparison:

> I say to you:
> When a person strikes you on the right cheek,
> turn and offer him the other.
> If anyone wants to go to law over your shirt,
> hand him your coat as well.
> Should anyone press you into service for one mile,
> go with him two miles.
> Give to the man who begs from you;
> do not turn your back on the borrower.[54]

The text in Q must have read roughly like this. It is a carefully planned four-part composition of sayings which builds toward an anticlimax. In other words, the worst evils — which range from an inordinate request and pressure to the threat of a lawsuit and naked violence. Other factors also show that this is a carefully composed redactional composition of individual sayings. Yet we need not take an interest in the literary history and tradition of the total composition. The important point is that the four-part composition of sayings reflects in its individual parts the provocative speech and the radical ethic of Jesus with regard to the renunciation of violence. There is a widespread consensus in New Testament exegesis that in this text we hear Jesus himself speaking. We need to examine the four sayings somewhat more closely.

Loaning is discussed at the end of the anticlimax. Presumably it is a question of finances. Someone comes and wishes to borrow money. This is not an injustice, but it is unpleasant. It could even be an imposition, for a devout person in Jesus' day was not permitted to take interest. The context also suggests that the prospective borrower exerts pressure. But Jesus says, "Do not turn your back on the borrower."

The saying before this speaks of begging. The situation is not described more concretely, but the passage may be concerned with professional beggars. If we realize how widespread and how obtrusive begging can be in the Middle East, we can imagine what is demanded here. Once again the context requires that we presuppose a certain pressure from the beggar. The beggar becomes burdensome; he acts aggressively. But Jesus says, "Give to the man who begs from you."

Force comes into play at the next level of the anticlimax. The Greek text uses a verb (*aggareuō*) which is a technical term for the extortion of penal labor and menial service by an occupying power. There is every reason to suppose that the situation of Palestine, occupied by the Romans, is envisioned in this third saying. The Roman cohorts claimed the right to force a Jew to accompany them as a guide or as an unpaid porter (cf. Mark 15:21). Jesus says that if someone forces you to go *one* mile in this fashion, then do double that: go two miles.

The next case is more serious. Someone is on the verge of losing the only shirt he owns. The pressure goes so far as a threat to bring matters before a judge. Perhaps it is a question of collecting a deposit, perhaps one of reparation for damage—the concrete situation remains open. In any case the victim is a poor man who possesses only a single shirt and a single cloak. The cloak could not be taken away from him—that was already established legally in Exod. 22:25–26—for on cold nights the poor had to cover themselves with their cloaks. They had nothing else. Jesus says not to go to court about the shirt. Let it be taken away immediately, and even give your cloak along with it.

211901

At the beginning of the anticlimax stands the worst case of all. While the other cases are concerned with increasing pressure, perhaps even with covert, hidden violence, the issue now is the outbreak of open and brutal violence of a sort which must also be considered a severe personal affront. It is explicitly said that the first blow falls on the *right* cheek, not on the *left*. The blow must then have been struck with the back of the hand, not the inside. In the Middle East, being struck with the back of the hand was considered an extraordinarily serious affront. Jesus says to allow oneself to be offended brutally, and even to offer one's foe the other cheek.

The *intention* of the four sayings is unmistakable. Jesus' listeners are told to renounce all legal sanctions and all retribution. Do not answer violence with violence. When injustice is done to you, do not remain passive, but take the first step toward your foe. Answer pressure or brutality with overflowing goodness. Perhaps in this way you can win over your adversary.

These injunctions acquire special force in that they do not portray relatively unusual, extraordinary events. The instances they depict are taken from the everyday life of Jesus' listeners and presuppose a whole range of hidden or open violence, from minor disturbance to direct use of force.

This last observation is a very telling argument against interpretations which seek to understand Matt. 5:39–42 in a purely metaphorical way. Obviously Jesus provides no casuistry. And obviously the text does contain metaphorical elements which are particularly evident in the subordinate clauses. "Go a second mile," "give your cloak as well," "turn the other cheek,"—these transform the passive endurance of injustice into an active going to meet one's enemy, even into being concerned with one's enemy and seeking to make him a brother. To this extent the language is metaphorical; here as in many other places Jesus speaks with provocative, prophetic exaggeration. But this does not alter the fact that he is concerned with *real* examples of conduct which are to be applied as such and which, as examples, illuminate analogous cases. Jesus does in fact forbid the use of violence, and he is convinced that anyone who accepts his word can live without recourse to violence and retribution.

The so-called *charge to the missionaries* shows how necessary it is to avoid either watering down Jesus' injunction to renounce violence or weakening it through subtle interpretation. In all probability this passage stems from the mission of the Twelve into all parts of Israel.[55] We have already discussed the prophetic symbolic action which stands behind this mission (cf. I: 2). From the perspective of the history of tradition, the charge to the missionaries belongs in the complex of "missionary discourse," which can be found in four places in the synoptic gospels: Mark 6:7–11‖Luke 9:2–5, and Luke 10:2–16‖Matt. 10:5–42.

In the charge to the missionaries, Jesus commands the twelve disciples, who are to journey through Israel in pairs to proclaim the arrival of the reign of God, not to take with them money, a knapsack, a second cloak, sandals or a staff. In Luke (9:3; cf. Matt. 10:9–10) this is worded as follows:

> Take nothing for your journey, no staff, nor bag, nor bread, nor money; and do not have two tunics.

The charge to the missionaries can also be understood in a metaphorical sense, and some exegetes have deliberately done so. It is possible to speak of the missionary's *inner poverty* or of something similar. But this misses the real meaning of the text. First of all, this text has the form of an *instruction* which gives very concrete, binding directives. Second, in the ancient world and in early Judaism we know that the equipment of peripatetic philosophers, itinerant preachers and members of certain religious groups was often carefully chosen and sometimes even precisely regulated. Mention may be made of Pythagoras, the peripatetic Cynic philosophers, the Essenes and John the Baptist. In such cases, dress and equipment had symbolic significance. They were intended to say something about the nature of the person or group involved.[56]

In its oldest form the charge to the missionaries is extraordinarily rigorous. It is completely inconceivable without presupposing that the messengers were welcomed with hearty hospitality when they arrived at a home in the evening. In our context, however, the absolute defenselessness which is indicated by their equipment—more exactly, by their lack of equipment—is much more important. In Palestine a staff served not only as a support while walk-

LORETTE WILMOT LIBRARY

NAZARETH COLLEGE

ing, but also as a poor man's weapon against robbers and wild animals. Swift escape while barefoot was impossible. Thus the renunciation of staff and sandals led to defenselessness and entailed nonviolence; it had to become a demonstrative signal of absolute readiness for peace. It is therefore appropriate to find in the same context the words, "Behold, I send you out as sheep in the midst of wolves" (Matt. 10:16∥Luke 10:3).

It would be a serious exegetical error not to interpret the concrete elements of the charge to the missionaries literally. This gives us an important methodical indication of how to interpret Matt. 5:39–42. The charge to the missionaries can be interpreted literally only if we take seriously the missionary discourse's social context in the hospitality and helpfulness of the new family of Jesus which was emerging everywhere. Everywhere in Israel there were those who had accepted Jesus' message and let their lives be transformed by the reign of God. Everywhere in Israel others were won for the kingdom by the Twelve. God's eschatological peace, which rested on Jesus' new family, descended upon all of these people. It is for this reason that Jesus' messengers are told (Luke 10:5–7; cf. Matt. 10:10–13):

> Whatever house you enter, first say, "Peace be to this house!" And
> if a son of peace is there, your peace shall rest upon him; but if not,
> it shall return to you. And remain in the same house, eating and
> drinking what they provide, for the laborer deserves his wages.

The rigor of the charge to the missionaries cannot be understood unless the background of the emerging new family of Jesus is considered. Nor can the radical character of Jesus' injunction be understood unless its social context is kept in mind: the circle of disciples, the new family of Jesus' brothers and sisters, the Israel which is to be gathered, the sons of peace.

The radical ethic of renouncing violence is thus addressed neither to isolated individuals nor to the entire world, but precisely to the people of God which has been marked by the preaching of God's reign. This insight is of great importance for the contemporary debate about peace, a debate which becomes stronger daily. One party to this debate takes the position that renunciation of violence is possible only for an *individual* who has no responsibility for others; the other side would prefer in principle for all political and social action in the world to follow the rules of the Sermon on the Mount. But neither of these positions really does justice to the gospel.[57]

The thesis that renunciation of violence is possible only for an individual who has no responsibility for others is basically false. It corresponds neither to the practice of the early church nor to the will of Jesus, who thought in a manner eminently related to society. He always had in mind *Israel* or the *community of disciples* which was the prefiguration of the Israel in which the reign of God was to shine. Jesus' requirement of absolute nonviolence was thus directly related to society; it had public character.

Yet his preaching was not addressed to nations, to states, to society in general. Jesus was never concerned with this audience; he did not address them. He did not seek to establish contact with Herod Antipas or Pontius Pilate in order to tell them how they should govern. The most he would have said to people of this sort is what the author of the Fourth Gospel quite appropriately formulated in these words (John 18:36):

> My kingship is not of this world; if my kingship were of this world, my servants would fight, that I might not be handed over to the Jews.

We must note the language carefully. There is no reference to *heaven*. Jesus' kingdom is indeed *in* this world. But it is not *of* this world, that is, it does not conform to the structures of this world.

If Jesus' kingdom did conform to the structures of this world, then even in that kingdom one would have to fight for one's rights — with force if necessary. But according to Jesus, other laws obtain where the kingdom of God is present and where it has already begun to appear. The true people of God, the true family of Jesus, is not allowed to impose anything through force — *neither internally nor externally*. Members of that people cannot fight for their rights with the means of force which are customary in society and which are often even legitimate. Followers of Jesus should rather suffer injustice than impose their rights through violence. They should give to anyone who asks. They should be willing to let themselves be forced. They should not only give up their only shirt, but even their only cloak. They should let themselves be slapped in the face rather than strike back.

It must be stressed once again that with all this Jesus sought not only to express an inner attitude, but also to address concrete practice within a new social order. As Mark 10:42–45 has already shown us, Jesus understood the people of God which he sought to gather as a *contrast-society*. This in no way means that he envisioned the people of God as a *state* or a *nation*, but he did understand it as a community which forms its own sphere of life, a community in which one lives in a different way and treats others in a different way than is usual elsewhere in the world. We could definitely describe the people of God which Jesus sought to gather as an *alternative* society. It is not the violent structures of the powers of this world which are to rule within it, but rather reconciliation and brotherhood.

6
THE LIGHT BURDEN

Is nonviolence in the harsh and uncompromising sense of Matt. 5:39–42 at all viable? The question applies not only to nonviolence, but in principle to all elements of Jesus' moral instruction. His ethic definitely is radical — and not only as far as the specific ethic of discipleship is concerned (cf. II: 3). Can an ethic that radical be lived? A great deal of thought has been devoted to this question, which is generally treated under the rubric of the possibility of fulfilling the Sermon on the Mount.

One of the most influential answers to this question, offered especially since the time of Immanuel Kant and German Idealism, is that Jesus' demands are nothing other than *instruction for the proper attitude of heart*. His requirements, often quite demanding, are said to be really concerned with only one thing, the inner attitude of sacrificial love.

Now it is certainly not false to say that Jesus was concerned with the proper attitude. For him, sin does not begin when the deed is complete, but rather right in the human heart. It is from within, from the human heart, that all evil comes: acts of fornication, theft, murder, adultery, greed, maliciousness (cf. Mark 7:21-23). In the words of Luke 6:45:

> The good man out of the good treasure of his heart produces good, and the evil man out of his evil treasure produces evil.

Jesus described in numerous metaphors how the heart, the innermost part of man, had to be in order.

So the various types of an *attitudinal ethic* do have a valid point. But this correct insight must not lead to considering the concrete performance of Jesus' commands as less important. It can be shown that Jesus attributed decisive importance precisely to "doing" (In Greek, *poiein*). As early as Q, the first programmatic discourse, which Matthew later used as the basis of his Sermon on the Mount, ended with a parable aimed entirely at the actual deeds of Jesus' listeners (cf. Matt. 7:24-27‖Luke 6:47-49). It ran something like this:

> Who is the man like who hears my words and puts them into practice? He is like the wise man who built his house upon rock. When the rainy season set in, the torrents came and the winds blew and beat upon his house. It did not collapse; it had been founded upon rock.

> But who is the man like who hears my words and does not put them into practice? He is like the foolish man who built his house upon sand. The rains fell, the torrents came, the winds blew and beat against his house. It collapsed and was completely ruined.

This parable, which uses the same imagery as rabbinic parables and is organized according to the same structure, presupposes the conditions of the Palestinian mountains. Those building houses did not lay foundations, but rather built on rock. Rain, flood and storm stand for divine judgment, not for the vicissitudes of life. In a rabbinic milieu, the parable would begin with the words: "Who is the man like who can display many good works and who has studied much Torah? He is like a man who . . ."[58]

The close proximity of the parable of the house on rock to rabbinic parabolic material is of great importance for its interpretation, for it makes clear that in Matt. 7:24-27 the teaching of Jesus takes the place of the Torah. Now the Torah was Israel's order of life, its social order. Matt. 7:24–27 must, therefore, be concerned with Jesus' words as an order of life and society for the eschatological people of God. It is clear that one cannot do justice to a social order simply with a pure attitude. For the people of God to exist as a community, its social order has to be put into practice. So the parable says that it would be a catastrophic mistake merely to listen to the word of Jesus. His word has to be *done*.

It is astonishing how stubbornly the theme of *doing* Jesus' teaching can be found at all levels of the sources of the synoptic tradition. Let us note again Jesus' saying in Mark 3:35, "Whoever *does* the will of God is my brother, and sister, and mother." A brief narrative from Luke's special material (11:27–28) is also particularly instructive. In translations it usually bears the heading, "Praise of the Mother of Jesus":

> As he said this, a woman in the crowd raised her voice and said to him, "Blessed is the womb that bore you, and the breasts that you sucked!" But he said, "Blessed rather are those who hear the word of God and *keep it*!"

If Semitic linguistic practices are taken seriously, this passage is at most a very indirect praise of Jesus' mother. Jesus himself, not Mary, is the object of the exclamation of wonder. Jesus is pronounced blessed with a typical Semitic expression. As a polite Jew, he responds to the compliment—for that is what it is—with a compliment in return, "Blessed rather are those who (now, from me) hear the word of God!" The woman from the crowd had of course listened to all that Jesus had said. But, in a way that is characteristic of Jesus, he also corrects the woman's compliment. The important thing, he says, is not to praise him, but solely to hear in his word the word of God *and to keep it*.

Insistence on keeping his word, or God's word, is typical of Jesus. It is also expressed in other texts (cf. esp. Matt. 21:28–32). Jesus was always concerned with concrete practice; in this he stood on biblical, Jewish ground. This aspect of Jesus' teaching is so certain that attempts to reduce his teaching to a pure ethic of attitudes have no chance at all of winning acceptance among contemporary exegetes.

Can the Sermon on the Mount be fulfilled? There is another, very different answer to this question which has been developed in Protestantism (though it is far from being accepted by all Protestant theologians). This answer begins with Jesus' insistence on doing his word and asks who can really love an enemy, refrain from resisting violence, be absolutely truthful and not even look covetously at a woman. Only one individual has ever lived in that way, Jesus himself. Jesus, it is said, fulfilled these requirements vicariously for all others. Confronted with the Sermon on the Mount, others can only fail and acknowledge their guilt. But this is precisely the point of the Sermon on the Mount. It destroys human self-security. It judges us mercilessly and exposes the true human situation. In this way it enables us to expect nothing from ourselves and everything from God.

This interpretation clearly draws from Paul's comments about the role of the Mosaic Law (Rom. 3:20 and 7:7–13), a theological key with which to unlock the Sermon on the Mount and wrest meaning from it. The position just described seems to have theological support in Paul. Its mistake lies in applying in a facile manner Pauline statements about the Law and about man under the Law to the Sermon on the Mount. The Sermon on the Mount stands on the same level as what Paul considers Christian instruction (*paraklēsis*), not on the level which the Law of Sinai occupies for Paul. As we have seen, the Sermon on the Mount in Matthew and Luke has a programmatic introduction intended to make clear that all the demands which follow presuppose that God's salvation is already present in advance as an absolutely free gift. It is all the more true of Jesus himself that the liberating and salvific reality of the reign of God is in principle a presupposition of all demands (cf. Mark 1:14–15).

Jesus' ethical instruction must be interpreted against the horizon of his preaching of the reign of God.[59] Only in this way can the problem of the possibility of fulfilling the Sermon on the Mount be answered appropriately. The question is whether the gospel of the reign of God imposes intolerable demands, or whether the rule of God exerts a fascination which removes the burden and the difficulty from all the demands which it implies. The answer is obvious. The point is made particularly well by the double parable of the hidden treasure and of the precious pearl (Matt. 13:44–46*):

> The kingdom of heaven is like a buried treasure which a man found in a field. He hid it again, and *rejoicing* at his find went and sold all he had and bought that field. Or again, the kingdom of heaven is like a merchant's search for fine pearls. When he found one really valuable pearl, he went back and put up for sale all that he had and bought it.

Jesus does not say that the kingdom of God is as precious as a buried treasure or a valuable pearl. He rather compares the reign of God to two whole stories in which a poor laborer finds a buried treasure and a merchant comes upon an extremely valuable pearl. What is the decisive point of the two stories? It is neither two men's *grim efforts* to uncover a treasure or a pearl nor their *heroic separation* from their possessions. The men do give up everything and act in a radical manner, but they do so without bitterness and without heroism. They behave like men who have made a great *discovery* and have had extraordinary luck in doing so. The attraction of what they have found overwhelms them and permeates everything they do. "*Rejoicing* at his find . . ." is the decisive theme of the double parable. A profound joy, an absorption by the discovery, makes it automatic for both men to sell all their possessions. They have no need to think things over first.

Jesus here depicts the fascinating appeal which the arrival of the reign of God exerts. The reign of God which is now coming to the world, which is actually already in its midst, is so appealing and so fascinating that it is not at all difficult to change one's life and to live from now on enthralled by what has been found.

The parables of the treasure and of the pearl provide us with a key to understanding the existence of Jesus and his new family. Every really good text which a person speaks or writes is always to a certain extent autobiographical. This principle applies also to our double parable. Jesus tells something about the basic experience of his own life and that of his disciples—though with the greatest reticence and tact. It is a story of the blessed, fascinating discovery for the sake of which Jesus and his disciples have given up everything. To do so was not a heroic decision. To live from then on completely under the demands of the reign of God did not make them tortured, bitter or downtrodden. Instead they experienced a new ease and a profound freedom known only to those captivated by truly important things. The burdens of their lives became light. Jesus, or perhaps one of his followers, expressed this basic experience in another text, the so-called "cry of the savior" (Matt. 11:28–30):

> Come to me, all who labor and are heavy laden, and I will give you rest. Take my yoke upon you, and learn from me; for I am gentle and lowly in heart, and you will find rest for your souls. For my yoke is easy, and my burden is light.

A text from wisdom literature, Sirach 51:23–27, stands behind this call. The Old Testament author tells people to bow their necks under the yoke of *wisdom* and to take on its *burden*. He promises that they will find *rest* in wisdom.

It is important to note that in Jesus' day the "wisdom" which comes from God and illuminates human beings had long since been identified with the Torah (cf. as early a text as Sirach 24:22–25). Instead of speaking of the "yoke of wisdom" the rabbis spoke of the "yoke of the commandments" and meant with this expression faithful obedience to the Law.[60] At the time of Jesus, "to bow your necks under the yoke of wisdom" meant to live faithfully and strictly according to the Torah. Only when this background is recognized is it possible to grasp the profound new interpretation which takes place in Matt. 11:28–30. "Jesus' yoke" replaces the Torah; his word, his teaching take the place of the Law of Sinai.

It is said of this teaching of Jesus, which replaces the social order of Sinai, that it is a yoke which does not oppress, a *light burden*. Why? Because Jesus is gentle and humble of heart. Unlike the rulers of the nations, he does not seek to dominate and overpower his followers (cf. Mark 10:42). He is the servant of all. He lives not for himself, for his power and his interests, but completely and exclusively for God's sake, for God's kingdom. In the background of this passage, which must not be taken in an individualized way, there stands once again the kingdom of God as liberating, healing and invigorating reality. The text is certainly not easy to interpret. Yet one thing is clear: Jesus' teaching is not a law which judges us mercilessly and enables us only to say, "God, be merciful to me, a sinner." It is an easy yoke and a light burden which enables us to breathe freely.

No one who seeks to survey the extended and moving discussion of recent centuries about the problem of fulfilling the Sermon on the Mount—only a few of the many attempts at a solution have been mentioned here—can avoid a mixed impression. On the one hand, the discussion, which still continues today, is understandable. Jesus' demands are radical and uncompromising. The Sermon on the Mount resists every effort to co-opt it for a cheap Christianity.

On the other hand, there is the inescapable impression that the entire discussion has proceeded from a much too narrow experiential basis. The question whether the demands of Jesus can be fulfilled is not one which can ultimately be answered by an individual, especially an individual sitting at a desk. Jesus' ethic is not directed to isolated individuals, but to the circle of disciples, the new family of God, the people of God which is to be gathered. It has an eminently social dimension. Whether or not this ethic can be fulfilled is something that can only be determined by groups of people which consciously place themselves under the gospel of the reign of God and wish to be real communities of brothers and sisters—communities which form a living arena for faith, in which everyone draws strength from each other.

Are our parishes communities of this sort? Do they have any consciousness of community, the kind of consciousness possible only when a community knows that it has its own history before God? Are they not all too frequently a collection of many individuals, each one of whom hardly takes notice of the others?

The social context in which Jesus placed his demands and in which they become viable has to a great extent slipped away from us. Jesus did after all turn to the people of God and gather disciples around himself, in order to make Israel the true people of God. It is impossible to discuss the fulfillment of the Sermon on the Mount without taking all this into consideration.

If we really wish to know if the Sermon on the Mount can be lived, we need to ask the groups and communities in which Christians not only live alongside one another but have undertaken a journey together as the people of God. These communities would certainly not conceal from us that in their midst too there is again and again failure and profound guilt. But they would also tell us how the ancient texts about the salvation of the reign of God suddenly came alive for them and how they experienced that all of this is true, that it is taking place in their midst, that the reign of God is infinitely fascinating, that Jesus' burden is light.

Moreover, even Paul could speak of the *burden* of Christians. He wrote to the Galatians (6:2):

Bear one another's burdens, and so fulfil the law of Christ.

He surely intended this to say that where the Christian community is a true community, where it sticks together, and where everyone helps one another, the "law of Christ" can be fulfilled.

7
THE CITY ON THE HILL

It was not very long ago that German Catholics at religious services enthusiastically sang a hymn which praised the church as a mighty fortress against which all foes contended in vain. Only in the last two decades have people gradually become conscious of the hymn's triumphalism. In the new *Gotteslob*, which has been the official hymn book in German-speaking countries since 1975, the hymn is published with four new verses which speak of the holy city on Mount Zion, of God's tent on earth and of the pilgrim people of God.[61] Only the first verse remains as it was:

> A house of glory overlooks
> a great expanse of land.
> Built of eternal stone
> by God's master hand.
> God, we praise you,
> God, we honor you.
> O let us all be safe
> in this house of yours.

The old wording of the hymn can be used to measure how much Western European ecclesial consciousness has changed in a very brief period. No one wishes to defend an *ecclesiology of glory* (*ecclesiologia gloriae*) any longer. In reaction to this, however, a diametrically opposite picture of the church has appeared — formulated initially by only a few theologians, but nesting in the subconscious of a much larger number of people. This idea envisions a completely invisible church, deeply embedded in human society, renouncing its own existence almost to the point of suicide, losing itself in the world in order to penetrate and transform everything. In the background is the image of the yeast which leavens all the dough but which in the end is completely used up. This understanding of the church is marked by a profound embarrassment at the history of the church since Constantine as a dominating institution; it is also characterized by an aversion to elitist and triumphalist thought, a longing for solidarity with all of humanity, and a determination to avoid forever one error of the past, the identification of the church with the kingdom of God.

In part this image of the church is of course correct and indispensable: renunciation of all ecclesial triumphalism; desire for solidarity with all people of good will; rejection of a naive identification of the church with the kingdom of God. The only question is if this reaction against an earlier triumphalism does not threaten to bring about a complete absorption of the church. Is not a serious illness of the present church — the fact that many Christian communities are hardly recognizable as communities and that Christians have increasingly accommodated themselves to the rest of society — being canonized with the aid of an appropriate ecclesiology? Is not a very dubious virtue being made out of the contemporary weaknesses of European Christianity? Is the idea that the church must immerse itself in the rest of society to the point of self-destruction really the right way to transform society? The gospel evidently takes a very different position on this issue. The decisive text in opposition to this view is Matt. 5:13–16:

> You are the salt of the earth; but if salt has lost its taste, how shall its saltness be restored? It is no longer good for anything except to be thrown out and trodden under foot by men. You are the light of the world. A city set on a hill cannot be hid. Nor do men light a

lamp and put it under a bushel, but on a stand, and it gives light to all in the house. Let your light so shine before men, that they may see your good works and give glory to your Father who is in heaven.

At first glance one might think that this text confirms the conception that the church must be so deeply submerged in society that it is scarcely recognizable. Isn't salt absorbed completely into food?

But to draw this conclusion would be to miss the point of the image completely. In reality the text speaks of a store of good, pure salt which is on hand at home and which does not decay (as often happened with salt from the Dead Sea, which contained a multitude of chemical by-products). The disciples, who are the subject of discussion and who according to Matthew represent the whole church, are to be prepared at all times to season the world, that is to make it tasteful and to preserve it from decay. The image probably extends even further. The church should not only make the world tasteful but also sanctify it before God. The following principle (Lev. 2:13) held good for Israel's cult:

You shall season all your cereal offerings with salt; you shall not let the salt of the covenant with your God be lacking from your cereal offering; with all your offerings you shall offer salt.

If this cultic function of salt is part of the background, the text intends to say that the church, as God's holy people in the world, has simply through the mere fact of its existence the task of sanctifying the rest of the world (cf. 1 Pet. 2:9).

The images of the light and of the city would fit extremely well into this interpretation. The two images belong together in Matthew's composition. It is not a matter of just any city, but of the holy city, the eschatological Jerusalem, which the prophets foretell will one day be raised above all mountains and illumine the nations with its light (cf. Isa. 2:2–5). In Isa. 2:3–4 the Torah, which goes forth from Zion and whose plausibility is evident to all nations because it is truly lived in Israel,[62] corresponds to the good deeds of Matt. 5:16. In Matthew the place of the Torah is taken by the order of life and of society which is proclaimed by Christ in the great programmatic discourse on the mountain. In Matthew, however, it is no longer the case that the nations journey to Zion to participate in the true Israel; rather, the disciples will journey into the whole world in order to make disciples of the nations (Matt. 28:19–20). The visible movement is in the opposite direction; but the telling force of the eschatological social order of the people of God, which convinces the nations and is accepted by them, remains constant. "What is meant is precisely that according to God's will Jesus' followers will transform the whole of humanity through their lives. More and more people will join the community of those who orient themselves on the will of God."[63]

The church which is described here is anything but an elitist community, which revolves around itself or cuts itself off from the world. It is the salt of the earth, the light of the world, a city visible from afar. It lives a social order which is plausible to humanity (Matt. 5:16). It is church for the world. *But it is all of this precisely by not becoming the world or by being dissolved in the world; it rather achieves this effect by preserving its own contours.*[64] This conclusion is shown not only by the images of the salt, the light and the city, but also by the context in which Matt. 5:13–16 stands. The passage is immediately preceded by the beatitudes, which surely do not depict an accommodated society, and immediately followed by the new Torah of the people of God, which begins with a description of the better justice.

If Matt. 5:13–16 is read in its context and against its Old Testament background, it is clear that the radiant city on the hill is a symbol for the church as a contrast-society, which precisely as *contrast-society* transforms the world. If the church loses its contrast character, if its salt becomes flat and its light is gently extinguished (or, as the text puts it, the lamp is put under a bushel basket, so that it goes out), it loses its meaning. It will be despised by others ("trampled underfoot"), and society will no longer be in a position to recognize God ("give praise to your heavenly Father").

In the preceding paragraphs, Matt. 5:13–16 was deliberately interpreted as a text of the evangelist. For this reason it was possible and necessary to speak of the church. But did the historical Jesus think in the same way? That he did cannot be assumed without investigation. Matt. 5:13–16 uses older material, but on the whole it is a Matthean composition. Does our text correspond to the preaching and the intentions of Jesus? In any case, extensive connection with the historical Jesus can be established. This will be shown in three steps in what follows.

1. Behind Matt. 5:13 stands a metaphor of salt, which seems to have been used by Jesus as follows (cf. Luke 14:34–35; Mark 9:50):

> Salt is good; but if salt has lost its taste, how shall its saltness be restored? It is fit neither for the land nor for the dunghill; men throw it away.

Whom Jesus addressed here is disputed. Was it a word of warning to his disciples? Its point would then have been that if they ceased to be salt, that is if their discipleship lost its radiance, then their existence as disciples would be worthless and they would be despised by others. But it is more reasonable to think of the saying as a threat directed against Israel. Its point would then be that if Israel ceased to be salt, that is, if it no longer corresponded to its responsibility of being a holy people, if it did not do the will of God at the decisive moment, it would forfeit its existence as God's people. It would be cast out and trodden underfoot by the nations. With a metaphor of this sort, which has been passed on in isolation from its original context, it is hardly possible to determine now which of the two possible interpretations is correct. But this question is really not that decisive. However the image of salt is interpreted, it refers in any case to a *contrast function for others*. The salt must have strength to season others. It does not make much difference whether Jesus said that of Israel or of his community of disciples. Matthew had good reason to relate the saying to the true Israel.

2. Behind Matt. 5:14b seems to stand an older saying which the evangelist combined with a word about light (cf. Mark 4:21; Luke 8:16; 11:33). It read as follows:

> A city set on a hill cannot be hid.

Though formulated as a general *principle of everyday experience*, this saying is scarcely conceivable without the theology of

Zion which is present in the Old Testament and in early Judaism. The presence of the motif of the *pilgrimage of the nations* in Jesus' preaching (cf. I: 5) confirms this point. If this motif does stand in the background, the saying about the city on the hill must be interpreted in the light of Jesus' preaching of the reign of God. As far as Jesus is concerned, the rule of God certainly no longer lies in an absolute future; it is already breaking into the present. In the same way, it is impossible for the eschatological city of God to be an absolutely future reality. It shows itself already in the group of disciples who follow Jesus. Together with Jesus, the disciples are already the city on the hill. This is the presupposition of the saying preserved in Matt. 5:14b. But as it is formulated in this text, the saying also presupposes a situation in which questions and doubts have been raised. "Is this small, unimposing circle of disciples really the eschatological Israel, the city on the hill of which the prophets spoke? The reality falls far short of the promise!" Jesus could have responded to objections of this sort with the general principle of experience contained in Matt. 5:14b. "Even if the beginnings are small and unimposing, nonetheless the city of God has already begun to shine forth. *And a city set on a hill cannot remain hidden.* So fear not, the radiance of the city will indeed be noticed." For Jesus to formulate a principle of general experience along the lines of Matt. 5:14b would presuppose on the one hand his conviction that the holy city had already begun to shine in the movement of gathering which he had initiated, and on the other hand questions and doubts on the part of his listeners, perhaps even on the part of the disciples themselves.

3. A very similar situation is presupposed by the so-called "parables of growth," which offer important confirmation for our interpretation of Matt. 5:14b. Contained in this category are the parables of the *sower* (Mark 4:3–9), of the *seed which grows automatically* (Mark 4:26–29), the *mustard seed* (Mark 4:30–32), and the *leaven* (Luke 13:20–21). In all of these parables a small, unimposing or even fragile start is contrasted with a wonderfully rich and glorious ending. The farmers bring in a great harvest; the small bit of yeast leavens seventy-five pounds of dough; a bush a yard high, in whose shade birds nest, grows from a tiny mustard

seed. Jesus told the parables of growth because he encountered questions and doubts. People must have objected that what he and his disciples were about had nothing to do with the reign of God, that when God's rule arrived, all Israel would be transformed, the Gentiles would be expelled from the land, and all would be glorious. To such objections Jesus may have retorted: "Just as surely as a rich harvest results in your gardens and fields from a small beginning, so too will the full glory come from what your eyes now see and your ears now hear (cf. Luke 10:23–24). The reign of God is already in your midst (cf. Luke 17:21), and no one can impede God's work. The radiance of the eschatological city of God shines already, and no one can destroy it. Fear not: its radiance will not remain hidden."

Our interpretation, which brings Matt. 5:14b and the parables of growth into close proximity to one another, does presuppose that according to Jesus the reign of God is not present in isolation only in his own activity, but also in the activity of his disciples, and even in the community of disciples as such. This point should never have been doubted,[65] for not only Jesus but also his disciples proclaimed the reign of God (cf. Luke 10:9, 11). Not only Jesus, but also his disciples, healed the possessed (cf. Mark 3:15). Anyone who restricts the hidden reality of the reign of God to Jesus alone and excludes the disciples from its symbolic presence has neither taken seriously the mission of the disciples nor grasped that according to biblical Jewish thought the kingdom of God must have a people. Rudolf Schnackenburg is quite correct in commenting that "the community which forms around Jesus, the Messiah, is just as much a sign of the present power of the reign of God as are his word and actions, his forgiveness of sins, his exorcisms and his cures."[66] For Jesus the disciples were a symbolic initiation of the completed presence of the kingdom. The early church later formulated this *in pneumatological language*. The faithful's existence in the Holy Spirit was an anticipation of eschatological fulfillment. We must be consistent. Just as, according to the understanding of the early church, all Christians possess the Spirit, so too even before Easter all those in Israel who let themselves be gathered by Jesus are living signs of the presence of the reign of God.

Our historical inquiry behind Matt. 5:13–16 — a study whose scope had to be broadened — has surely shown that Matthew in no way made up the fascinating interpretation which he gave the church in this text. He was able to draw on older traditions about Jesus which already pointed in the same direction. Jesus *did not* speak of the church. But he did gather around himself, in the midst of Israel and for Israel, people who were for him the new family of God, the true Israel, the eschatological city of God. For Jesus, the reign of God shone already in these people; the future kingdom was already symbolically present in them.

In recent decades, it has rightly been stressed frequently that neither the community of disciples nor the church may be equated with the kingdom of God.[67] Anyone familiar with the history of the idea of the reign of God among the Christian churches knows how necessary that emphasis was. But if this corrective shares responsibility for the ever-widening chasm between church and kingdom in our current consciousness, new corrections are appropriate. A decisive element of Jesus' eschatology, one which distinguished him from all apocalypticists, was that the rule of God was already becoming present reality in Israel — visible and tangible, though not perfected. If this is correct, a valid ecclesiology must hold firmly that the reign of God must also be a present reality in the church and in Christian communities: visible, tangible, capable of being experienced, even though not yet perfected. The situation of people at the time of Jesus must also be the situation of people today (cf. Luke 10:23–24∥Matt. 13:16–17):

> Blessed are the eyes which see what you see! For I tell you that many prophets and kings desired to see what you see, and did not see it, and to hear what you hear, and did not hear it.

8
JESUS' WILL FOR COMMUNITY

Here a brief summary is in order before proceeding. Our survey of the synoptic tradition has surely shown how strongly Jesus was concerned with community. Obviously he did address individuals; obviously he did insist that each individual decide in freedom and constantly reevaluate whatever decision was made. But Jesus was not concerned with a collection of individuals; he was concerned with Israel.

After a history of more than a millenium, the people of God could neither be founded nor established, but only *gathered* and *restored*. It was precisely this that Jesus sought. But the eschatological thrust of the concept of *gathering the people of God*, a term now used increasingly in New Testament scholarship to express Jesus' intention with regard to Israel, must be taken seriously. It is not just any movement of gathering and awakening, but the *eschatological* gathering of God's people. The central content of Jesus' preaching, after all, was that with his appearance the time was fulfilled. The ancient promises for the last days had become reality. The reign of God had begun to arrive. In this eschatological situation, Israel had to grasp the salvation it was offered; it had to repent and let itself be gathered for the reign of God.

When the greater part of Israel rejected this call, Jesus concentrated his attention on his disciples more than he had previously. But for him the circle of disciples was anything but the holy remnant of Israel; still less was it a replacement for Israel. It rather represented the whole of Israel, which right then could not be gathered as a whole; at the same time the disciples were an anticipation of what eschatological Israel, fully gathered, should one day be. Even in Israel's moment of crisis Jesus did not abandon the claim on Israel as a whole that he had raised in the beginning with the prophetic sign of the institution of the Twelve.

This complete concentration on Israel, which reached its climax at the Last Supper (cf. I: 7), in no way excluded a universalism of salvation. On the contrary! The conception of the pilgrimage of the nations demonstrates that Jesus saw the role of Israel in the universal horizon of the tradition of Isaiah. Israel was not chosen for its own sake, but as a *sign of universal salvation* for all nations. The reign of God in its final form was for Jesus certainly a universal reality which transcended the Israel of his day. But this did not mean that the rule of God would be established worldwide in one fell swoop. It would not fall from the clouds; it would rather be mediated historically. It would be established by shining forth from one concrete people, specifically Israel, and by thus revealing its nature in the world. The reign of God is in no way something elusive and unattached; it is bound to a concrete people, the people of God. How could the rule of God come to the world without being accepted—more concretely without being accepted by people who in their social relationships could bring to light the social dimensions of God's rule?

Precisely to the degree that the people of God let itself be grasped by God's rule it would be transformed—in all dimensions of its existence. It would become a contrast-society. This in no way meant that it would become a theocratic state, but rather that it would become a family of brothers and sisters, just like the family Jesus had gathered in his circle of disciples.

What was foreshadowed in and beyond Jesus' circle of disciples as the initiation of eschatological Israel was more than an ideal community, more than a society hidden in the heart (*societas in cordibus*). According to the will of Jesus, different social relationships obtain in it (i.e., in the actual circle of disciples) than in the rest of society. There is no retribution; there are no structures of domination. This alone makes it clear that we are dealing with a very concrete social reality.

Jesus' ethic was aimed toward an eschatological people of God renewed precisely in this sense. It was not directed toward the isolated individual, for isolated individuals are simply not in a position to exemplify and to live the social dimension of the reign of God. Nor was Jesus' ethic directed to the world as a whole. A new order of society and of life could have been imposed on the world as a whole only by force. But that would have contradicted the very nature of God's rule. Only one path remained opened: that God begin at some place in the world, in one people, to create something new. When this people remained unmoved, God began with an even smaller group, the new family of disciples gathered around Jesus.

But is the picture which we have developed in the first two units of this book accurate? That question is ultimately decided by whether or not it is possible to incorporate all the texts of the synoptic tradition into this picture without doing violence to them.

There is also a second criterion. How did the early church, at whose beginning stood eyewitnesses and immediate followers of Jesus, act with regard to community? Its practice and its self-understanding are the oldest and best interpretation now available to us of what Jesus intended. We shall therefore proceed to investigate the early church (III). Obviously, a comprehensive presentation of the self-understanding of the New Testament communities is not possible within the framework of this book. All we can do is to take samples in places whose particular importance is evident from what we have already seen (I and II).

III

The New Testament Communities in the Discipleship of Jesus

1
THE CHURCH AS THE PEOPLE OF GOD

The disciples' self-understanding after Easter was manifested first of all in their *conduct*. It can be determined from their concrete actions. The most striking event is that the disciples left Galilee, even though the first Easter appearances took place there, assembled in Jerusalem and remained in the capital. The Christian movement spread from Jerusalem, not from Galilee. It was centered in Jerusalem for a number of years. Its earliest community developed in Jerusalem, not in Galilee.

The reason for this striking action of the disciples was their eschatology. They were convinced that they stood in the midst of the last things. As a result, they awaited the definitive revelation of the reign of God in Jerusalem, the place where, according to Jewish belief, the last events would run their course.[68]

Precisely because the disciples interpreted their own existence *eschatologically*, they faced that task of summoning once again the whole of Israel to conversion. Since the parousia of the Son of Man was expected momentarily, the conversion of the people of God was the most urgent command. The Acts of the Apostles depicts the Christian preaching of repentance to unbelieving Israel paradigmatically in four discourses of the apostles (Acts 2:14–40; 3:12–26; 4:8–12; 5:29–32). Although the structure of these addresses comes from the author of Acts, there is no reason to doubt the fact of post-Easter preaching of repentance to Israel.

The concern which the community of disciples had for Israel is also shown by the phenomenon of early Christian baptism (cf. Acts 2:38–42). This baptism was considered an eschatological sacrament for Israel. The people of God was to be sealed in preparation for the coming end, in order to enable it to endure the judgment of the Son of Man. The situation of John's baptism was picked up under new conditions. Early Christian baptism also served the eschatological gathering and preparing of Israel.[69]

Another phenomenon also throws light on the self-understanding of the early church. The circle of the Twelve was reconstituted after the departure of Judas Iscariot by the election of a new member (cf. Acts 1:15–26). This addition can be understood only on the basis of the original function of the Twelve. They were eschatological witnesses *for* or *against* Israel (cf. I: 2). The moment that people were once again offered the possibility of repentance, on the basis of Jesus' atoning death, it was necessary for the Twelve to become "symbolic" again, that is to be complete in its reference to the twelve-tribe people.[70]

The reconstitution of the Twelve, the offer of baptism and the return of the disciples to Jerusalem establish that *the eschatological gathering of Israel, initiated by Jesus, was continued by the post-Easter community of disciples in faithfulness to Jesus.* But the movement aimed at the gathering of Israel now stood within the framework of the new possibility of repentance established by Jesus' atoning death. The changes which Jesus' death had brought about in the salvific situation must not be ignored in considering the movement of gathering. From now on the situation of Israel was marked by Jesus' sacrifice of his life for the people of God. In this changed situation it was no longer sufficient to preach the *kingdom of God* as Jesus did. Now *Jesus' death* also had to be preached as the basis of the possibility of new repentance on Israel's part. The new salvific situation was manifested very dramatically in early Christian baptism. The early community drew on John's baptism, but performed its own baptism "in the name of Jesus" (cf. Acts 2:38); the baptized Israelite was drawn into the salvation given and established in Jesus. The movement of gathering which Jesus has initiated thus continued, but it continued under a *christological* sign.

The early church was well aware of the implications of this practice, so significant from a theological perspective. It shows that the community in no way saw itself as a *sect* distinguished from Israel only through its concrete messianic faith and otherwise fully absorbed by Judaism. The renewed intention of gathering Israel presupposes that the community of disciples saw itself as the *true Israel*. This is also clear from two self-designations which can be traced back as far as the earliest community in Jerusalem.

The Christian community in Jerusalem called itself the "*ekklēsia* of God" (cf. 1 Cor. 15:9; Gal. 1:13). In Greek, *ekklēsia* meant a public assembly, the popular assembly of the political community. But in many texts, including some important ones, the Septuagint had used *ekklēsia* to translate *qahal*, the assembly before Yahweh of the Old Testament people of the covenant. Deut. 23:2–9 and the history of its early Jewish interpretation are especially important. Here *ekklēsia* is understood as the true people of God, separated from all unholiness and impurity. If the earliest Christian community called itself the "*ekklēsia* of God" against this background, it must have seen itself as the chosen people of God, the true Israel.[71]

Closely related to *ekklēsia* is the concept of "the saints," which also reaches back to the time of the earliest community in Jerusalem (cf. especially Acts 9:13; Rom. 15:25). This concept, already fixed as a technical term, was found and applied to *ekklēsia*. The term had been used since Daniel 7 to refer to the eschatological people of God.[72]

We do not know exactly when the disciples in Jerusalem first referred to themselves as the "saints" and as the "*ekklēsia* of God." But both terms must go back to the early days of the initial community in Jerusalem, since they are connected with the post-Easter movement of gathering which has been described above. Both terms betray an extraordinary self-consciousness. As early as shortly after Easter, this community understood itself as the true Israel, the eschatological people of God. A self-consciousness of this sort would be inconceivable had Jesus not previously appeared with the claim of gathering Israel in view of the approaching reign of God.

Another phenomenon is at least as noteworthy as the early

church's immediate appropriation of the idea of the people of God. The idea of the people of God was retained even in the historical phase in which the early communities were opened to the nations by the acceptance of uncircumcised pagans, resulting in a single church *of Jews and Gentiles*. Not only the Jewish Christian communities in Palestine but also the new mission communities, in which Gentile Christians were soon a majority, considered themselves the people of God.

Theological reflection on this extraordinary phenomenon was primarily the work of Paul. He reflected on the question of Gentile Christians belonging to the people of God chiefly under the rubric of descent from Abraham (cf. Romans 4; Galatians 3). Paul presupposed as self-evident that anyone who wished to participate in salvation must belong to the people of God, must be the "seed of Abraham." But how did one become Abraham's seed, Abraham's descendant? It was not enough to be circumcised, nor simply to observe the Law of Sinai. To become Abraham's seed it was necessary to *believe* as Abraham did. All who believe in Christ are the true descendants of Abraham, the true people of God.

It is astonishing how thoroughly Pauline theology is permeated by concepts which are strictly related to the idea of the people of God and which can be understood only when that is recognized.[73] The privileges of Israel belong to all who believe in Christ, without distinction between Jewish and Gentile Christians. Abraham is their father (Rom. 4:12); they are his heirs (Gal. 3:29); they are the children of the promise (Gal. 4:28); they are the elect (Rom. 8:33); they are the beloved (Rom. 1:7); they are the children, the sons of God (Rom. 8:16; Gal. 3:26).

It is necessary to remember with regard to all these concepts that Paul did not understand them in a diffuse individualistic sense. Without exception they belong to the field of imagery of the "people of God." The reference to being God's children must not, for example, be equated with the Stoic idea that all human beings are children of God. What is meant is rather a relationship which according to Jewish beliefs belongs only to the people of God and its members:

Beloved (of God) are the Israelites, for they have been called children of God. A special love has been made known to them, that they might be called children of God, for it is written: "You are the sons of the Lord your God" Deut. 14:1) (Rabbi Akiba, *Aboth* III.15).

But Paul's consistent broadening of the honorary titles of the old people of God to apply to the church of Jews and Gentiles is much more comprehensive than this. Believers in Christ stand under the new, eschatological covenant of God (2 Cor. 3:6); their countenance reflects the glory of the Lord, the glowing radiance of his powerful presence which accompanied the fathers of Israel through the desert and then found its final resting place in the temple (2 Cor. 3:18); the communities of those who believe in Christ are the temple of God, filled with the Holy Spirit (1 Cor. 3:16); they are God's plantation (1 Cor. 3:5–9), God's building (1 Cor. 3:9). They are even the true circumcision (Phil. 3:3), for circumcision is something that happens in the heart through the Spirit (Rom. 2:29).

Paul never directly calls the church the "true Israel"— he would have had to speak of "Israel according to the Spirit." But the content of that phrase is nevertheless constantly expressed indirectly in his writings. The same is true of the authors of other books of the New Testament. Anyone who addresses Christians as "the twelve tribes in the Dispersion" (James 1:1) understands the church as the true Israel of God.

It is surely not necessary to continue with observations of this sort. But one more point should be added. The *proof from Scripture*, so prevalent everywhere in the New Testament, unquestionably presupposes the conviction that the church is the true Israel, for it announces the Christian community's claim upon Scripture. Beyond this, it expresses the church's claim to possess the true understanding of Scripture, an understanding granted by the Spirit (cf. 2 Cor. 3:14–16).

The Christian communities' claim to be the true Israel also created a problem which must not be overlooked here. This claim inevitably suggested denying to an Israel which did not believe in Christ the role of the people of God and a further function in salvation history.

This theological step with such serious consequences was in fact taken as early as the first century by a number of New Testament authors — most decisively by Matthew and Luke.[74] Matt. 21:43 provides the clearest textual reference:

> Therefore I tell you, the kingdom of Goa will be taken away from you and given to a nation producing the fruits of it.

This disqualification of the synagogue from salvation history was quite problematic in theological perspective (to abstract for the moment from the horrible persecutions of the Jews which it favored). Jesus sought the gathering of the *entire people* of God and held to his mission to the whole of Israel even in his death. His community of disciples was not envisioned as a *substitute* or *replacement* for Israel; it was rather to remain open to Israel and constantly directed toward the whole of Israel. It was to prefigure eschatological Israel, to represent symbolically what really should have taken place in Israel as a whole. In view of Jesus' stubborn claim on *the whole of Israel*, any ecclesiology which fails to work out the permanent relationship of church and synagogue in salvation history must be called into question as unfaithful to Jesus.

Fortunately there is present in the chorus of New Testament theologies at least one voice which holds clearly and decisively to the role in salvation history of the Israel which does not yet believe in Christ. That author is Paul, specifically in the three chapters of Romans which are dedicated to Israel (Romans 9 — 11). Here Paul declares as clearly as possible that not all who come from Israel are Israel (9:6). Only those who believe in Christ are Israel (9:30 — 10:21). Nevertheless, the history of all who believe in Christ remains inseparably bound to the history of the *other Israel*. Paul illuminates this connection from diverse angles.

1. It was precisely through Israel's failure that salvation came to the nations (11:11). It was precisely through Israel's failure that the Gentiles were brought into Israel's history of election (11:13–24).

2. Israel's failure is depicted to the church as a permanent warning. No one who is called may become arrogant; God will spare an unbelieving church no more than he has spared unbelieving Israel (11:20–22).

3. Israel's failure confers a stable, indestructible hope. The church can learn from Israel that God is faithful and that he never withdraws his grace. Despite its failure, Israel remains called

(11:29). It is not rejected (11:1), but forever loved by God (11:28). One day it will again become the true Israel (11:26–27) and then through its salvation it will bring life to the entire world (11:12).

4. In the meantime the church has above all the task of making Israel jealous (11:11, 14). By this Paul means that the church must live its messianic existence so convincingly that Israel will abandon its reserve and come to faith. The unbelief of Israel is thus a permanent question for the church, as it asks if the church makes real in a credible manner its existence as people of God.[75]

Thus according to Paul the church cannot exist without Israel. It is not only that the church, as a grafted branch, lives from the power of the ancient olive tree, Israel (Rom. 11:17). The church also learns from guilty Israel to recognize both the danger of arrogance on the part of those chosen and the irrevocability of God's electing love. Beyond this, Israel alone can continually place the church before the radical question: does it actually live out its messianic existence? For this reason, the church would lose its identity if it were to forget its permanent relationship to Israel.

Now that the full force of the statements of Romans 9–11 has been presented, this section may be summarized. After Easter, the disciples resumed the gathering of Israel which had begun with Jesus. Taking seriously Jesus' idea of the circle of disciples as the prefiguration of eschatological Israel, they understood themselves as the true Israel. When the church finally stood in danger of disqualifying unbelieving Israel from salvation history, Paul worked out the permanent relationship of church and synagogue and in this way unerringly held fast to the ordering of the community of disciples to the whole of Israel, along the lines of Jesus' thought.

2
THE PRESENCE OF THE SPIRIT

The early church's understanding of itself as the true Israel was not an ideological claim unsupported by reality. It was supported by a history of concrete experiences: Jesus' own movement of gathering, which had led to division in Israel, and above all the overpowering manifestations of the Spirit, which had occurred abruptly in the post-Easter community. According to Scripture, the coming of God's Spirit is an eschatological phenomenon. The Spirit is described as *God's gift to the eschatological community*, and even as God's power which truly creates eschatological Israel (cf. Isa. 32:15; Ezek. 11:19; 36:26-27; 37:14; Joel 3:1-2). The moving and profoundly unsettling experiences of the Spirit must have deepened the awareness, already established by Jesus, that the eschatological fulfillment was taking place, that the true people of God was being assembled in their midst. It is no accident that Luke (Acts 2:17-19) cites Joel 3 (in slightly altered form) in a prominent part of his description of the Pentecost events:

> And in the last days it shall be, God declares, that I will pour out my Spirit upon all flesh, and your sons and your daughters shall prophesy, and your young men shall see visions, and your old men shall dream dreams; yea, and on my menservants and my maidservants in those days I will pour out my Spirit; and they shall prophesy. And I will show wonders in the heaven above and signs on the earth beneath.

In all likelihood, this text was used at a very early stage to interpret the charismatic phenomena (prophecy, visions, healings) occurring within the community as gifts of the Spirit to the true, eschatological Israel. It is impossible to discuss the self-understanding of the early church without considering its consciousness of the living presence of the Spirit in its midst. The early church experienced the Spirit in a variety of ways. In what follows, only one particular type of charismatic event, healings, will be discussed. In our context, we are not seeking to provide a comprehensive description of the early church, but only to examine its faithfulness to Jesus and its continuity with him.

We have already seen (I: 3) that healings of the sick cannot be eliminated from Jesus' life. They stand in close connection to his preaching of the kingdom. The rule of God comes not only in word, but also in deed. It grasps the whole of our existence; we never exist as isolated individuals. The society which surrounds us is part of us. For this reason, Jesus' healing miracles cannot be seen solely as actions on behalf of individuals. They are always concerned with the people of God. Many diseases are curable only if the environment of the sick person is also healed. An individual's illness is always the manifest wound of a sick society. The linking of disease and milieu is especially apparent in instances of possession, which are in all probability mostly time-conditioned psychosomatic objectifications of the compulsions and inhumanities of a diseased society.[76] When the reign of God becomes present, its healing power must not only reach deeply into human corporeality but also extend deeply into the social dimension of human existence. It must free people for new community. It must liberate from the isolating and destroying demons of a sick society. It must free people from possession.

Only from this perspective can the mixture of preaching and therapy in Jesus' life be truly understood. As Luke 9:1–2 reports, he sent the Twelve not only to preach, but also to heal:

> And he called the twelve together and gave them power and authority over all demons and to cure diseases, and he sent them out to preach the kingdom of God and to heal.

The fascinating thing is that this linking of preaching and healing was preserved in the early church. After Luke depicts the first public appearance of the apostles of Pentecost — right after Peter's major address is completed — he appends a summary: "and fear came upon every soul; and many wonders and signs were done through the apostles" (Acts 2:43). Following this summary, Luke immediately portrays a specific miracle by way of illustration, the healing of the cripple in the Temple by Peter and John (Acts 3:1–10).

According to Luke, not only the apostles but all the great preachers worked wonders: Stephen (6:8), Philip (8:6–8, 13), Barnabas (15:12) and Paul (13:6–12; 14:3, 8–18; 16:16–18; 19:11–12; 20:7–12; 28:1–6, 8–10). The Acts of the Apostles are filled with miracle stories and summary notices of the miraculous activity of the preachers. The healings and exorcisms, which Luke is able to draw from diverse traditions, support the preaching as "accompanying legitimating signs."[77] The show the irresistible power of the gospel, which no one can impede. But they also show that the gospel is a liberating and healing power. While unbelieving Israel is unable to produce wonders (Acts 19:13–16), miracles abound in the true people of God (cf. also Acts 5:12–16; 9:17–19, 32–35, 36–43).

Luke's telling of these stories is not a later embellishment, a romanticized picture of the church's infancy. The author of Hebrews, who was completely independent of Luke, saw things in exactly the same way. Right at the beginning of the epistle he warns his readers not to disregard the gospel through which they have come to believe. Then (Heb. 2:3–4) he speaks of this gospel as follows:

> How shall we escape (God's judgment) if we neglect such a great salvation? It was declared at first by the Lord, and it was attested to us by those who heard him, while God also bore witness by signs and wonders and various miracles and by gifts of the Holy Spirit distributed according to his own will.

According to Hebrews as well as Luke, miracles belong to the apostolic preaching as accompanying signs (cf. also Mark 16:20). They witness to the truth of the gospel. The author of Hebrews is not thinking only of an extrinsic, in a sense *juridical*, confirmation of the message. The wonders which accompany the gospel also make clear that God's "salvation" (2:3) is now real, a tangible reality. The community can already taste the powers of the age to come (Heb. 6:5).

Paul shows how widespread the ideas of Acts and Hebrews were in the early church. He never says anything critical about miracles. Instead he automatically presupposes that wherever a Christian community lives on the basis of the gospel, miraculous powers exist. For Paul, *charisms of healing* are just as evidently present in a community as charisms of prophecy or leadership. As he writes in 1 Cor. 12:28 (cf. also 12:9–10):

> And God has appointed in the church (*ekklēsia*) first apostles, second prophets, third teachers, then workers of miracles, then healers, helpers, administrators, speakers in various kinds of tongues.

When a community accepts the gospel, a new reality, reaching deeply into the corporal dimension, is set free. Paul is therefore convinced that wonders are a constitutive part of preaching the gospel (cf. 1 Cor. 2:4–5; 2 Cor. 12:12; 1 Thess. 1:5). J. Jervell has quite correctly pointed out that this aspect of Pauline missionary activity is generally overlooked or even suppressed.[78] The contemporary picture of Paul is one of the apostle as a man of the *word alone*. The historical reality was quite different. At the end of

Romans (15:17–19), Paul looks back at his apostolic activity in the East and mentions — almost in passing reference to something self-evident — the wonders which everywhere accompanied his preaching of the word:

> In Christ Jesus, then, I have reason to be proud of my work for God. For I will not venture to speak of anything except what Christ has wrought through me to win obedience from the Gentiles, by word and deed, by the power of signs and wonders, by the power of the Holy Spirit, so that from Jerusalem and as far round as Illyricum I have fully preached the gospel of Christ.

The Letter to the Galatians is also instructive. In Gal. 3:5 Paul asks if the Galatians have received salvation by *following the law* or by *accepting the gospel*. He is able to presuppose without discussion that the Galatians have in fact received salvation. How do the Galatians know that salvation is present among them? Through the Spirit that they have received. And how do they know that they have received the Spirit? Through the wonders that have taken place and still are taking place in their midst. As Paul writes (Gal. 3:1–5):

> O foolish Galatians! Who has bewitched you, before whose eyes Jesus Christ was publicly portrayed as crucified? Let me ask you only this: Did you receive the Spirit by works of the law, or by hearing with faith? Are you so foolish? Having begun with the Spirit, are you now ending with the flesh? Did you experience so many things in vain?— if it really is in vain. Does he who supplies the Spirit to you and works miracles among you do so by works of the law, or by hearing with faith?

Galatians 3:1–5 expresses a perspective which is extremely important for us. *Miracles in the communities are not to be described only as accompanying legitimating signs of the preaching of the gospel, but also as signs of the presence of the Spirit.* These two realities are obviously intimately connected, for it is faith in the gospel which confers the Spirit. Yet it is nonetheless necessary to emphasize the inner connection between the presence of the Spirit and the wonders which occur in the communities. This shows anew how faithfully the basic elements of Jesus' public activity were perpetuated in the early church. How was this so?

The characteristic element of Jesus' preaching lies in the fact that the eschatological events are no longer located solely in the future. The reign of God is already breaking in. It is already present to the eyes of those who grasp the signs of the times. As Luke 11:20 indicates (cf. also 17:21), its presence is shown above all in Jesus' miracles of healing:

> But if it is by the finger of God that I cast out demons, then the kingdom of God has come upon you.

We can even say as a rule that whenever Jesus speaks of the *presence* of the reign of God he has his mighty deeds and wonders in mind. The presence of the kingdom manifests itself for Jesus above all in the liberation of those afflicted by illness and possession.

Did the early church preserve the decisive characteristic of Jesus' preaching, the idea that the eschatological events had already begun, that the longed for salvation is already becoming present? The answer is an unqualified Yes. The New Testament communities held firmly to the tension between the *already* of the presence of salvation and the *not yet* of the perfection still awaited. The early church rarely spoke of the presence of the *reign of God* (but cf. Rom. 14:17; 1 Cor. 4:20). The decisive experience in which it really grasped the presence of the gift of salvation was the experience of the *Spirit*. God's eschatological Spirit had already been poured out; he was already active in the communities in a multiplicity of charisms. Where Jesus spoke of the presence of the reign of God, the early church spoke of the presence of the Spirit. The language thus changed as a result of the experience after Easter. But the basic line of Jesus' message was continued. The future of eschatological salvation had already begun.

It was thus no accident that Jesus' wonders were perpetuated in the early church by the miracles of preachers and charismatics. And it was above all no accident that they were described as wonders *in the power of the Spirit* (cf. Acts 2; 13:9; 1 Cor. 12:9–10; Gal. 3:5). Signs and wonders belong to the essence of the New Testament communities, just as they were essential to the preaching of Jesus. When God's salvation became present, disease and possession had to yield.

Christian communities today would do well to reflect on why wonders no longer occur in their midst — or why no one speaks of the wonders which do occur. Of course we have to speak of miracles today in a much more nuanced way than the early Christians did. We also have to realize that there is a historically conditioned structural change in the procedural occurrence of miracles. A concrete healing is always in part the unconscious psychosomatic structuring of a very particular expectation, influenced by the age and milieu in which it happens. Nonetheless, when Christian communities are again transformed into true communities, wonders will begin anew.

3

**THE ELIMINATION OF
SOCIAL BARRIERS**

In the previous section we encountered Joel 3:1–5. This text evidently played an important role in the early church's self-understanding. It is highly unlikely that Luke was the first to use it to interpret the Pentecost events. Joel 3:1–5 could have mediated to the earliest community the definitive insight that the ecstatic and prophetic phenomena—which had been occurring abruptly in its midst since Pentecost[79]—signified the *eschatological outpouring of the Spirit*. But the text of the prophet Joel not only aided an eschatological interpretation of glossolalia and prophecy; it also made intelligible a *social* phenomenon of which they were becoming increasingly aware. The disciples of Jesus who had assembled in Jerusalem were increasingly becoming a *community*, one in which all were grasped by God and therefore also stood in a new relationship among themselves, a relationship which excluded privileges and discrimination.

Joel announced this new social structure of the people of God by saying that when Israel was revivified God would pour his Spirit upon the *entire* people. All Israel would become a "people of prophets."[80] From then on, being gifted with the Spirit would no longer be the privilege of an individual prophet or a group of prophets. All in Israel would become bearers of the Spirit— women as well as men, young as well as old, slaves as well as the free. As Luke states in Acts 2:17–18*:

It shall come to pass in the last days, says God, that I will pour out a portion of my spirit on all flesh. Your sons and daughters shall prophesy, your young men shall see visions and your old men shall dream (prophetic) dreams. Yes, even on my servants and handmaids I will pour out a portion of my Spirit in those days, and they shall prophesy.

It is evident that the prophet is concerned not only with the eschatological coming of God's Spirit, but also with the conferral of the Spirit on the entire people of God and the elimination of all social differences. As the context makes clear, "all flesh" does not mean humanity as a whole but the people of God, with all its groups and in its entire range. Israel's social barriers will be dismantled by the Spirit; the overpowering experience of the Spirit will lead to new community. This social dimension of Joel's prophecy is not suppressed in Acts 2, but rather extended. It is explicitly stated (through expansion of the Old Testament text) that the servants and handmaids will not only receive God's Spirit, but also themselves prophesy.

Earlier we developed the thesis that the *presence of the Spirit* in the early church corresponds to the *presence of the reign of God* in Jesus (cf. I: 7; III: 2). If this principle is correct, the removal of social barriers in the eschatological people of God (of which the earliest community became conscious by reference to Joel 3) must have begun in Jesus' preaching of the reign of God. The new reality which took form through the Easter experience of the Spirit in the earliest community must have been a continuation of what had already begun in Jesus.

This is in fact the case. It was characteristic of Jesus that he constantly *established community*[81] — precisely for those who were denied community at that time, or who were judged inferior in respect to religion. Jesus made clear through his word and even more through his concrete conduct that he did not recognize religious-social exclusion and discrimination. The reign of God permitted no "classes"; it was in principle open to all within Israel who accepted Jesus' message.

Jesus sought to make Israel a *reconciled community*. He therefore turned to rich (Luke 19:1–10) and poor (Luke 6:20), to the educated (Luke 14:1-6) and uneducated (Matt. 11:25-26), to the rural population of Galilee (Mark 1:14) and the urban residents of Jerusalem (Matt. 23:37), to the healthy and the sick (Matt. 4:23), to the just (despite Mark 2:17) and to sinners (Luke 19:10). We must even say that Jesus took the side of the poor (Luke 7:22), the hungry (Luke 6:21), those mourning (Luke 6:21) or burdened (Matt. 11:28), the ill (Mark 3:1-6), sinners (Mark 2:17), tax collectors (Matt. 11:19), prostitutes (Matt. 21:31-32), Samaritans (Luke 10:25-37), women (Matt. 5:31-32) and children (Mark 10:13-16) — because it was these groups which were denied equality or even refused community in contemporary Jewish society. The words of Mark 10:14, "Let the children come to me, do not hinder them; for to just such belongs the kingdom of God," all too often misused sentimentally, seek to make clear that in God's kingdom all are *recipients* and that when the reign of God arrives no one can be disqualified as religiously inferior.

So much for Jesus' praxis! Before we proceed to the early church, to test if it continued this praxis, a serious objection must first be addressed. Did not Jesus, despite his bold actions which went far beyond contemporary consciousness, conduct himself in a restrictive manner on one particular point, namely in relation to women? He called no women into the circle of the Twelve, and he celebrated the decisive paschal meal before his death with men alone. Did this not seriously depreciate the role of women in the reign of God? And did it not set decisive tones for the later pattern of official ecclesial structures?[82]

Failure to keep in mind that Jesus' constitution of the Twelve was a *symbolic prophetic act* will result in false judgments on this question. The twelve disciples represented Jesus' claim on the twelve-tribe people (cf. I: 2). The earliest community took this symbolic dimension so seriously that it immediately restored the full complement of twelve after the loss of Judas (Acts 1:15-26) — for otherwise the sign would have lost its symbolic force. Now the sign would have lacked symbolic force in exactly the same way if Jesus had accepted women into the circle of Twelve. The names of the twelve tribes are the names of the twelve sons of Jacob: Reuben, Judah, Levi, Joseph, Benjamin, Dan, Simeon, Issachar,

Zebulon, Gad, Asher and Naphtali (Ezek. 48:30–35). In a symbolic prophetic action whose existence depended on immediate intelligibility these tribes simply could not be symbolized by women — at least not in a patriarchal milieu. Had Jesus undergone this risk, he would have robbed his own symbolic action of its luminosity and plausibility.

It is also immediately apparent why Jesus celebrated his last paschal meal exclusively with males. In principle the paschal meal was a family meal. The pilgrims visiting Jerusalem for the feast formed meal communities (*chaburot*) with ten to twenty members; each group slaughtered and consumed a lamb. An association formed for this purpose could consist exclusively of men, but normally women also belonged.[83] But in this particular case, Jesus did not allow any of the women who had journeyed to Jerusalem with him (Mark 15:40–41) to participate in his *chabura*; as Mark (14:17–18*) tells us, he celebrated the paschal meal exclusively with the Twelve:

> As it grew dark he arrived with the Twelve. They reclined at table and ate.

What was the reason for this disturbing exclusion of women? The answer can only be that at the Last Supper the symbolic dimension, which had already played an extraordinary role in Jesus' public life, reached its final intensity. Jesus interpreted bread and wine as his own life which would be given in death. His death is for the "many" (Mark 14:24):

> This is my blood of the covenant, which is poured out for many.

We have already seen that the word "many" refers primarily to Israel (cf. I: 7). At the Last Supper Israel was present not only on the level of the interpreting word but also on the level of sign, *in the person of the Twelve*. It was to the Twelve and to no one else that Jesus handed the bread and wine in a solemn gesture intended to make clear that the sacrifice of his life, demonstrated in the presentation of bread and wine, was on behalf of the twelve-tribe people of Israel. Here too the luminosity of the symbol would have been destroyed if Jesus had celebrated his last paschal meal with an arbitrary number of companions or with a mixed *chabura* of men and women.

If we take seriously these symbolic actions, which Jesus always performed in a precise manner, then it follows from our observations that the absence of women from the Twelve and from the Last Supper has absolutely no implications for the role which Jesus attributed to women in the people of God. Their absence was conditioned solely by the fact that the Twelve represented the tribes of Israel — and tribes simply could not be represented by women, at least not in the Near East at that time.

The role which, according to Jesus, women played in the inbreaking reign of God must therefore not be determined by reference to the symbol of the Twelve, but rather by reference to the composition of the circle of disciples. There it is clear that Jesus integrated women among his students with an astonishing freedom and without regard for the expectations of contemporary Judaism. (Mark 15:40–41) reports at the end of the crucifixion scene that Jesus was accompanied by female as well as male disciples:

> There were also women looking on from afar, among whom were Mary Magdalene, and Mary the mother of James the younger and of Joses, and Salome, who, when he was in Galilee, followed him, and ministered to him; and also (looking on from afar) many other women who came up with him to Jerusalem.

On the basis of additional information, Luke was in a position to modify this list of names. In 8:1–3 he writes:

> Soon afterward he went on through cities and villages, preaching and bringing the good news of the kingdom of God. And the twelve were with him, and also some women who had been healed of evil spirits and infirmities: Mary, called Magdalene, from whom seven demons had gone out, and Joanna, the wife of Chuza, Herod's steward, and Susanna, and many others, who provided for them out of their means.

The older report in Mark 15:40–41 is decisive for us. Its comment that women (only three of whom are mentioned as representatives of the rest) *served* Jesus (attended to his needs) during his activity in Galilee is itself an indication that the passage refers to female disciples. We saw earlier (II: 1) that according to Jewish understanding a disciple *assisted and served* his teacher. Even more important is that fact that Mark uses the verb *akolouthein* ("to follow"), thus specifying the event which underlies the service with precisely the same word with which the language of the early church characterized the life of Jesus' disciples. The only conclusion which can be drawn from this is that Jesus called women as well as men and brought them into the service of the reign of God.

So both men *and women* belonged to Jesus' circle of disciples. According to the will of Jesus, the disciples were the start of the eschatological people of God. How the community of the true Israel was envisioned was to become representatively visible in the disciples. Jesus showed through the automatic integration of women into the circle of those who followed him that *in the new order of the reign of God, which would become reality in the eschatological people of God, there would be no discrimination against women — just as there would be no discrimination against the poor, the unsuccessful, or children.*

Did the early church preserve this program? Paul at least assumed it homogeneously into his theology and even deepened it. He wroted in Gal. 3:26–29*:

> Each one of you is a son of God because of your faith in Christ Jesus. All of you who have been baptized into Christ have clothed yourselves with him. There does not exist among you Jew or Greek, slave or freeman, male or female. All are one in Christ Jesus. Furthermore, if you belong to Christ you are the seed of Abraham, which means you inherit all that was promised.

It is important to see the decisive statement of 3:28 in its context. For this reason I have cited the entire passage. The context shows at once that Paul is not concerned here with humanity as a whole, but rather with the descendants ("the seed") of Abraham; he is concerned with the heirs to the promise to Abraham, with true sonship (cf. III: 1). In a word, he is concerned with the *people of God*, with that people of God which is here specified unambiguously as a unity in *Jesus Christ*. That means that he is concerned with the church. The church is the true, eschatological people of God, which comes to life through faith and baptism. Those who believe in Christ and let themselves be incorporated into the body of Christ through baptism (the text speaks of being clothed with Christ) become a new community in Jesus Christ, a community in which the oppositions which prevail in the rest of society are removed. In 1 Cor. 12:12–13 the theme of the body is developed even more clearly and the motif of the Spirit is added:

> For just as the body is one and has many members, and all the members of the body, though many, are one body, so it is with Christ. For by one Spirit we were all baptized into one body—Jews or Greeks, slaves or free—and all were made to drink of one Spirit.

Just as in Joel 3, it is the Spirit who creates the new order. The new community, which exceeds all purely innerworldly possibilities, can be accomplished only through the abundant eschatological gift of the Spirit. Only in the Spirit is it possible to dismantle national and social barriers, group interests, caste systems and domination of one sex over the other. Religious and social dimensions simply cannot be separated from one another. What happens "before God" in the realm of faith has immediate social consequences in the church. The people of God, the church as Body of Christ, is a *social* reality.

In Gal. 3:28 and 1 Cor. 12:13 Paul speaks neither of the equality of all people in the sense of a general world citizenship, nor only of the equality of all believers "before God." He speaks rather of the "arrival of the new world of God in Christ, which has already begun in the community"[84]—with concrete social consequences for the people of God.

In Gal. 3:28 and 1 Cor. 12:13 Paul draws upon Joel's prophecy and Jesus' praxis of the reign of God with breathtaking boldness. But this is not simply the formulation of a program. The concrete praxis of the Pauline missionary communities stands behind the cited texts (to which Col. 3:10–11 should be added).

There is no longer Jew or Greek. How much Paul struggled to integrate fully uncircumcised Gentile Christians into the people of God need not be shown here in detail. In this regard Paul radically brought to a conclusion what the Hellenists had already begun before him (cf. Acts 11:19–26). He withstood Peter to his face when Peter broke off the table fellowship which he had been practicing with Gentile Christians in Antioch (Gal. 2:11–21). According to Paul, the unity of the church as expressed in Gal. 3:28 was at stake, along with much else, in Peter's conduct. What Peter did was, according to Paul, equivalent to establishing an opposition between Jews and Greeks in the midst of the people of God.

Paul not only stubbornly defended the freedom of *Gentile Christians* from the law; he also worked tirelessly to bring ecclesial communion with the *Jewish Christians* in Judea, who observed the law, to visible expression. For him the concrete sign of this communion was the collection for Jerusalem (Gal. 2:9–10) in which he invested an enormous amount of time (cf. 2 Corinthians 8–9) and which eventually cost him his life. Paul verified with his entire existence that "there is no longer Jew or Greek."

There is neither slave nor free: this statement did not remain mere theory. It is true that Paul never sought to oppose the ancient institution of slavery on a general social level. Not only would he have had no possibility of success but a struggle of this sort also could not have stood within his intentions. What he was decisively concerned with was the community: where it assembled *as community*, where the eschatological people of God was present, the distinction between slaves and free could no longer be permitted. How this worked out concretely is not described in Paul's letters, because the communities already knew what it meant. But the letter to Philemon does give us a point of reference.

A pagan slave, Onesimus, had run away from a Christian named Philemon. Onesimus had sought refuge with Paul and had been converted by him to the Christian faith. Although Paul would have liked to keep Onesimus with him, he sent him back to his master—"no longer (only) as a slave but more than a slave, *as a beloved brother*" (Philemon 16). That Onesimus had in the meantime been baptized did not necessarily change his status as a slave; but since he had become a "brother" to Paul and Philemon, that is a fellow Christian, something decisive had changed. From then on, Onesimus was "fully equal to his master in the service of the gospel."[85] He would participate in the assemblies of Philemon's "house church" (Philemon 1–2) and exchange the kiss of brotherhood with his master during this community's celebrations of the Eucharist.[86] This surely had effects outside the liturgy. Philemon was to treat Onesimus as his "beloved brother"—"both in the flesh and in the Lord" (Philemon 16*), that is, not only in the realm of faith and of the Christian community but also beyond this in everyday contact.

While we learn little from the New Testament about the concrete living of *Christian* slaves with their *Christian* masters,[87] it is clear that the full equality of slaves in the realm of the community was never disputed. Here there seems to have been no material for conflict. If we also take into consideration that the Christian communities of the first three centuries included a surprisingly large number of slaves and that slaves were not denied access to even the highest church offices,[88] something of the new eschatological order of the reign of God does come into focus.

The old objection that Paul was unfaithful to the core of his own message of justification in failing to mount an attack against the slave-holding society of the ancient world and its social structures has recently been revived.[89] This charge profoundly misunderstands a fundamental principle of biblical theology, one which we have already frequently encountered. The final goal is indeed the eschatological transformation of the entire world, but this transformation presupposes that the people of God first lives the new reality in its own midst. Furthermore, when Paul said that *in the Christian community* the distinction between slave and free no longer plays a role this did not leave the social structures of the ancient world untouched. The antisocial and corrupt systems of a dominant society cannot be attacked more sharply than by the formation of an *antisociety* in its midst. Simply through its existence, this new society is a much more efficacious attack on the old structures than any programs, without personal cost, for the general transformation of the world.

There is neither male nor female: this is the third pair of opposites. Is it not evident that at least in this respect the New Testament communities fell far short of the ideal? Did they not generally deny women access to ecclesial offices?

We must grant that wherever the classical ecclesial office — the office of bishop — emerged, women were excluded from the start. The office of presbyter in Jewish Christianity corresponded to that of the bishop, and it is very doubtful that women were ever considered "elders." When the classical threefold structure of *bishop, deacon, presbyter* developed, women participated only in the diaconate — and even that apparently only in the East, not in the West.[90] Exactly when women were forbidden to *speak* in public or *teach* in the congregation is still disputed. The answer depends on whether 1 Cor. 14:34–35 is seen as an interpolation into 1 Corinthians or not. Much speaks against the authenticity of this passage, especially 1 Cor. 11:5. In any case, toward the end of the first century the pastoral epistles insist that public teaching by women is not permitted (1 Tim. 2:11–12). Clear distinction from Gnosticism, necessary for the survival of the church, presumably contributed to this development. In any case it is certain that the programmatic declaration of Gal. 3:28 was not put into practice as early as the second century.

This negative finding must not lead us to ignore the beginnings of the church. Women played a much different role in the church *in the first few decades* than we are accustomed to from later periods. For example, at that time it was possible for women to act as *prophets* without having ecclesial opposition form immediately. The evangelist Philip had four daughters who spoke prophetically (Acts 21:8–9) — surely not in their rooms, but before the assembled community. In 1 Cor. 11:5–16 Paul presupposes without discussion that women speak prophetically in the liturgy. He insists only that they do so with their heads covered (with a hairstyle corresponding to custom?). Beyond this it is for Paul self-evident that the Spirit confers on everyone in the church whatever charism he wishes to grant (1 Cor. 12:11). Why should women not be given the charism of prophecy? For proper understanding of female prophecy in the early church it must also be remembered that prophecy at that time meant much more than foretelling the future. Prophecy was also interpretation of the present, judgment, admonition, consolation, preaching of the will of God, movement of the community to a particular goal willed by God. The broad spectrum of prophetic activity extended well into what we would now call leadership of the community.

The service of *missionary couples* was just as important as the prophetic activity of women in the early church. Here we must mention Peter and his wife (1 Cor. 9:5), Aquila and Prisca (Rom. 16:3–5), and Andronicus and Junia (Rom. 16:7). We are best informed about Aquila and Prisca.[91] They are also mentioned together, from which we may infer that they were both active in missionary work. With their loyalty and willingness to make sacrifices for the Pauline mission, they must have been an extraordinary source of help, so that Paul could say that all Gentile Christian communities were indebted to them (Rom. 16:4). He explicitly calls both of them his "collaborators" (Rom. 16:3). Against this background, it is also significant that Prisca is usually named *before* her husband (cf. Acts 18:18, 26; Rom. 16:3; 2 Tim. 4:19). H. J. Klauck rightly comments: "This finding is certainly not to be understood as courtesy . . . On the contrary, it breaks ancient convention, a fact which implies the special importance of this woman for the primitive Christian mission. She spread her far-reaching activity out from the base of her house community."[92]

Another missionary couple mentioned in the list of greetings in Romans 16 is Andronicus and Junia.[93] Like Aquila and Prisca they were Jewish Christians. Paul states that they had already come to faith before he did—"they were in Christ even before I was"—and that they were "respected among the apostles" (Rom. 16:7*). This can hardly be explained in any way other than that in their case, like Paul's, conversion and vocation were a single event. They apparently belonged to that larger group of apostles which according to 1 Cor. 15:7 had a vision of the risen Christ. For a time they conducted missionary activity together with Paul (perhaps from Antioch), and at some point were imprisoned along with him (Rom. 16:7).

Without exception, the fathers of the church took Junia to be a *female apostle*. Only since the Middle Ages has the name increasingly been interpreted as a man's name, since there was resistance to the idea that in the early days of the church a woman was an apostle and was even described by Paul as "respected among the apostles."

Prisca and Junia can show us that the missionary activity of women in the first century was not restricted to charitable services

or to the family sphere. The mention of Evodia and Syntyche in
Phil. 4:2–3 suggests the same point. Paul describes both women as
his "costrugglers for the gospel." In Rom. 16:6, 12, he says of other
women, Mary, Tryphaena, Tyrphosa and Persis that they have
"labored hard in the Lord." "Labor" is a technical Pauline term for
hard missionary work.[94]

We do well not to underestimate the role of women in Pauline
missionary work and in the early Christian Gentile mission as a
whole. Romans 16 casts a surprising flash of light on an area about
which we have almost no other reports. On the basis of what Paul
says there more or less in passing we can certainly conclude that
he was able to win a large number of women missionaries for his
mission and to make full use of women's charisms for preaching
the gospel. In this respect as well as others he put into practice the
program articulated in Gal. 3:28*, "There does not exist among
you male or female."

That the realization of Gal. 3:28 in the Pauline mission communities was at least reasonably successful depended not only on the
example of the apostle and the charismatic structure of his communities. It was also conditioned by the fact that at that time
Christians still assembled for the liturgy in relatively small "house
churches." As Peter Stuhlmacher rightly observes,

> The significance of early Christian "house churches" must not be
> underestimated. Paul himself had established "house churches," and
> lived and taught in them. For him not only the larger congregations
> but also the "house church" was the place where sociological and
> ethnic-religious barriers between Jew and Gentile, free and slave,
> men and women, high and low, educated and uneducated — all
> quite important in the ancient world — were broken and relativized
> by and in favor of the new binding of all Christians to Christ as the
> Lord (Gal. 3:27; 1 Cor. 1:26–28; 12:12–13). The "house churches"
> were places where the one, pluriform body of Christ, the commu-
> nity of the redeemed, developed from the common celebration of
> the Lord's Supper. Where this succeeded, it was really possible to
> speak without other-worldly enthusiasm of the community as the
> "new creation," that is, the anticipatory sign of the new world of
> God, and of the necessity and reality of a new life (Gal. 6:15–16;
> Rom. 6:4).[95]

4
THE PRAXIS OF "TOGETHERNESS"

We are in the process of examining samples of the New Testament letters to test if Jesus' praxis of the reign of God was perpetuated in the post-Easter church. The previous section showed that Jesus' intention of forming a reconciled society out of the fractured and diseased people of God was continued in the Pauline mission communities in the *togetherness* of Jew and Gentile, slave and free, man and woman.

This *togetherness* must now be pursued further—beyond the programmatic statement of Gal. 3:28. We could do this, for example, with reference to the concept of *community* (*koinōnia*), which was highly significant for the early church.[96] Nevertheless, this section will take as its point of departure a different concept, or perhaps we should say a different linguistic clue, one which allows the reality of *togetherness* to be grasped rather accurately and perhaps even more forcefully than the concept of ecclesial communion. I refer to the reciprocal pronoun "one another" (*allēlōn*).[97] Kittel and Friedrich's ten-volume *Theological Dictionary of the New Testament*, which treats even individual prepositions, does not consider *allēlōn* worth an entry, even though an important part of early Christian ecclesiology can be shown by reference to it. Consider the following list, which is far from exhaustive:

outdo one another in showing honor (Rom. 12:10)
live in harmony with one another (Rom. 12:16)
welcome one another (Rom. 15:7)
admonish one another (Rom. 15:14*)
greet one another with a holy kiss (Rom. 16:16)
wait for one another (1 Cor. 11:33)
have the same care for one another (1 Cor. 12:25)
be servants of one another (Gal. 5:13)
bear one another's burdens (Gal. 6:2)
comfort one another (1 Thess. 5:11*)
build one another up (1 Thess. 5:11)
be at peace with one another (1 Thess. 5:13*)

> do good to one another (1 Thess. 5:15)
> bear with one another lovingly (Eph. 4:2*)
> be kind and compassionate to one another (Eph. 4:32*)
> be subject to one another (Eph. 5:21)
> forgive one another (Col. 3:13*)
> confess your sins to one another (James 5:16)
> pray for one another (James 5:16)
> love one another from the heart (1 Pet. 1:22*)
> be hospitable to one another (1 Pet. 4:9*)
> meet one another with humility (1 Pet. 5:5*)
> have fellowship with one another (1 John 1:7)[98]

Even a quick glance at this list is enough to show that the linguistic structure of *togetherness* is located within the New Testament epistles in sections of *admonition* (*paraklēsis*). The use of the reciprocal pronoun is particularly frequent and varied in the authentic letters of Paul and in the other letters which stand in the Pauline tradition (Ephesians, Colossians, 1 Peter). There is only one exception. In the pastoral letters (1 Timothy, 2 Timothy, Titus), *allēlōn* never occurs in a positive sense — a clear sign that the responsibility of the members of the community for one another, so important a concern of the historical Paul, is no longer a theme of these letters.

In order to illustrate better the rich theme of *togetherness* in New Testament ecclesiology, we begin by taking one particular formula from our list, "build one another up" (1 Thess. 5:11).

One of the most important concepts of the New Testament lies behind the rubric "edification" (*oikodomē/oikodomein*).[99] This later had extraordinary effects in Pietism, though in that context there occurred a development which narrowed the concept in an individualistic manner to the interior religious life of the Christian personality. In contrast to this, Paul thought of *edification* primarily in connection with the local community, in which for him the church was present. A good part of Pauline ecclesiology can be unfolded with reference to the idea of *edification*.

The roots of the Christian term *edification* lie in the Old Testament, especially in Jeremiah. In this book the pair of concepts "build up and tear down" form a standard theme (cf. Jer. 1:10).

God can *build up* nations, but he can also *uproot* ("pluck up") them (Jer. 12:14–17). Above all, it is said (Jer. 31:27–28) that God will *build* Israel into a new community after the conclusion of the Exile:

> Behold, the days are coming, says the Lord, when I will sow the house of Israel and the house of Judah with the seed of man and the seed of beast. And it shall come to pass that as I have watched over them to pluck up and break down, to overthrow, to destroy, and bring evil, so I will watch over them to build and to plant, says the Lord.

The text shows that "build" means *to raise up, to bring to life*, and that it can be related directly to the people of God. This becomes even clearer in the oracle of Jer. 24:5–7*:

> I will regard with favor Judah's exiles whom I sent away from this place into the land of the Chaldeans. I will look after them for their good, and bring them back to this land, to build them up, not to tear them down; to plant them, not to pluck them out. I will give them a heart with which to understand that I am the Lord. They shall be my people and I will be their God, for they shall return to me with their whole heart.

As the opening verses of Romans (1:1–7) and Gal. 1:15 show, Paul understood his own vocation in the light of the call of Jeremiah. He takes from Jer. 1:4–10 the formula of *building up and tearing down*. He received from the Lord the power to "build up and not to destroy" (2 Cor. 10:8*; 13:10*) the Corinthian church. The edification or upbuilding of communities is his apostolic office. Paul distinguished further between the foundation of churches and their further edification. Others were to perform the further development; his real task was to be the first to lay everywhere the foundation, Christ (1 Cor. 3:6, 10; Rom. 15:20).

At this point it is important to call to mind Jesus' intention of gathering Israel (cf. I:1–8). It would seem that the Pauline concept of *edifying communities* is precisely analogous to Jesus' theme of *gathering Israel*. This would mean that Jesus drew more from Ezekiel, Paul more from Jeremiah. Jesus knew that it was God himself who gathered his people (Matt. 6:9). Nonetheless—this is his secret—Jesus himself gathered Israel (Matt. 12:30; 23:37). In exactly the same way Paul knew that the incorporation of the Gentiles is the great eschatological work of God (Rom. 14:20; 15:18; 1 Cor. 3:9). Nonetheless, the edification of Gentile Christian communities was Paul's foundational apostolic task. *Both Jesus and Paul were concerned with the gathering or building up of the one people of God which now, in the last days, was to be established definitively in accordance with God's irrevocable will.*

All of this should make clear that *edification* refers not to individuals who are to mature to spiritual personalities but to the church, which, for Paul, exists in concrete local communities. The matter is put very well by Philip Vielhauer: "The goal of the ways of God is not the pious individual, but the one, holy, catholic church, in the pregnant and radically eschatological sense of the New Testament; it is the church's creation and preservation, its promotion and realization, that Paul describes as *oikodomein*."[100]

The fascinating thing is that Paul speaks only very rarely of his apostolic authority to build communities. He mentions it really only when forced to do so by his opponents, such as those in Corinth (cf. 2 Cor. 10:7–9; 13:10). Paul speaks of edifying or building up the community much more frequently in connection with the *responsibility which all in the community have for one another.*

The responsibility of all for one another is manifested, for example, in the liturgy. As 1 Cor. 14:26 indicates, liturgy in that period took on a variety of forms in which the community could participate and in which quite varied charisms could come to bear:

> What then, brethren? When you come together, each one has a hymn, a lesson, a revelation, a tongue, or an interpretation. Let all things be done for edification.

The practice of speaking in tongues, or glossolalia, posed problems here. The reference is to praise of the great deeds of God in unintelligible ecstatic speech. Someone who speaks *in tongues* during the liturgy profits from what he does—Paul says he builds himself up—but it is of no benefit to others, for no one understands. But someone who speaks *prophetically* speaks intelligibly, and he "speaks to men for their upbuilding, and encouragement and consolation" (1 Cor. 14:2–4). Paul insists on a liturgy structured in such a way that it edifies the community (14:26). Ecstatic prayers are permitted only when they are followed by an interpretation for everyone (14:13, 27–28). Prophetic speaking must take place in turn, not all at once — again so that it will be intelligible for others (14:29–33).

All this makes clear that the edification of the community assembled for liturgy is the task of all those assembled, not solely of the leader of the assembly. (Moreover, Paul does not say a single word about any such leader in 1 Corinthians 14.) A goal of this sort can of course not be achieved without a highly communicative form of liturgy. But Paul's intention is precisely that a maximum amount of meaningful, constructive communication occur in the liturgy. He wants the participants in the liturgy to wait for one another, greet one another, encourage one another, console one another, admonish one another, teach one another and care for each other. In other words, the list, in reference to *allēlōn*, refers not only to the everyday life of Christians at that time, but also in large measure to the *liturgical conduct* which Paul hoped for and desired.

Seen from this perspective, a look at 1 Corinthians 14 is almost a glance at a different world. If Paul was so displeased at glossolalia which destroyed communication, what would he have said of the majority of our contemporary Central European liturgies, in which social communication hardly occurs at all — and where what does occur takes place in extremely ritualized form. Where among us does the normal person *attending* (even our vocabulary is revealing) the liturgy have the opportunity to edify the rest of the community through a word of encouragement, a teaching, a spirit-given insight or a psalm (a new psalm, personally composed)?

It is necessary to go even further. Even ritualized forms of communication such as the mutual kiss of peace frequently meet with indifference or rejection in our congregations. What would congregations today say if they were urged to express peace to one another as was the custom in early Christian communities: "Greet one another with a holy kiss" (Rom. 16:16; 1 Cor. 16:20; 2 Cor. 13:12; 1 Pet. 5:14)?

To be fair we must note that the new form of the kiss of peace has to some extent been received enthusiastically. A longing for a more human, more communicative form of liturgy stands behind this enthusiasm. Both the opposition mentioned above and this longing are signs that much is wrong with our liturgies. They produce being *next to one another*, but not *togetherness*. And that our liturgies repress community is in turn only a sign that much is wrong with communication in our congregations *outside* the liturgy. Communication generally occurs only in a reduced form. The content of the list with which this chapter began is frequently found in the private lives of Christians, but much less often on the level of the Christian community.

Now the earliest Christian communities no doubt often fell short of the Pauline standards (*paraklēsis*). The purpose of this book is certainly not to paint a romantic picture of the early church. Simply reading 1 Corinthians is an antidote for that. But it is not our guilt and our failure that are really dangerous. The real danger comes from the fact that we are no longer even aware that we fall short of what community and people of God are, according to the New Testament, supposed to be. We take for granted our huge, anonymous parishes, well administered but largely without communication, and perhaps even assume that this is God's will. We no longer even notice how little elementary requirements of New Testament community life, such as those mentioned in the following list, can occur at all in this type of parish:

> live in harmony with one another (Rom. 12:16)
> have the same care for one another (1 Cor. 12:25)
> build one another up (1 Thess. 5:11)
> confess your sins to one another (James 5:16)
> admonish one another (Rom. 15:14*)

Consider for a moment the last expression, "admonish one another." Paul wrote to the church at Thessalonica: "We exhort you, brethren, admonish the idlers" (1 Thess. 5:14). The context shows that Paul wanted to protect this warning against misunderstandings and exaggerations. The verse continues as follows:

> encourage the fainthearted;
> help the weak;
> be patient with them all.

But this clarification, while surely necessary, does not alter the fact that Paul considered mutual admonition within the Christian community to be necessary for its life. Rom. 15:14* shows this as well:

> I myself am satisfied about you, my brethren, that you yourselves are full of goodness, filled with all knowledge, and able to admonish one another.

A final text, Gal. 6:1, demonstrates how deeply the prescription of mutual admonition is anchored in Paul's *paraklēsis* (exhortation):

> Brethren, if a man is overtaken in any trespass, you who are spiritual should restore him in a spirit of gentleness. Look to yourself, lest you too be tempted.[101]

Here Paul introduces some very careful distinctions. Each individual (in the singular) should examine his own conscience. But all (plural) are to bring their brother or sister back to the right path. They are able to do this, for they are filled with the Spirit. Once again we see how seriously the fulfillment of Joel 3 was taken by the early church. The whole community has received the Spirit and is therefore both authorized to lead the guilty party to repentance and able to do so.

This practice of mutual admonition was not limited to the Pauline communities. This is shown by texts such as James 5:19–20 and *Didache* 15.3. In Matt. 18:15–17 the procedure for fraternal correction is even regulated as a three-stage process. Admonition should first take place in private; if that produces no results, then it should be repeated before two or three witnesses; finally, if that too is useless, the matter should be brought before the entire community.

The cited passages make clear that the early church did not consider serious offenses by an individual member of the community a private affair for the individual to take care of alone with God. The early church was rather convinced that such offenses weighed upon the entire local church, detracting from the community and weakening it.[102] This conception of sin surely presupposes a very intensive consciousness of community.

A further point must also be mentioned. Proper admonition requires much of the one who admonishes, for instance, the courage to allow *oneself* to be corrected on another occasion, and the knowledge that in a truly fraternal community conflicts absolutely must be resolved, not suppressed or artificially concealed. The courage to admonish others fraternally and the humility to let oneself be corrected are among the most certain signs of the presence of authentic community and of consciousness of community.

Once again, just as with the question of mutual edification, we must raise a question. Does anything like fraternal correction occur today in the average parishes of the major Christian churches? If not, why not? Is it not the reason that we often lack a consciousness of being a community before God, a community that belongs together, whose members are responsible for one another and have a common history of salvation and of failure?

Closer examination thus shows that the apparently insignificant *allēlōn* ("one another") provides a very strict criterion of the reality of community. The list at the beginning of this unit (III: 4) is anything but harmless. It implies a fundamental ecclesiological decision. Behind it stands ultimately Jesus' intention of leading the people of God to true community once again.

5
BROTHERLY LOVE

Jesus promised those who left their families in order to follow him on his journeys through Palestine that they would receive, in this age, a hundredfold in return. From then on God would be their Father (Matt. 23:9), and they would receive in abundance mothers, brothers, and sisters (Mark 10:29–30). As we saw above (cf. II: 1), this is the program of the *new family*. The new family was to encompass all who accepted Jesus' message of the reign of God and thus did the will of God; as Mark 3:35 indicates, it was not limited to Jesus' immediate followers:

Whoever does the will of God is my brother, and sister, and mother.

From the time that Jesus announced his new family a deep split ran through Israel. Families became divided. As Luke 12:53* shows, from then on there stood:

> father against son
> and son against father,
> mother against daughter
> and daughter against mother.

Eschatological Israel had begun, in the midst of the old people of God. Former family structures were eliminated or at least relativized.[103]

The early church remained true to Jesus on this point as well. It continued to practice and to think about the program of the new family. An important role in this process was played by early Christian apostles and itinerant missionaries, who handed on most intensively Jesus' radical ethic of discipleship and sought to embody it in their own lives.[104] They practiced the *tropous kyriou*, "the Lord's manner of life" (*Didache* 11.8). In later generations, the tradition of these itinerant missionaries was picked up and continued by Syrian ascetics, Irish and Scottish monks, Dominicans and Franciscans. The program of the new family was kept alive in the church chiefly through monasticism.

In the beginning, early Christian "house churches" were the place where, in addition to itinerant missionaries and their supporters, Christian brotherhood could be realized concretely. In each city where Christians lived one or more families made their homes available for the assembly of the community (cf. Acts 12:12; Rom. 16:5, 23; 1 Cor. 16:15, 19; Col. 4:15; Philemon 2). The owners of the homes (such as Prisca and Aquila) often conducted vital missionary activity; with self-sacrificing hospitality they made their house both the center of community life and a place of support for Christians who were traveling. This involved not only hosting missionaries traveling on behalf of a congregation (cf., e.g., 2 Cor. 8:23), but also welcoming Christians underway on their own accord, for example for business reasons. Extending hospitality to strange "brothers" played an extraordinary role in the early church.[105] The structure of the new, open family, which transcended its own boundaries in openness to the community, is exemplified in the families of those who placed their homes at its disposal. It was in the realm of "house churches" that brotherhood and sisterhood were lived concretely. When Matthew told his community, "Do not let yourselves be called Rabbi, for only one is your teacher and you are all brothers" (23:8*), "brother" was not only an ecclesiological hallmark of the community (church as brotherhood). Behind the saying stands the totally concrete practice in the communities of one addressing each other as "brother" and "sister." What with us today remains restricted to sects, religious orders, and "brothers in spiritual offices" was obviously in the early church a standard form of address within its communities. One's comrades in the Christian faith were "brothers" and "sisters."

From a linguistic point of view this was nothing new. The use of "brother" as a form of address had been introduced to Israel by the Deuteronomic reform. Fellow believers were addressed as "brother" in ancient cults, at Qumran, and in Judaism as a whole. But though the language was not new, its background was. The brotherhood and sisterhood of the early Christian communities were based on the eschatological outpouring of the Spirit. Experience of the Spirit meant experience of being a child of God, as was promised for the last days (Rom. 8:14–16; Gal. 4:5–7); consciousness of being God's beloved sons and daughters made Christians brothers and sisters of one another.

Addressing each other as brother and sister was evidently not only a pious practice; a spirit of brotherhood was also concretely tangible. Note once again what Paul wrote to Philemon (9–20) about the runaway slave Onesimus:

> I, Paul, an ambassador and now a prisoner also for Christ Jesus—I appeal to you for my child, Onesimus, whose father I have become in my imprisonment. (Formerly he was useless to you, but now he is indeed useful to you and to me.) I am sending him back to you, sending my very heart. I would have been glad to keep him with me, in order that he might serve me on your behalf during my imprisonment for the gospel; but I preferred to do nothing without your consent in order that your goodness might not be by compulsion but of your own free will. Perhaps this is why he was parted from you for a while, that you might have him back for ever, no longer as a slave

but more than a slave, as a beloved brother, especially to me but how much more to you, both in the flesh and in the Lord. So if you consider me your partner, receive him as you would receive me. If he has wronged you at all, or owes you anything, charge that to my account. I, Paul, write this with my own hand, I will repay it — to say nothing of your owing me even your own self. Yes, brother, I want some benefit from you in the Lord. Refresh my heart in Christ.

In our context it is not only important that this epistle offers a particularly concrete instance of the early Christian use of brother as an address. How Paul argues is equally significant. His argumentation rests on his identification with Onesimus. As Joachim Gnilka rightly states: "Accept him as you would me, charge his debt to my account, accepting him will make me happy, he comes as one who cared for me . . . Fulfilling Paul's request would be no more than fulfilling the requirements of Christian love. Philemon is therefore told that he stands in the same family relationships. He too is a brother; he too owes himself to the apostle and stands in his debt . . . As a Christian he is committed to fraternal love."[106]

Even more important than all this is the tone in which Paul writes. This brief Letter to Philemon makes clear something about earliest Christianity that is otherwise difficult to detect due to our lack of sources. It shows the freshness, the sincerity, the goodness which flourished wherever people experienced the new reality of sisterly and brotherly community which comes from the new beginning made possible by the Spirit. The early church's most beautiful word for the new reality which spread in the community given by God is *agapē* (love).

Examining this word more closely will prove especially useful in connection with our topic. When Christians nowadays speak of love and mean love for their fellow humans rather than love for God, or Christ, or a spouse, the word almost always has *universal* overtones. As is rightly often said, love for one's neighbor must transcend all limitations of group, nation, race or religion. Anyone who needs me is my neighbor. The varied factors which have led to this radical universalizing of the concept of love of neighbor cannot be investigated here. Decisive contributions to the process were in any case made by Jesus himself when, in the parable of the Good Samaritan (Luke 10:25–37), he redefined the concept of neighbor, and when (Luke 6:27-28) he called for love even of enemies:

> Love your enemies, do good to those who hate you, bless those who curse you, pray for those who abuse you.

A further factor is also important for our contemporary understanding of love of neighbor: the almost apocalyptic awareness, made possible through modern means of communication, of how many people in the world starve to death each day. The widespread response which religious fasting campaigns (such as *Brot für die Welt* [Bread for the World] and *Misereor* in Germany) have received from their inception shows that there exists a profound need among Christians to help the suffering throughout the world, no matter what their religion. At least in Central Europe, this is now the central reference point for the notion of "love of neighbor." To a large extent, the idea is separated from care for one's fellow believers within the church. Of course this does not mean that there is no longer love of neighbor within the Christian communities. But this love is now seen simply as an aspect of the great universal love directed toward all people in the world.

In view of contemporary Christian consciousness it comes as somewhat of a shock to realize as an exegete that in the New Testament—if we abstract from Jesus' saying about love of enemy—interpersonal love almost without exception means *love for one's brother in the faith, love of Christians for one another.*[107] There seems to be hardly anything else about the New Testament which is as intensively suppressed as this fact.[108]

We should actually be alerted to this reality by the occurrence, sometimes in combination, of such formulas as "love one another" (John 13:34; 15:12, 17; Rom. 13:8; 1 Thess. 4:9; 1 Pet. 1:22; 1 John 3:11, 23; 4:7, 11*, 12; 2 John 5), "love the brethren" (1 John 3:14, "love his brother" (1 John 2:10*; 3:10; 4:20*, 21), "love for the brotherhood" (1 Pet. 2:17*), "love the children of God" (1 John 5:2), "love to one another" (1 Thess. 3:12; 2 Thess. 1:3*; 1 Pet. 4:8*; cf. Rom. 12:10), and "love for the saints" (Eph. 1:15*; Col. 1:4*).

Far more important than this list is the observation that the New Testament letters normally use terms completely different from *agapē/agapan* (love/to love) to designate concern for people outside the church. Since this fact is important we will illustrate it with some examples. The most striking text is 1 Pet. 2:17, where the author distinguishes with particular care:

> Honor all men. Love the brotherhood. Fear God. Honor the emperor.

This is obviously a highly rhetorical construction whose formulations should not be pressed; the author surely thinks that one should also love God. But the fourfold admonition, so carefully constructed, nonetheless shows that a different terminology is suited for conduct within the community (second and third parts) than for conduct which extends beyond the community (first and fourth parts).

1 Thessalonians is also important for our question. 1 Thess. 3:12 is the only place in the New Testament (apart from Jesus' command of love of enemies in Luke and Matthew) where the object of *agapē* also includes non-Christians, those outside the community. "May the Lord make you increase and abound in love *to one another and to all men.*" But even in the following two chapters Paul distinguishes more precisely. When concerned with the church he formulates as follows (4:9–10):

> But concerning love of the brethren (*philadelphia*) you have no need to have any one write to you, for you yourselves have been taught by God to love one another; and indeed you do love all the brethren throughout Macedonia. But we exhort you, brethren, to do so more and more.

A little later (5:15), when concerned with conduct which transcends the churches, he formulates differently:

> See that none of you repays evil for evil, but always seeks to do good to one another and to all.

This striking distinction between "loving" and "doing good' has an exact parallel in Galatians 5 – 6. On the theme of "love" Paul writes as follows (5:13–15):

> For you were called to freedom, brethren; only do not use your freedom as an opportunity for the flesh, but through love be servants of one another. For the whole law is fulfilled in one word, "You shall love your neighbor as yourself." But if you bite and devour one another take heed that you are not consumed by one another.

The command of love, taken from Lev. 19:18, clearly stands here in a context which considers only the conduct of members of the community among themselves. Here, as elsewhere in Paul, the "neighbor" is one's fellow believer.[109]

In the following passage (Gal. 5:16 – 6:8) Paul continues his instructions on proper conduct within the community. Only beginning with Gal. 6:9*, toward the conclusion of the whole admonition, does he turn his attention to non-Christians, those outside the community. Significantly (just as in 1 Thess. 5:15) this takes place under the rubric "doing good," not under that of "love."

> And let us not grow weary of doing good, if we do not relax our efforts, in due season we shall reap our harvest. So while we have the opportunity, let us do good to all – but especially to those of the household of the faith.

The reference to "those of the household of the faith" obviously means fellow Christians. Here Paul considers the community as a family of believers, whose members conduct themselves differently within the family than with those outside. Some theologians have taken offense at this and held it against Paul. H. Weinel spoke of an "ecclesial constriction of love," and H. Preisker of "detracting from the unlimited living fullness of love."[110] It is clear that the apostle is being criticized by these authors on the basis of our modern concept of love of neighbor. But is this contemporary concept also that of the Bible? Before we venture an answer to this question let us first look at Romans 12 and 13.

A new subdivision of the admonition begins with Rom. 12:9. Under the motto, "let love be genuine" (12:9), this section first treats proper conduct with the community. Beginning with 12:14, conduct with regard to non-Christians enters the picture, and from 12:17 on this becomes the exclusive topic. The look outward lasts until 13:7. Within the entire section concerned with those outside the community (12:17 – 13:7) the rubric "love" is never mentioned. We do find the charge already familiar to us from 1 Thess. 5:15 and Gal. 6:10: "Be attentive to the good with regard to all" (12:17*). In Rom. 12:18–21, this is expanded through further statements:

If possible, so far as it depends upon you, live peaceably with all. Beloved, never avenge yourselves, but leave it to the wrath of God; for it is written, "Vengeance is mine, I will repay, says the Lord." No, "if your enemy is hungry, feed him; if he is thirsty, give him drink; for by so doing you will heap burning coals upon his head." Do not be overcome by evil, but overcome evil with good.

Paul here provides his longest explanation of the command to love one's enemies. But in doing this he makes no use of the concept "love." He adheres instead to the high ethical standards of an Old Testament admonition about treatment of an enemy (Prov. 25:21–22), which also avoids the rubric "love," although its content coincides completely with the conduct toward an enemy that Jesus required.[111] The concept of *love* recurs in Paul only in Rom. 13:8–10. As in Gal. 5:14, Lev. 19:18 is cited: "'You shall love your neighbor as yourself'" (Rom. 13:9). As in Gal. 5:14, this can only refer to *brotherly love*, for the passage speaks of *mutual* love (Rom. 13:8*). "Mutual love" presupposes a clearly defined group and stands in contrast to love "for all" (cf. 1 Thess. 3:12). It should be noted as well that in Rom. 15:2 "neighbor" undoubtedly refers to *fellow believer* (cf. also Eph. 4:25; James 2:8; 4:12).

The transition in Rom. 13:7–8 causes difficulties for this interpretation of Rom. 13:8–10. In verse 7, Paul speaks of what Christians owe civil authorities (taxes, tolls, respect, honor). In the next verse (13:8*), he continues as follows:

Owe no debt to anyone except mutual love.

The context (verse 7) and the construction of the sentence would lead the reader to conclude that the passage speaks of love for all human beings. But this is absolutely excluded by the concept of "mutual love."[112] The only possible way to interpret verse 8 is that Paul speaks first of what is owed to all. One must not fail to pay this in full. But there is something else which one can never fully satisfy, with which one is never finished—love. This presupposes a different realm—the realm of *togetherness*, of community. And so Paul changes his point of reference; from verse 8b on he speaks again of conduct with regard to fellow believers.

Thus Romans 12 and 13 also confirm the point that *when the New Testament speaks of interpersonal love it means almost exclu-*

sively fraternal love within the communities. The Johannine literature, in which this phenomenon has always been recognized, in no way stands alone. John's Gospel and Letters simply reflect with particular clarity what is true of the entire New Testament.

If all this is correct, a further question is inevitable. Did not the New Testament communities betray the position of Jesus? Jesus explicitly insisted on *loving* enemies. Should not the apostolic instruction have preserved this terminology? Two points must be kept in mind on this issue.

First, the *reality* which Jesus intended with love of enemy is clearly present in the New Testament letters. The communities are told: "Bless those who persecute you" (Rom. 12:14; 1 Pet. 3:9*), "do not return evil for evil" Rom. 12:17*; 1 Pet. 3:9), "overcome evil with good" (Rom. 12:21), and "if your enemy is hungry, feed him" (Rom. 12:20). In content this is exactly what Jesus meant with love of enemy. The idea of blessing persecutors even derives from a saying of Jesus (Luke 6:28; Matt. 5:44). Men like Paul and the author of 1 Peter simply hesitate to describe the listed forms of conduct as "love."

Second, Jesus' position would be misunderstood if it were defined in an undifferentiated manner as *universal philanthropy*.[113] Jesus stood completely on the foundation of the Old Testament, where one's neighbor is first of all one who lives nearby and who shares the same faith. Jesus did relativize the concept of neighbor by making clear that anyone in need becomes one's brother. But this meant precisely that the fraternal love which has its basic and permanent location in the people of God must extend to anyone who is in need. While the concept of neighbor is thus radically opened, it does not become a "universal abstraction."[114] The constant opening of fraternal love retains its basis in the people of God, which first of all lives out within itself what love of neighbor means. It is precisely preserving this basis that makes it possible to go beyond the boundaries of the community.

If matters are examined without prejudice, the early church was following in the footsteps of Jesus — probably more exactly than we do. The New Testament communities never considered capitulating to naive dreams of "all men becoming brothers" or of "millions being embraced." In a very realistic manner they sought to achieve fraternal love within their own ranks and constantly made simultaneous efforts to transcend their boundaries. In this fashion an ever increasing number of people was drawn into the fraternity of the church, and new neighborly relationships became possible.

6
THE RENUNCIATION OF DOMINATION

Jesus emphatically rejected, as far as his community of disciples was concerned, domination and the structures of domination which are customary in society. In a community of *brothers* no *fathers* are permitted to rule. The rule of God does not imply the rule of humans. Did the early church take seriously this program of a new society without domination? Is it in any case possible to achieve a society of this sort?

One thing at least can be said. The early church clearly recognized Jesus' intention of not founding the true Israel on a basis of human domination; it expressed this intention in an important text, preserved this text, and passed it on. The passage now stands in a prominent place in the Gospel of Mark. It is immediately preceded by the story of a request of James and John, the sons of Zebedee (Mark 10:35–38*):

> "Teacher," they said, "we want you to grant our request." "What is it?" he asked. "See to it that we sit, one at your right and the other at your left, when you come into your glory." Jesus told them, "You do not know what you are asking. Can you drink the cup I shall drink or be baptized with the same baptism that I will be baptized with?"

The scene almost evokes the imagery of a novel. A new king has mounted his throne and begun his reign. He has his highest officials take their places, also on thrones, at his right and left. They are to rule and to judge along with him. James and John were obviously interested in very real power in the approaching reign of God; they wanted to guarantee their place in time before others got there first. The other members of the Twelve understood this quite accurately, and were disturbed at Zebedee's sons.

The text with which we are concerned (Mark 10:42–45) follows this scene. It is a short speech which surely mirrors rather exactly the historical Jesus' opinion of human domination. As the text stands, however, it is a post-Easter composition which reflects on problems of domination in the church:

> You know that those who are supposed to rule over the Gentiles lord it over them, and their great men exercise authority over them. But it shall not be so among you; but whoever would be great among you must be your servant, and whoever would be first among you must be slave of all. For the Son of man also came not to be served but to serve, and to give his life as a ransom for many.

As has been mentioned, the text alludes to problems of domination within the church. The issue is the basic structure of ecclesial offices which are defined in reference to Jesus' existence in service to others. It is presupposed that authority and power must exist within the church. But this authority must not be domination of the sort that is exercised in the rest of society. Elsewhere rule is exercised all too frequently in the interests of the rulers. In the people of God, on the other hand, authority must derive completely from *service*. Within the church only one who abstracts from oneself and one's own interests and lives a life for others can become an authority.

But the text goes much further than this. Although this is not explicitly mentioned, we must proceed from the fact that selfless sacrifice for others also exists in the rest of society. While there are tyrants, there are also rulers who put the interests of the common good first in the exercise of their office. Yet even they must enforce or defend the welfare of society by the use of force—with the instruments of power given them by the law. In the divine contrast-society which our text has in mind, even this is not allowed. The authority discussed here may not compel even what is legitimate and right. All it can do is bear witness and in extreme cases die for its cause. It is anything but fortuitous that Jesus' sacrifice of his life for the many is mentioned at the conclusion of the passage (Mark 10:45). Jesus did not use means of force to advance his message. He did not even organize the movement which he evoked in Israel. He was only a witness, and he made his disciples witnesses.

When others took steps to do away with him by violence because of his message, he preferred to let himself be killed than to answer the violence of his enemies with violence in return. That is Jesus' authority. It is a *paradoxical authority* to the very last, an authority which in its unprotectedness and vulnerability turns any other type of authority upside down.

On the basis of Jesus' conduct, Mark 10:42–45 defines with disturbing consistency every possible form of authority within the church. Nonviolence, renunciation of domination and consequent vulnerability are irrevocably embedded in the church and its offices by the praxis of Jesus.

So the program was recognized clearly. It was recognized by Matthew (20:25–28) and Luke (22:24–27) as well as by Mark. Luke even developed the *ecclesial reference* of the passage more strongly than Mark (cf. Luke 22:26). But did the early church also live in accord with this program which differed so sharply from the customary forms of human desire to dominate? At the very least it did not forget the program. However much it fell short of Mark 10:42–45, it always at least recognized that this represented the point of decision, the criterion which determined if it was really the true people of God, God's counter-society in the world.

Paul above all others was the living conscience of the early church on this point. He possessed a very explicit knowledge of his apostolic authority— much more explicit than some exegetes wish to recognize.[115] Paul was in no sense merely a fatherly "advisor" or just a "charismatic judge" in extreme situations, as K. Wegenast has claimed.[116] In his monograph on concrete individual commands in Pauline paranesis, W. Schrage has shown how extensively Paul issued regulations for his communities *by virtue of apostolic authority*: "The authoritative, commanding aspect must indeed not be overemphasized (cf. 2 Cor. 1:24; 8:8), but neither may it be suppressed by reducing the apostolic directives to tactful recommendation and pieces of good advice."[117]

It is true that Paul was primarily a preacher of the gospel; but in this preaching we encounter God's command as well as his mercy. For this reason the apostle gave binding directives for the moral life of the individual and for the common life of the community with the same authority that he proclaimed the gospel. These directives could even extend into the juridical realms; the apostle could make decisions in the spirit of the risen Lord and could establish laws.[118]

So Paul was well aware of the apostolic authority (*exousia*) which had been conferred on him by Christ himself. But that is only one side of the coin. Paul's exercise of this authority was almost always limited in a distinctive way; it was integrated into the structure of service (*diakonia*). For this reason his exercise of apostolic authority raised no suspicions of dominating the community; it had the character of self-sacrificing service.[119] Paul preferred to come to Corinth "with love and a gentle spirit" (1 Cor. 4:21) than with harshness. He could have insisted in Thessalonica on the weight of his authority "as apostle of Christ," but instead treated the Thessalonians "lovingly, like a mother fondling her children" (1 Thess. 2:7*). He could have commanded Philemon in the "freedom which he possesses in Christ," but prefers to "appeal in the name of love" (Philemon 8*) instead. Despite the grave disputes which he had with the Corinthians he wrote to that community: "We are not lords over your faith, but coworkers on your joy" (2 Cor. 1:24*).

Now texts like this could be just empty words. For this reason it is important that our sources are not limited to individual formulations of this sort. Even the *form* of Paul's letters proves how little he wished to be lord over the faith of the churches. From a literary point of view, his letters are among the most extensive and most personal letters preserved from the ancient world. This results from the fact that Paul did not primarily *issue decrees*, but rather *argued* with deep theological engagement. He sought to convince his communities; he wrestled for their agreement so that they could participate in the decision with the aid of the insight they had gained. Paul took seriously the freedom and responsibility of his communities.

It is not only the first, *argumentative* part of his letters that shows he did not merely decree and command, but also their second, *admonitory* section (*paraklēsis*). Paul's *paraklēsis* is indeed instruction and directive, but it is simultaneously appeal, encouragement, admonition, consolation, invitation, even request.[120] All of this is implied by the Greek word *parakalein*, so characteristic of the second half of Paul's letters (cf. esp. Rom. 12:1). When Paul gave instructions his very personal requests, which came from the heart, always stood in tension with his directives and constantly permeated them.

Even more telling than the form in which Paul wrote is the way in which he treated his coworkers. This can frequently be seen in his letters. Even the word "coworker" (*synergos*) is significant. The word is not only used relatively frequently by Paul,[121] it also received from him a distinctive linguistic twist. With this word Paul designated the men and women who labored together with him in joint missionary activity. In an outstanding study of Paul and his coworkers, W. H. Ollrog has shown that the Pauline form of mission should be described as "collaborative mission"—which was by no means always the case in the early church.[122] Ollrog also demonstrated that in view of his many collaborators Paul made the "common work" (*ergon*) the "core which guaranteed unity," not his own person. Paul himself was "coworker" in this endeavor (1 Cor. 3:9), and he treated other coworkers as mature and autonomous partners, not as his assistants.[123]

Paul's failure and defeats were also part of his praxis. The apostle's sufferings were not due only to persecutions from without, but also to his constant "anxiety for all the churches" (2 Cor. 11:28). In a number of local churches, above all in Corinth, Paul seems to have been only partially or only temporarily successful in achieving his theological conception of community. This was not due only to the fact that after the conflict in Antioch, Jewish Christian delegates constantly invaded his mission territory and disrupted the communities; it came also from Paul's unwillingness to keep his communities immature, which led him to leave them an extraordinarily broad room for charismatic activity. Paul sought free obedience and bound the charisms to the reason of the Spirit and of love[124] — and in doing so undertook a great risk. But this was precisely the risk of authority without domination in the following of Jesus. The church will always find it necessary to choose between the security of bondage and the risk of liberty.

Paul reflected on this alternative more than anyone else. He knew very well that an authority required to renounce domination would very quickly be brought close to the cross of Christ. His apostolic service was realized in weakness, a weakness that, as 2 Cor. 4:10–12 indicates, had much to do with the helplessness of the crucified Christ:

> [We are] always carrying in the body the death of Jesus, so that the life of Jesus may also be manifested in our bodies. For while we live we are always being given up to death for Jesus' sake, so that the life of Jesus may be manifested in our mortal flesh. So death is at work in us, but life in you.

The weakness and helplessness of apostolic existence (cf. also 1 Cor. 4:9–13) is also its power and its strength: "When I am weak, then I am strong" (2 Cor. 12:10). To what extent was this true? Even *service* can subtly be transformed into *domination*. The bearer of authority can avoid this most abysmal of all temptations only by grasping failures and defeats as a co-dying with Christ. Only in this impotence does service become completely selfless and achieve a power able to overcome all obstacles. Only in such cases can a preacher truly say with Paul (2 Cor. 4:5):

> For what we preach is not ourselves, but Jesus Christ as Lord, with ourselves as your servants for Jesus' sake.

It is one of the church's tragic blind spots that it again and again seeks to protect its authority (which is certainly necessary and legitimate) through *domination*. In reality it undermines its authority in this way and does serious harm to the gospel. True authority can shine forth only in the weakness of renouncing domination. True authority is the authority of the Crucified. Paul knew this better than anyone else; for this reason he constantly connected the paradox of his apostolic authority with the paradox of the Crucified and Risen One. It is astonishing how intensely the substance of Mark 10:42–45 reappears in Paul.

Must we go on to add that service of the churches in the impotence of the cross of Christ is by no means merely a matter of *inner attitude* or *proper disposition* on the part of the office holder? It would be disastrous to interpret Mark 10:42–45 and its parallels merely on the basis of an individual or attitudinal ethic. New Testament texts of this sort are always concerned with the concrete *form* of ecclesial office, which must not reflect the world's structures of power and domination.

The temptation to dominate and to force one's way was of course not limited to office holders. Members of the community in Corinth brought legal action against one another in civil courts. As 1 Cor. 6:5–6 shows, Paul was profoundly upset at such actions:

> Can it be that there is no man among you wise enough to decide between members of the brotherhood, but brother goes to law against brother, and that before unbelievers?

According to Paul, Christians are not allowed to take their legal cases before a pagan court. They must settle their legal affairs within the community itself. That is the first point Paul makes to the Corinthians about matters of this sort. But then he raises a more radical question and continues as follows (1 Cor. 6:7):

> To have lawsuits at all with one another is defeat for you. Why not rather suffer wrong? Why not rather be defrauded?

At precisely this point in Paul's argumentation, Jesus' spirit breaks through (cf. II: 5). No struggle for rights is acceptable within the true people of God. Anyone who conducts such struggles introduces the structures of pagan society into the people of God and thus obscures the character of the church as a contrast-society.

Repudiation of *struggling for rights* does not mean that there is no place for *law* within the church. That would be just as foolish as to insist that authority and institutions are not permitted within the church. In the long run such goals would lead to an *invisible church*, which would have nothing at all in common with the New Testament concept of church. It is obvious that there must be law within the church, for otherwise the church would not be the "people of God" or the "body of Christ," a socially tangible "realm of Christ's rule in the world." But in comparison with secular law, church law can be *law only in an analogous sense*. It must in every particular be transformed and relativized by the spirit of Jesus. While it can exclude neither authority nor binding quality, it cannot be supported by institutions which have to enforce this law by means of force. It can only be supported by communities which *unanimously*[125] and *in free obedience* place themselves under such law and live according to it. On a human basis, such unanimity is impossible. But it is possible as a *miracle* worked ever anew by God's Spirit.[126] Where God is at work things suddenly succeed which otherwise constantly fail despite all moral efforts. It becomes possible to keep others in mind, to exercise trusting concern for others, and to find unity.

7
THE CHURCH AS CONTRAST-SOCIETY

The notion of a contrast-society, and even more that of a counter-society, which have been used frequently in this book, have probably met with confusion and even resistance on the part of some readers. They are in fact not biblical concepts. The *reality* which the terms envision fills the Bible from beginning to end. But this reality largely escapes us; we no longer recognize it in the Bible. For this reason we are forced to make use of new terms to make possible the appearance of the reality with which the Bible is concerned, one which is present under the cover of a vocabulary which strikes us as merely edifying and insignificant.

In the Bible the people of God is always understood as a contrast-society. People of God means something different from the national structure in, for example, the time of Solomon or the Hasmoneans. People of God is not equivalent to the state of Israel. But neither is people of God merely the spiritual community of the pious, who await salvation as the quiet ones in the land. People of God is rather the Israel which knows itself to be chosen and called by God in its entire existence—which includes all of its social dimension. As Deut. 7:6–8 makes clear, people of God is the Israel which, according to God's will, is to distinguish itself from all the other peoples of the earth:

> For you are a people holy to the Lord your God; the Lord your God has chosen you to be a people for his own possession, out of all the peoples that are on the face of the earth. It was not because you

were more in number than any other people that the Lord set his
love upon you and chose you, for you were the fewest of all peoples;
but it is because the Lord loves you, and is keeping the oath which
he swore to your fathers, that the Lord has brought you out with
a mighty hand, and redeemed you from the house of bondage, from
the hand of Pharaoh king of Egypt.

The people's conduct must correspond to the liberating action
of God who chose Israel from all nations and saved it from Egypt.
Israel is to be a *holy* people with a social order which distinguishes
it from other nations. In the words of Deut. 7:11:

> You shall therefore be careful to do the commandment, and the stat-
> utes, and the ordinances, which I command you this day.

There are thus two grounds for Israel's being a *holy* people.
First, there is the electing love of God who chose Israel from all
nations to be his own people. But, in the second place, Israel's holiness also depends on whether it really lives in accordance with the
social order which God has given it, a social order which stands
in sharp *contrast* with those of all other nations. This connection
is expressed trenchantly in the so-called "holiness code" (Lev. 17 –
26), in texts such as Lev. 20:26:

> You shall be holy to me; for I the Lord am holy, and have separated
> you from the peoples, that you should be mine.

That God has chosen and sanctified his people in order to make
it a contrast-society in the midst of other nations was for Jesus the
self-evident background of all his actions. The difference between
Jesus and the texts cited from Leviticus and Deuteronomy lies only
in the fact that for Jesus, on the basis of the prophets' message,
everything stood within an *eschatological* perspective. God's past
deeds receded in favor of his approaching eschatological action, in
which he would restore or even reestablish his people, in order to
carry out definitively and irrevocably his plan of having a holy
people in the midst of the nations.

Jesus' movement of gathering cannot be understood at all apart
from this background. It aimed at the true, eschatological Israel
in which the social order of the reign of God would be lived. It is
true that Jesus never called for a political, revolutionary transfor-

mation of Jewish society. Yet the repentance which he demanded as a consequence of his preaching of the reign of God sought to ignite within the people of God a movement in comparison to which the normal type of revolution is insignificant. Think for example of Jesus' call for absolute renunciation of violence (cf. II: 5). This renunciation of violence was not merely a matter of inner attitude; it was concerned with concrete actions. Nor was it merely intended for individuals; it presupposed a group of people who together would take nonviolence seriously. This is even more clear as far as renunciation of domination (cf. III: 6) is concerned. Nonviolence and renunciation of domination can be realized only within the complex of social reality; it is precisely this reality they seek to transform. Jesus' call for nonviolence and renunciation of domination implies the perspective of a new *society*, one which stands in sharp contrast to secular societies marked by the will to overpower and control.

Jesus also spoke bluntly in the "prayer for gathering" of the Our Father, a prayer which incorporates the entire Old Testament theme of holiness. We have already seen (cf. I: 4) that the prayer, "Hallowed be thy name," means nothing other than "Gather and renew your people; let it again become the true people of God." Against the background of Deut. 7:6–11 and Lev. 20:26 we can now be more precise. "Hallowed be thy name" also means "Gather to yourself a renewed people that is truly holy, so that the reign of God can shine forth and your holy name may stand in its full glory before the eyes of all peoples."

Did the early church grasp this intention of Jesus? Did it perpetuate it? Did the church understand itself or, more accurately, did the New Testament communities understand themselves as a fundamental *contrast* to paganism, as a holy people which had to be different from pagan society? This question has special importance since for centuries now the Christian churches have scarcely had the feeling of being in contrast to society. Only sects or mission churches can really grasp what it means to believe in opposition to the rest of society. In the popular Christian churches, a sense of this has broken through only intermittently—for German Catholics in the *Kulturkampf* of Bismarck's day and for portions of German Catholicism and Protestantism in the resistance to the

Third Reich. On the whole the consciousness of churches in Western Europe has become assimilated in a disturbing way to the rest of society and its structures. *Resistance* or *refusal* has occurred only sporadically. Western European Christians are no longer aware that the church as a whole should be an alternative type of society; at most this has again slowly penetrated their consciousness in the past few years.

Things are quite different in the New Testament. There the knowledge that the church is God's contrast-society in the midst of the rest of society found expression in a variety of concepts and even in extended compositions. An example of the latter can be found in Eph. 5:8:

> *For once* you were darkness, but *now* you are light in the Lord; walk as children of light.

In this passage two states of affairs, past and present, are sharply contrasted with each other. *Once* the believers addressed here were "darkness"; *now* they are "light." "Darkness" is a metaphor for their former existence as pagans, "light" a metaphor for their current existence in the church. "In the Lord" means life *within the realm of Christ's rule,* and that, in the tradition of Pauline vocabulary, is the church. A command in the imperative follows the statements in the indicative. Christians are in principle "light," but they must also act in their lives in accordance with what they are.

Similar constructions are so common in the epistles that it is possible to speak of a fixed pattern,[127] which has been called the "Once and Now" pattern.[128] It is not always worded as briefly as in Eph. 5:8; often it is pursued at greater length and in more detail. Titus 3:3–6 provides an example:

> For we ourselves were *once* foolish, disobedient, led astray, slaves to various passions and pleasures, passing our days in malice and envy, hated by men and hating one another; *but when* the goodness and loving kindness of God our Savior appeared, he saved us, not because of deeds done by us in righteousness, but in virtue of his own mercy, by the washing of regeneration and renewal in the Holy Spirit, which he poured out upon us richly through Jesus Christ our Savior.

In this passage *Once* and *Now* are again contrasted. But this time the *Once* of pagan existence is described with a whole *catalogue of vices*, not one single concept. Related to this is a second construction which early Christian preachers used to contrast pagan society and the church. They simply opposed in lengthy lists the insoluble problems of paganism and life in the power of the Holy Spirit. One of the most beautiful examples is Col. 3:8–14:

> But now put them all away: anger, wrath, malice, slander, and foul talk from your mouth. Do not lie to one another, seeing that you have put off the old nature with its practices and have put on the new nature, which is being renewed in knowledge after the image of its creator. Here there cannot be Greek and Jew, circumcised and uncircumcised, barbarian, Scythian, slave, free man, but Christ is all, and in all. Put on then, as God's chosen ones, holy and beloved, compassion, kindness, lowliness, meekness, and patience, forbearing one another and, if one has a complaint against another, forgiving each other; as the Lord has forgiven you, so you also must forgive. And above all these put on love, which binds everything together in perfect harmony.

It is obvious that this text contrasts a negative list (anger, quick temper, malice, insults, foul language, lying) with a positive one (mercy, goodness, humility, meekness, patience, love). The negative list is intended to characterize pagans, the positive list Christians. The middle portion of the text shows that the passage is not concerned merely with the virtues of individuals. It is rather concerned above all with pagan society as a whole, for it compares this society to the new society of God in which the old lines of social separation between Greek and barbarian, Jew and Gentile, slave and free are radically abolished (cf. III: 3).

The category of *the new*, which is introduced in Col. 3:8–14 to define the existence of the baptized, is also particularly instructive. The *new man* in Christ is contrasted with the *old man* (cf. also Eph. 2:15; 4:24). The invasion of something radically new into an old, decrepit world is a favorite theme of eschatology; the fact that the replacement of the old man by the new man is an eschatological event shows the motif of new creation in all possible clarity. This motif also shows why the early church was able to distinguish so sharply between *Once* and *Now*. God has brought about the eschatological turn in Christ; he has created his people anew in Christ. Therefore, as 2 Cor. 5:17 states:

Therefore, if any one is in Christ, he is a new creation; the old has passed away, behold, the new has come.

Let us repeat that *being in Christ* means living within the realm of Christ's rule—and that realm is the church. Just like Titus 3:3–6, 2 Cor. 5:17 refers to baptism through which the individual is incorporated into the body of Christ, the church. Such incorporation not only affects the *interior* aspects of the baptized person; for Paul it has radical consequences which extend far into the social dimension.

Christ died in order to "rescue from the present evil age" (Gal. 1:4*) all who believe. There is not the slightest indication that Paul means future assumption of believers into heaven with his reference to rescue from the present age. What he means is rather the profound separation from the world which takes place through faith and baptism. The baptized person is rescued from the world to the realm of Christ's rule. The world, called here an "evil age," is more than just the summation of many individuals who do evil. It is simultaneously the potency of evil which has been deposited in social structures by the sins of many and which has perverted the world into a realm of the power of evil. Since the church lives from Christ's salvific deed, it is rescued from this world, that is, it need no longer live in the bondage of evil and according to the false structures of pagan society. For this reason Paul writes as follows (Rom. 12:2*):

Do not make yourselves like the structures (literally, the form) of this age, but be transformed by the renewal of your mind.

Since force of habit usually causes all of these texts to be interpreted in a quite onesided way with reference to the inner renewal or even moral rearmament of individual Christians, we must repeat again the point made earlier. Romans 12:2 and many other texts are not concerned only with the transformation of inner attitudes or with new motivation; above all, they are not concerned only with the individual. Renewal of mind is rather a matter of the eschatological turn which has brought about in the midst of the world a *new creation* wherever the church has come into being as the realm of Christ's rule. This new creation grasps not only the spirit of the church, but also its body, its form—or, as we really have to say today, its structures. In other words, Rom. 12:2 says that the form and spirit of the churches must not be adapted to the form and spirit of the rest of society.

We have already seen in one concrete instance what consequences this principle has for Paul. Christians are not permitted to take even their private legal disputes before pagan judges. Even conflicts of this sort affect the whole community; they must therefore be settled within the community itself (cf. III: 6). This principle draws an extremely sharp dividing line between church and society, a line which admits of no blurred borders. The division finds verbal expression in Paul's distinction, without any hesitation, between "believers" and "unbelievers" (1 Cor. 14:22; cf. 1 Cor. 6:1–2, 6). Who among us would dream of applying such linguistic distinctions in our own environment? Paul here distinguishes as a matter of principle—on the basis of the new reality which has begun in the midst of the world with Christ and the church. In this sense he is even prepared to distinguish between those "inside" (1 Cor. 5:12) and those "outside" (1 Cor. 5:12–13*; 1 Thess. 4:12*).

Paul never distinguishes between "practicing" believers and Christians who belong only nominally to the community; being Christian and belonging to the visibly assembled community are for him evidently equivalent.[129] Beyond this, being Christian also requires correspondence between the sanctification received in baptism and the moral life of the baptized. If too great a gap opens between the two, Paul insists that the appropriate consequences be drawn. A case in point is 1 Cor. 5:9–11:

> I wrote to you in my letter not to associate with immoral men; not at all meaning the immoral of this world, or the greedy and robbers, or idolaters, since then you would need to go out of the world. But rather I wrote to you not to associate with any one who bears the name of brother if he is guilty of immorality or greed, or is an idolater, reviler, drunkard, or robber—not even to eat with such a one.

A fundamental biblical principle, which we might term the *sanctity of the community*, is expressed in this very harsh instruction which—taken in isolation—awakens suspicions that Paul would not even recommend extending Christian mercy to those who offend. The church is not only sanctified through Christ's redemptive deed; it also has to practice this sanctity through a corresponding life. Otherwise it conforms to the world. Paul had no difficulty in applying to the community in Corinth a provision of the Law intended to assure the sanctity of the Old Testament people of God: "You shall purge the evil from your midst" (cf. Deut. 17:7*; 1 Cor. 5:13*). This too shows the sharp contrast of church and world.

We sense this profound opposition only in the Johannine writings. But closer inspection shows that Paul draws the boundary just as sharply as the Johannine material. The passage cited below is taken from the Gospel of John (17:14–19). It is a portion of Jesus' so-called *High Priestly Prayer*. The text speaks of the disciples who in the Fourth Gospel represent the entire church:

> I have given them thy word; and the world has hated them because they are not of the world. I do not pray that thou shouldst take them out of the world, but that thou shouldst keep them from the evil one. They are not of the world, even as I am not of the world. Sanctify them in the truth; thy word is truth. As thou didst send me into the world, so I have sent them into the world. And for their sake I consecrate myself, that they also may be consecrated in truth.

Once again it is essential to translate correctly the almost mythical language of John's Gospel and the formulas which have become too familiar to us. "They are not of the world, even as I am not of the world," surely means that with Christ something completely new has entered history, something which human society could never produce on its own. Christ is someone absolutely different and new, in whom the holiness and truth of God have become definitively present in the world. Wherever his word is believed and life is based on his truth, something new and different, the sacred realm of truth, emerges in the midst of the world. Those who have been sanctified by Christ and live in his truth are therefore sharply distinguished from the rest of society, from its deceit, its institutionalized untruth. They will be hated by others since they expose the social construction of reality as deceit. The world has structured itself in such a way that God no longer figures in its interpretation of reality. The moment that Christ and the community of disciples which follows him lives the true, God-given construction of reality, the deceit of the world collapses. To the extent that human beings love the truth, they too will come to faith and join the community of disciples. But insofar as they wish to remain "world," they must react with hatred and persecution in order to be able to hold fast to their deceit. As John 15:18–19* shows, this is not only the private lie of their lives, but also the deceit of a society which has surrounded itself with a false reality:

> If you find that the world hates you, know it has hated me before you. If you belonged to the world, it would love you as its own; the world hates you because you do not belong to the world, because I chose you out of the world.

The Gospel of John thus also reflects a wide distance between the world and the community of disciples. It is important that the concept of *sanctification of the disciples* appears precisely in the context in which this distance is formulated (John 17:17,19). This not only shows how the basic lines of the Old Testament continue in the New, but also makes definitively clear that the concept of *sanctification of the community* is the central concept with which the Bible formulates in its own language its conception of *the people of God as a divine contrast-society to the world*. The church is a holy nation (1 Pet. 2:9); it is a holy temple of God (1 Cor. 3:17*); it is sanctified and purified through the baptismal bath of water (Eph. 5:26*); the faithful are sacred branches on the noble olive tree of Israel (Rom. 11:16–17*); they are called by God to holiness (1 Thess. 4:3*).

More important than anything else is the fact that Christians called themselves "the saints." Originally this term was a self-designation on the part of the earliest community in Jerusalem (cf. Rom. 15: 25,26,31; 1 Cor. 16:1; 2 Cor. 8:4; 9:1,12). It was later adopted by all the communities, even in the Gentile church. For Paul "saints" is actually a synonym for "church" (cf. Rom. 1:7; 16:15; 1 Cor. 1:2; 2 Cor. 1:1; 13:12; Phil. 1:1; 4:22). The word remained the real self-designation of Christians until the Montanist crisis; from that time on its use gradually waned. Later Christians no longer held themselves "to be holy, but rather possessed holy martyrs, holy ascetics, holy priests."[130] There are some indications that the fourth century addition to the Apostles' Creed, (I believe) in the communion of saints, originally meant *communio* with the entire church, not only communion with the saints in heaven.[131] If this is so, it means that here too, just as with the word "spiritual," we encounter an instance of the dangerous narrowing of concepts so characteristic of later ecclesial development. In any case, in the New Testament all members of the church are still considered "holy," "spiritual," "brothers and sisters."

To us the early Christian self-designation as "the saints" is almost embarrassing. It sounds a bit like the "latter-day saints." But the word once expressed much of what was meant by "contrast-society." The church understood itself to be the sacred people of God's possession, a people with a pattern for life which differed from that of the world. Consider the consciousness which stood behind 1 Pet. 2:9:

> But you are a chosen race, a royal priesthood, a holy nation, God's own people, that you may declare the wonderful deeds of him who called you out of darkness into his marvelous light.

This text shows again how vital the Old Testament (cf. esp. Exod. 19:6) remains in the New. But it also shows that the primary issue is not the private holiness of the individual Christian. The point is that an entire people give witness to God's plan for the world. This people can indeed be small, as long as it fulfills its task with a cheerful heart. As R. Riesner has rightly said, "The decision to prefer to remain a minority with an unambiguous identity (rather than to secularize the church) is the presupposition of activity which will change the world."[132] What is decisive is not the size of the city, but the fact that it rests on the mountain. There it becomes the light of the entire world. Paul came very close to Matt. 5:14–16 when he wrote as follows to the church at Philippi (2:14–15):

> Do all things without grumbling or questioning, that you may be blameless and innocent, children of God without blemish in the midst of a crooked and perverse generation, among whom you shine as lights in the world.

We conclude our long list of texts with this citation from Philippians. The list could be extended much further. The entire New Testament sees the church as a contrast-society which stands in sharp contrast to the world. We must ask with regret how this fact could for centuries be so thoroughly suppressed in Christianity. Surely, this mechanism of suppression could ultimately function, not because the New Testament's call to holiness was overlooked, but because it was consistently narrowed to refer either to the private holiness of the individual Christian or to particular groups such as priests and religious.

Perhaps it is a blessing that the illusion of living in a completely Christian society has been definitively and thoroughly demolished in our day. It may sharpen our vision that the church must go its own way.

Even more effective, however, may be the fact that our world at present is coming ever closer to its own definitive self-destruction and that it evidently does not have the strength to question or abandon its social construction, one based chiefly on domination and mistrust. Precisely this dreadful need should finally force Christians to show the world that an entirely different form of society would be made possible by God. This, of course, cannot be made possible through instruction, but only through concrete actions.

8
THE SIGN FOR THE NATIONS

The image of the church which has been sketched in the previous section raises many questions. How can communities whose self-understanding reflects such a great contrast to the rest of society come to terms with the mission command of Matt. 28:19: "Go therefore and make disciples of all nations"? Does not this commitment to universal mission require a deep unity with the situation of peoples throughout the world? Beyond this, how does consciousness of contrast and of distance from the world come to terms with the statement of John 3:16: "God so loved the world that he gave his only Son"? If this statement is taken seriously, does it not require a complete abandonment of oneself, just as God has given his own Son in love for the world?

Seen from this perspective, is it not inevitable that communities whose self-understanding is profoundly marked by *contrast* to a pagan society and which wish precisely to preserve their own distinctive traits will fall into a spiritual ghetto and become sects? Will not their horizon rapidly narrow in an unacceptable manner? Will they not always circle around themselves? Will they not quickly cultivate an elitist mentality of election, a mentality which is repulsive, miserable and, in any case, unchristian? Will they not quickly develop the consciousness which we encounter in 2 Cor. 6:14 – 7:1? (This passage seems quite out of place in 2 Corinthians. It interrupts the connection between 6:13 and 7:2; quite possibly it does not derive from Paul; it is considered by many exegetes to be one of the most dubious texts of the New Testament.)

Do not be mismated with unbelievers. For what partnership have righteousness and iniquity? Or what fellowship has light with darkness? What accord has Christ with Belial? Or what has a believer in common with an unbeliever? What agreement has the temple of God with idols? For we are the temple of the living God; as God said,

> "I will live in them and move among them,
> and I will be their God,
> and they shall be my people.
> Therefore come out from them,
> and be separate from them, says the Lord,
> and touch nothing unclean;
> then I will welcome you,
> and I will be a father to you,
> and you shall be my sons and daughters,
> says the Lord Almighty."

Since we have these promises, beloved, let us cleanse ourselves from every defilement of body and spirit, and make holiness perfect in the fear of God.

Recent works have sought to show that this text derives from Qumran.[133] The community at Qumran did in fact live in isolation; it even pulled back from the rest of Judaism. It considered itself the *true sanctuary* and the *heavenly Jerusalem* already become reality. That it represented "the most radical and also the most impressive attempt" of early Judaism "to actualize God's holy community"[134] is beyond question. But Qumran also cultivated a truly repulsive elitist attitude; it separated itself from others and withdrew from society. Even if there are many grounds for doubting that 2 Cor. 6:7 – 7:1 comes directly from Qumran, does not the inner relationship of this text to the Qumran writings show very clearly what dangerous consequences must follow from the conception of the church as a contrast-society?

Although the foundations for an answer to this question have already been laid (cf. I: 5; II: 7), the entire problematic will be unrolled again here. We do this because accusations of being *elitist* and *sectarian*, of *betraying Christian universalism*, occur in stereotypical fashion whenever the New Testament church is described as a contrast-society.

Beginning with 2 Cor. 6:14 – 7:1, we can proceed from the observation that this text has much in common with the self-understanding of the Qumran community; such commonalities can moreover also be found elsewhere in New Testament instruction (*paraklēsis*).[135] They are caused to certain extent by the fact that, like the early church, the people at Qumran sought to gather the true Israel, form God's sacred community and be constructed as an eschatological temple in the Spirit – that they sought, in short, to make central elements of the Old Testament fruitful in their own situation and to take them with radical seriousness. No Christian can criticize the Qumran community for that. At least in this respect, after all, the early church did exactly the same thing. Perhaps we should in general refrain from using the term "sect" *all too quickly* wherever a "people's church" or a "great church" is not found. It could be that "sects" exist at all only because their larger sisters have suppressed central elements of the Bible.

Beyond this, it is worthwhile to put together all the content of 2 Cor. 6:14 – 7:1 which can also be found in Paul. Paul too distinguishes sharply between *believers* and *unbelievers* (1 Cor. 6:1). Paul too uses the antonyms *light* and *darkness* when he wishes to distinguish the church from pagan society (1 Thess. 5:4–8). Paul too contrasts the *righteousness* of Christian existence with the *lawlessness* of pagan life (Rom. 6:19). Paul too calls the church the *holy temple of God* (1 Cor. 3:17).

The really decisive difference between the insertion of 2 Cor.

6:14 – 7:1 and the authentic Paul is the requirement of *ritual* holiness: "be separate from them . . . touch nothing unclean . . . purify yourselves from every defilement of flesh and spirit" (2 Cor. 6:17; 7:1*). Requirements of this sort suggest an extreme Jewish-Christian group whose members still fulfill all the Old Testament prescriptions for purification. Now this *ritual* dimension of the Old Testament standards for sanctification has in fact been abolished since Jesus (cf. Mark 7:1–23). But this is far from meaning that the requirement of holiness is in general abolished. Jesus simply traced it back from a reified, pre-personal level to its authentic meaning – to what it always meant, the holiness of the people of God itself.

Theologians generally speak in this regard of *inner personal* holiness as contrasted with *external ritual* holiness. But it is necessary to examine this distinction very closely. In the Bible even holiness separated from externals and things, means much more than just an inner quality inhering in the soul or in the moral individual. In the Bible holiness always includes the public, social dimension, which is connected inextricably to the personality of the individual. Not only the human heart must be holy, but also living conditions, social structures and the forms of the environment in which people live and which they continually construct. In all probability, reified, ritual holiness in the Old Testament and in Judaism always intended this. We must be extremely careful about reducing the requirement of holiness to the *purely moral*. In no case may the *social* dimension be lost.

The New Testament obviously knew why it referred to the believers of a church as "the saints," why it spoke of the "holy people" and why it called the church a "holy temple." In all of these expressions "holy" always connotes "separated." Not separated in a ghetto, in religious self-satisfaction or in cultural or intellectual isolation, but separated to a different style of life and to new forms of life which realize what God wants society to be, in contrast to the structures of a sick society that is far from God.

Seen from this perspective, the fragment incorporated in 2 Cor. 6:14 – 7:1 is perhaps not a highly exotic plant in the garden of New Testament writings. Perhaps it made its way into the Pauline corpus, through human error and divine providence, to force us to recognize that the Christian church really has to be a contrast-society—with its own social forms and an alternative style of life.

What then about Matt. 28:19? Does it not say there is an absolutely universal sense, "Go, teach all nations" (Matt. 28:19*)? Does not a commission of this sort require profound unification with the situation of peoples all over the world? It is indeed a universal commission. The universality of the commission corresponds to the universal rule of Christ who, according to Matthew's Gospel, issued this missionary command to his disciples (cf. Matt. 28:18). But the Greek text is often incorrectly translated (in German contexts, this error is due to the influential tradition of Luther's Bible). The Greek does not say, "Teach all nations," but "make disciples of all the nations"—and that is something different. Matthew in no sense wished to say that the church should instruct all nations. Such instruction does take place constantly today. Modern means of communication make it possible to disseminate ecclesial social doctrine and other teachings all over the earth. Nor would I completely question the legitimacy of this impressive accomplishment. But Matthew had something quite different in mind. He said that all nations should be made "disciples."

Like "the saints," "the disciples" is a self-designation of the earliest Christian communities (cf. Acts 6:1,2,7; 9:1, 19,25,26,38; 11:26; 13:52). To make disciples of the nations can only mean to have the number of Christian communities in the world increase—until one day all nations have become church. Matthew does not say *how* this is to take place. There is not a word in his text about missionary propaganda. Probably he envisioned the growth of communities in the world then known and recognized in the way that it actually took place in the first century. The apostles, and others as well, founded individual communities from which the church then grew to an ever increasing number of communities—chiefly through the attraction which they exercised on pagan society.

So it is not "teach all nations," but rather "make all nations (communities of) disciples." *Teaching* is not discussed until Matt. 28:20, and even then not in a general sense, but with a specification: "Teach them to carry out everything I have commanded you."

At issue is not dogmatic teaching, but the manner of life which Jesus had offered the true Israel as the praxis of the reign of God. Matthew certainly thought in this connection of the Sermon on the Mount (Matthew 5−7), in which he had drawn together−from disparate traditions stemming from Jesus−the social order of the eschatological people of God.

The magnificent conclusion of Matthew's Gospel can be summarized as follows. The apostles are to take care that there emerge everywhere in the world communities of disciples in which Jesus' praxis of the reign of God (or, as we might also say, the social order of the true Israel) is lived in radical faithfulness to Jesus. Matthew does develop a worldwide, universal concept. But he never loses sight of the concrete communities in which alone the "new justice" of the Sermon on the Mount (Matt. 5:20*) can be lived.

Universalism, worldwide thinking, and broadness of horizon can never be called into question in the church. On this point Matthew, Paul, John and all the other New Testament authors speak unambiguously. But this is far from settling *how, in what way*, and *with what strategy*, the reaching of all peoples, discussed in Matt. 28:19-20, is to occur.

We have already seen that Jesus himself, following a significant group of prophetic motifs, abstracted completely from any idea of *mission* among the nations. He limited himself to the gathering of Israel. Of course we have also seen that this limitation in no way excluded universalism. Jesus thought in the Old Testament category of the pilgrimage of the nations. He presupposed as self-evident that at the moment the reign of God arrived in Israel the nations would come on their own accord to obtain a share in the fascination of God's rule. His task could only be to gather Israel in view of the near reign of God and to let the kingdom shine forth in a particular part of the world through this gathering. *Jesus' complete concentration on Israel is thus not a lack of universalism, not a limited horizon, not retreat from the world; on the contrary, it is the essential presupposition for the possibility of the reign of God reaching all peoples.* As J. Munck has rightly stated, "Jesus came precisely to Israel because his mission was for the entire world."[136]

Moreover, *election* must also be understood in this sense. The election of a single people from the many nations does not imply preference for one over the others or discrimination against the others in favor of the chosen one; election of one people takes place *for the sake of the others*. The chosen people is to become a sign to the other peoples of what God plans to do with the world as a whole.

Anyone who accuses such a conception of having a narrow view or an elitist mentality of election not only disavows the praxis of Jesus but also shows that he or she cannot move beyond temporally conditioned conceptions of mission, which are at most those of modernity, not of early Christianity. The word "mission" is not used as frequently now as it was in the nineteenth century. In its place many Christians speak of "transforming the world." Here we presuppose that they mean "transforming the world" in a Christian, not a Marxist, sense. In any case, what has been said above about mission also applies to Christian efforts to transform the world. It does not correspond to the New Testament unless it has its basis in the people of God. The world can be changed only when the people of God itself changes. It is not possible to liberate others unless freedom radiates within one's own group. It is not possible to preach social repentance to others unless one lives in a community which takes seriously the new society of the reign of God.[137]

But did the early church think along these lines? Here again— now for the last time—we must ask if the New Testament communities perpetuated what Jesus began. We have already taken into consideration Matt. 28:19–20, which in this regard must be considered an ecclesial product. In the following pages we shall examine four samples above and beyond Matthew 28: Acts 15, Luke 2, Romans 9–11, and the Letter to the Ephesians.

These samples will show how exactly the early church continued along Jesus' path. The church did not lose from sight the model of the pilgrimage of the nations; rather, on the basis of this model it ordered its own missionary experience into a larger perspective of salvation history. At first that seems to be a contradiction, for the complex of motifs concerned with the pilgrimage of the nations knows nothing like mission. In this respect the early church did in fact change something in comparison to Jesus. After a temporally limited phase in which it was again concerned immediately with the gathering of Israel,[138] the early church conducted missions in the strict sense—first in Samaria, then also among non-Jews. What is decisive, however, is that even these missions outside Israel remained ordered into the framework of "Israel and the nations," and this in such a way that the real dynamic of the idea of mission came from the notion of the symbolic presence of the people of God among the nations. It is now time to examine our samples.

1. Within Luke's presentation of the apostolic council there is an address of the Lord's brother James, which begins as follows (Acts 15:13–18):

> Brethren, listen to me. Simeon has related how God first visited the Gentiles, to take out of them a people for his name. And with this the words of the prophets agree, as it is written,
>
>> "After this I will return,
>> and I will rebuild the dwelling of
>>   David, which has fallen;
>> I will rebuild its ruins,
>> and I will set it up,
>> that the rest of men may seek the Lord,
>> and all the Gentiles who are called by my name,
>> says the Lord, who has made these
>>   things known from of old."

We need not be concerned with the rest of this speech; the only thing important for us is the citation from Amos. Nor need we be interested in whether the historical James actually delivered this address and cited Amos 9:11–12 in the process. Much speaks against this. But neither did Luke compose James' entire address freely; he drew on older traditions. The citation from Amos, in the unusual form in which he cites it, probably also came to him from an older tradition, one which interpreted the missionary experiences of its own ecclesial context on the basis of Amos 9:11–12.

It is odd that the story of these experiences begins by stating that Israel (the collapsed hut of David) will be rebuilt. Obviously this does not mean a national renewal of the Jewish state. The issue is rather the reestablishment of the people of God, initiated by Jesus and continued after Easter by his disciples. It is God himself who thus rebuilds *in the church* dispersed and fallen Israel.

Now the decisive point is that *the restoration of Israel occurs in order that the Gentiles also seek the Lord* (cf. Acts 15:17). After all, his name has been invoked over them, which means that they have long since stood under his rule. Yet they can find God and enter the reign of God only if Israel is rebuilt. Absolutely nothing is said of any activity of restored Israel. Instead it is said that as soon as Israel is renewed the nations can begin to seek the Lord. They will find him in Israel. Surely we can explicate this by saying that as soon as Israel appears among all other societies of the world as the properly *constructed* (this is the precise terminology of the text) society, pagan society will be able to seek and find God — in Israel, the divine model society, which will then be completely transparent toward God.

Those who handed on this text of Amos obviously knew that active missionary efforts were necessary for all this. But they also knew that this missionary effort would change nothing among the nations unless the people of God itself stood as a transformed society in the background of the mission. The mission received its credibility through the concrete social construction of the people of God which conducted it.

2. For our second sample we turn to Simeon's prayer of thanks in Luke 2:29–32:

> Lord, now lettest thou thy servant
>   depart in peace,
> according to thy word;
> for mine eyes have seen thy salvation
> which thou hast prepared in the
>   presence of all peoples,
> a light for revelation to the Gentiles
> and for glory to thy people Israel.

This short hymn is much older than the Gospel of Luke. Just like the Magnificat (Luke 1:46–55) and the Benedictus (Luke 1:68–79), it reflects a very early ecclesiological self-consciousness. The communities which spoke in these terms understood themselves as the eschatological people of God; they called themselves "Israel" with no hesitation.[139] Presumably they must have been Jewish-Christian communities in Palestine. They said of themselves (through the mouth of Simeon) that they had seen salvation—had seen what many prophets and kings had wanted to see and yet had not seen (Luke 10:23–24). Salvation had appeared in their midst.

Obviously this salvation referred to Jesus. But not Jesus alone. The radiant salvation included the new reality which had come with Jesus—the presence of God's reign in Israel, the messianic renewal of the people. The messianic salvation conferred by God now shone forth in God's people, the church, to all nations; it was a light to illumine the Gentiles, but at the same time glory for Israel.

The hymn is formulated completely in the language of Second Isaiah (cf. Isa. 40:5; 42:6; 46:13; 49:6; 52:10); there is at least an allusion to the motif complex of the pilgrimage of the nations. Although there is not even the slightest mention of mission, the messianic salvation which erupts in Israel shines *before the countenance of all peoples*. We can even ask if "glory of Israel" does not mean the "riches of the nations," which the Gentiles bring from all over the world on their trip to Zion (cf. Isa. 60:11–13). It is striking that the illumination of the Gentiles is mentioned first, the glory of Israel only afterwards. But that issue can remain open. It is in any case certain that our text brings the messianic salvation which shines in the people of God and revelation to the Gentiles into close connection with one another. Insofar as it does this it is related to Acts 15:13–18.

3. If we ask Paul what significance the existence of the church has for pagan society in his writings, he gives different answers. He can for example say that God in Christ has reconciled the world to himself and that the church is now the place where reconciliation, which has already occurred in principle, is to be realized concretely. God has therefore charged the church with the service of reconciliation. The church is the place where, in a new creation, God has inaugurated reconciled society (2 Cor. 5:17–21). But Paul can also say that a life of the church according to the gospel becomes for the world a *sign of its downfall* (Phil. 1:27–28). The

church can thus be either a salvific or a judging sign for pagan society, depending on how that society responds to the symbolic life of believers. Even more important for our question is the apostle's wide-ranging reflection on salvation history — his reflection on God's faithfulness to his covenant and on the fate of Israel in Romans 9—11. What Paul says there is completely unintelligible apart from the Old Testament motif complex of the pilgrimage of the nations.

In principle, the course of salvation history should have been such that an Israel *believing* in Christ would have brought about the salvation of the nations. (Paul presupposes this "regular" course of salvation history for Romans 9—11, without formulating it explicitly.) But the reality was different. Apart from a *holy remnant* (Rom. 11:1-7), the majority of Israel took offense at its Messiah (9:32-33) and did not believe the gospel (11:20). Yet this failure did not end Israel's mediation of salvation. When it did not mediate salvation to the nations through its *faith*, it did so through its *unbelief*. The gathering of Israel yielded to the mission to the Gentiles; missionaries to Israel became missionaries to the nations; through the failure of Israel salvation came to the pagans (11:11). God does not let his plans be frustrated by human beings.

Salvation, then, is now with the Gentiles. But God does not think only of them. He granted salvation to the nations not for their sake alone, but also in order to make Israel jealous (10:19). The direction of the pilgrimage of the nations is now reversed. In principle, the salvation which shines forth in Israel ought to entice the nations into the people of God. But now, since Israel did not believe, God has let messianic salvation radiate in the Gentile church and has made a nonpeople into a people (9:25) — precisely in order that Israel become jealous. The plausibility of the messianic society, now taking form in the Gentile church, is to attract Israel and make it envious.

Paul is deeply convinced that God's strategy with his people will prove successful. As soon as messianic salvation among the nations achieves the "critical mass" known only to God,[140] all Israel will be saved (11:26) — obviously because it will then finally be able, because of the messianic attraction of the Gentile church, to believe in Jesus as the Messiah. At this point the schema of the pilgrimage of the nations recurs, this time in its original direction. As Rom. 11:12,15 suggests, in the eschatological hour at which Israel as a whole comes to faith (due to the messianic attraction of the Gentile church) the effect on pagan society, still unbelieving, will be immense:

> Now if their trespass means riches for the world, and if their failure means riches for the Gentiles, how much more will their full inclusion mean! . . . For if their rejection means the reconciliation of the world, what will their acceptance mean but life from the dead?

The only reason all of Paul's lines of reasoning are so difficult for us to follow is that even their details presuppose the motif of the pilgrimage of the nations. Even without pursuing these details individually, it should still have become clear that *for Paul the fate of the nations is indissolubly linked to the way of Israel; conversely, the fate of Israel is linked to the way of the nations.* It is not a question of the individual Jew or the individual pagan. The issue is rather the messianic existence of the Gentile church, or of Israel; it is a matter of the plausibility of a realized messianic society. Only in this way can, in each case, the other side be gained.

Yet the decisive point in Romans 9 – 11 is that Israel remains as the real locus of salvation. The Gentiles are grafted onto the noble olive tree of Israel (11:17), not the reverse (11:18). Paul even says in a prominent text, 11:25–26, that the full number of Gentiles will *enter*— in other words, by coming to faith through the Christian mission the Gentiles make entrance into the eschatological salvific community of Israel.[141] In this text the Gentiles' acceptance of the gospel and their entrance into the church are equated with the journey of the nations to Zion. Paul is probably not alone in holding this view (cf. also Luke 2:30–32 and Acts 15:16–17). The first steps of the Gentile mission were perhaps possible only because the early church considered Jesus' resurrection as the beginning of the eschatological events and therefore expected the *addition* of the Gentiles promised by the prophets.

4. Finally, there is the Letter to the Ephesians. The great theme of this letter is the *church*. The church is the true Israel in which Gentile Christians, once foreign to the community of Israel (2:12),

are now fellow citizens of the saints and members of the family of God (2:19).

Up to this point the ecclesiology of this letter is largely identical to the understanding of the church then current. The specific characteristic of Ephesians is that it rethinks the traditional picture of the church from a new point of reference, one much discussed in the Hellenistic thought of the day—a philosophy of the cosmos. The church is now no longer only the people of God; it is a cosmic body which reaches into heaven (2:5-6) and which is animated by its head, the risen and exalted Christ (1:22-23). An overabundant fullness of blessing streams from Christ, the head, into the body of the church (1:3,23). This fullness of blessing enables believers to grow steadily toward their heavenly head (4:15) and to build up the body of the church in love (4:16). Christ the head is not only the principle of the church's life, but also the ruler over all cosmic powers (1:20-22). He not only fills the church with his fullness of blessing, but also pervades the universe with his power (4:10) and draws it ever more into the sphere of his rule. The church is obviously the dimension through which Christ fills the universe (1:23). In any case, it is through the church that the wisdom of God is proclaimed to the cosmic powers (3:10).

In order to make clear at once how intensively Ephesians reflects on the relationship of *church and world* we need only translate into contemporary idiom the language, so strange to us, which was at that time current among educated people. Pagan society appeared to be an abysmal place dominated by principalities and powers, as Eph. 2:1-3 states:

> And you he made alive, when you were dead through the trespasses and sins in which you once walked, following the course of this world, following the prince of the power of the air, the spirit that is now at work in the sons of disobedience. Among these we all once lived in the passions of our flesh, following the desires of body and mind, and so we were by nature children of wrath, like the rest of mankind.

Behind mythical images of this sort stands a profound awareness, which we have unfortunately lost, that every human society lives not only from contemporary decisions but also from the evil potential of an unresolved and unredeemed past, a past which affects the present as a frightful force. Ephesians wishes to say that in the midst of this pagan society, dominated by enslaving powers, a new sphere of freedom has been opened by Christ. Christ rules over all powers and forces of society. But he cannot rule without his body, the church. The church is the place in which the freedom and reconciliation opened in principle by Christ must be lived in social concreteness.

For the author of Ephesians, the striking point is that missionary preaching of the gospel to the Gentiles no longer figures *as a current task*. The church of our day is the *result*, but no longer the *bearer* of mission. On the contrary, as Eph. 4:13–16* shows, the *inner growth* of the church has an absolutely crucial significance:

> So we should all become one in faith and in the knowledge of God's Son, and form that perfect man who is Christ come to full stature. Let us, then, be children no longer, tossed here and there, carried about by every wind of doctrine that originates in human trickery and skill in proposing error. Rather, let us profess the truth in love and grow to the full maturity of Christ the head. Through him the whole body grows, and with the proper functioning of the members joined firmly together by each supporting ligament, builds itself up in love.

The decisive task of the church is thus to build itself up as a society in contrast to the world, as the realm of Christ's rule in which fraternal love is the law of life. It is precisely through the church's doing this that pagan society will grasp God's plan for the world. Ephesians (3:10) expresses this too in mythical terms:

> . . . that through the church the manifold wisdom of God might now be made known to the principalities and powers in the heavenly places.

We can surely rephrase this. It is precisely through the church's being what it is by virtue of Christ that the church will grow of its own accord in pagan society and that Christ will be able to fill all things through the church.

If this is correct, Ephesians offers us something very similar to the model of the pilgrimage of the nations, though it does so in a completely different terminology and against a completely different horizon of thought. The people of God grows into society, without conducting mission, through the fascination which it exerts. The church is then quite simply the *efficacious sign* of the presence of God's salvation in the world.

Our samples from Acts 15, Luke 2, Romans 9–11 and Ephesians have surely made clear that the idea of church as contrast-society does not mean contradiction of the rest of society *for the sake of contradiction*. Still less does church as contrast-society mean despising the rest of society due to elitist thought. The only thing meant is contrast *on behalf of others* and *for the sake of others*, the contrast function which is insurpassably expressed in the images "salt of the earth," "light of the world," and "city on a hill" (Matt. 5:13–14). *Precisely because the church does not exist for itself, but completely and exclusively for the world, it is necessary that the church not become world, that it retain its own countenance.*

If the church loses its own contours, if it lets its light be extinguished and its salt become tasteless, then it can no longer transform the rest of society. Neither missionary activity nor social engagement, no matter how strenuous, helps anymore. The following recent report from India will serve to illumine the entire problem forcefully once again.

> *The village pastor of Silvepura*, near Bangalore, is a priest with missionary concerns. He purchased an automobile with German funds; evenings, after completing his parish work, he used to drive through the neighboring villages. He would stop in the market places, gather the children and the resting farmers around himself, and show them films (the vehicle was equipped for this) or perform small magic tricks. Then he would speak about Christ. One evening an elderly man, a Hindu, stood up and said: "Dear Pastor, we have listened with interest, yes, with respect, to your words about Jesus Christ. We love Christ and honor him as a unique man and as God. We also like to read the Bible, when we have time and are not too tired. But, pardon me for saying this, this does not make us want to become Christians. Don't we know your parishioners? Don't we know how they live? How much hostility and enmity, how much drunkenness and deceit there is among them? They live no better than we do.' That was the story of the pastor of Silvepura."[142]

That about exhausts the subject. Of course this concluding text could itself lead to a misunderstanding, to the deepest and worst of misunderstandings. Should the church be some sort of moral institution, should it see its ideal in moral rearmament, should it develop in the direction of an ethical-moral performance society? That too would deprive the church of its inmost characteristics.

What makes the church the divine contrast-society is not self-acquired holiness, not cramped efforts and moral achievements, but the saving deed of God, who justifies the godless, accepts failures and reconciles himself with the guilty. Only in this gift of reconciliation, in the miracle of life newly won against all expectation, does what is here termed contrast-society flourish.

What is meant is *not* a church without guilt, but a church in which infinite hope emerges from forgiven guilt.

What is meant is *not* a church in which there are no divisions, but a church which finds reconciliation despite all gulfs.

What is meant is *not* a church without conflicts, but a church in which conflicts are settled in ways different from the rest of society.

What is meant, finally, is *not* a church without the cross and without passion narratives, but a church always able to celebrate Easter because it both dies and rises with Christ.

IV

The Ancient Church in the Discipleship of Jesus

We have just attempted (III) to make clear that the early church accepted the decisive lines of Jesus' praxis of the reign of God and perpetuated them appropriately and objectively even where external conditions had changed. This presentation in no way tried to claim that the New Testament communities never fell short of Jesus and failed. Still less was it maintained that the early church really exhausted and completely realized the critical potential which had been placed irrevocably in the world through Jesus' gathering of the true Israel in distinction from all other societies. But is was claimed that the New Testament communities — on the whole — recognized Jesus' intentions; they passed on Jesus' word and at least began to put it into practice, so that it was engraved permanently into the church and would remain identifiable for all time. Had this not been the case, it would be impossible to explain how this critical potential has, even to the present day, continually produced repentance and movements of societal change both within the church and outside it.

Here we shall now show at least in principle that this foundational reception of Jesus' praxis of the reign of God continued *beyond* the New Testament communities *into* the age of the ancient church. This can indeed be shown only *in part*, for an attempt to do so comprehensively would exceed the competence of a New Testament scholar. But an attempt of this sort is absolutely necessary, for it is not unusual to find today among ecclesial office-holders (and elsewhere as well) a strange devaluation of the New

Testament. The New Testament communities are seen mostly as a slightly exotic testing ground for ideas and structures that were not yet fully mature; they were channeled into the paths willed by God only through later ecclesial and dogmatic development. In the first century, it is often said, many things were still in an experimental stage, and some utopian practices of the beginning period showed very quickly that they could not be actualized in concrete reality.

In contrast to this, we will show that the boldness and "foolishness" of what we have called a contrast-society extended far *beyond* the early church *into* the third century and marked the form of the ancient church so unmistakably that no one can speak in this regard of pure utopias, much less of purely New Testament utopias.

1
THE PEOPLE FROM THE PEOPLES

The Fathers speak continually of God's gathering the church from all peoples and from the ends of the earth. In doing this, they consciously adopt the biblical idea of the *eschatological gathering of God's people.* The well-known Eucharistic prayer from the *Didache* (10.5) reads as follows:

> Remember, Lord, thy Church, to deliver it from all evil and to make it perfect in thy love, and gather it together in its holiness from the four winds to thy kingdom which thou hast prepared for it.[143]

The allusions to the Our Father are quite obvious; reference is made not only to its seventh petition ("deliver us from evil") but also to the second ("hallowed be thy name"). The second petition of the Our Father is understood in a profound way as a prayer for the gathering of God's people (cf. I: 4).

How vital the notion of "people of God" was for the Fathers is also shown by the author of *1 Clement* (29.1—30.1), when he writes as follows:

> Let us then approach him in holiness of soul, raising pure and undefiled hands to him, loving our gracious and merciful Father, who

has made us the portion of his choice for himself. For thus it is written: "When the most high divided the nations, when he scattered the sons of Adam, he established the bounds of the nations according to the number of the angels of God. His people Jacob became the portion of the Lord, Israel was the lot of his inheritance." And in another place he says "Behold the Lord taketh to himself a nation from the midst of nations, as a man taketh the first-fruit of his threshing-floor, and the Holy of Holies shall come forth from that nation." Seeing then that we are the portion of one who is holy, let us do all the deeds of sanctification.[144]

It is not only presupposed here that the church is the true Israel; the biblical connection between the concept of the people of God and the notion of sanctification is also clearly recognized. That the church is the chosen people, God's own property, has the inevitable consequence that it must be holy among the nations — fundamentally different, in other words, from the other societies in the world.

The idea of the election of the church from among the nations occurs once again toward the end of *1 Clement* (59.3–4) in "General Intercessions" which once had a place within the Roman liturgy and which correspond to our "Prayer of the Faithful":

Thou dost multiply nations upon earth and hast chosen out from them all those that love thee through Jesus Christ thy beloved child, and through him hast thou taught us, made us holy, and brought us to honour. We beseech thee, Master, to be our "help and succour." Save those of us who are in affliction, have mercy on the lowly, raise the fallen, show thyself to those in need, heal the sick, turn again the wanderers of thy people, feed the hungry, ransom our prisoners, raise up the weak, comfort the faint-hearted; let all "nations know thee, that thou art God alone," and that Jesus Christ is thy child, and that "we are thy people and the sheep of thy pasture."[145]

The syntactic structure of the last sentence confronts us with a question which can scarcely be settled on the basis of this text, but which on the whole is very important. Does Clement intend to say that Jesus himself is revealed as the Messiah, and that God himself is revealed through the Messiah, through the credible existence of the people of God in the midst of the peoples? Put in different words, does Christ become recognizable only through the church and God recognizable only through Christ? That would be an idea with serious theological consequences; an allusion to it is made in the Gospel of John (cf. 17:21), and it is not foreign to the Fathers (cf. IV: 8 below). But this question can remain open as far as our passage is concerned. Quite apart from the answer to this question, it is obvious that this text is conceived and formulated on the basis of the idea of the people of God. The afflicted people mentioned in the General Prayer are not all the afflicted in the world, but the oppressed, starving and imprisoned members of the *people of God*. It is for them that one prays first and most extensively. Only at the end of the General Prayer does attention turn to peace in the world and the well-being of rulers (cf. *1 Clement* 60.4–61.2). This text alone is sufficient to make clear that the church's extraordinarily strong sense of community, which we encountered again and again in the New Testament, was continued in the ancient church.

2

THE RELIGION OF HEALING

The "General Intercessions" of Clement of Rome include a petition for healing the sick members of the people of God (*1 Clement* 59.4.) This introduces a second theme which persists from Jesus' praxis of the reign of God through the New Testament communities into the age of the ancient church. The consciousness of the *presence of the Spirit* which filled the early church did indeed gradually recede. But care for the sick, healings, and the exorcism of demons continued. All of this is embedded in a rich terminology which describes Christ as *physician*, the sacraments as *medicaments*, and the Christian faith as a religion of *healing*. This medical-theological vocabulary has been discussed at length by Adolf von Harnack.[146]

The extraordinary role which healing miracles played in the ancient church has been described much less frequently. Origen takes for granted the presence of healing miracles in Christian communities (*Contra Celsum* 1.67; 2.33; 3.28; 8.58), and states explicitly that he saw with his own eyes many who had been cured (*Contra Celsum* 2.8; 3.24). He can even say that Jesus' miraculous deeds "created" the church (*Contra Celsum* 2.51).

For Gregory the Great, the kingdom of God becomes visible in the miracles which occur in churches at the tombs of the saints.[147] Although Gregory belongs to a much later period, it is still instructive that he is able to bring the kingdom of God into contact with divine deeds of power in the people of God. This procedure is thoroughly in the spirit of the Gospels.

Augustine dedicates an extended section of his *City of God* to miracles (22.7-10). He is concerned above all with recording formally the healing miracles which had occurred in the churches of his day. He wants to show that miracles were not limited to the days of Jesus and the apostles, but that they were still occurring in Milan, in Carthage, in Hippo – all over the world. According to the *City of God* (22.8), there is need to record them and to read them to the congregations, in order to protect them from human forgetfulness:

> For miracles are still being performed in his name, both through his sacraments, through prayers, and through the relics of his saints. But these miracles do not have the same light of publicity, so as to be known with the same renown as the former. For the canon of sacred Scripture, which it was obligatory to close, explains why those miracles are rehearsed everywhere and fixed in the memory of all peoples, while these later miracles are known only where they are performed and there scarcely by all the people of the city or other local group.[148]

The Fathers did know that external miracles achieve their final conclusiveness only in the repentance of the people of God, itself caused by miracles (cf., e.g., *Contra Celsum* 3.28–30). Only the *history of the effects* of wonders shows their derivation from God. The Fathers also knew that the most profound miracle of the church did not consist in people being healed of their infirmities but in their ability – against all human expectation – to break with their pagan past and to begin a new life in Christ. Thus Cyprian (*Ad Donatum* 4) reports that he considered "putting off the old man" to be impossible:

> Afterwards when I had drunk of the Spirit from heaven a second birth restored me into a new man; immediately in a marvelous manner doubtful matters clarified themselves, the closed opened, the shadowy shone with light, what seemed impossible was able to be accomplished.[149]

Consequently, the fact that people received from God the power to die as martyrs for their faith was considered the greatest miracle. The death of martyrs was therefore described as a second baptism, as the definitive putting on of the new man, as the awakening of new miraculous powers in the church. According to the end of the *Passion of Perpetua and Felicitas* (21), the existence of martyrs is an undeceiving witness that the presence of the Spirit still perdures in the church.

3
CHRISTIAN FRATERNITY

The notion of fraternity, deeply rooted in the New Testament communities, also continued in the ancient church. As Clement (*1 Clement* 2.4–6) wrote to the church at Corinth:

> Day and night you strove on behalf of the whole brotherhood that the number of his elect should be saved with mercy and compassion. You were sincere and innocent, and bore no malice to one another. All sedition and all schism was abominable to you. You mourned over the transgressions of your neighbours; you judged their shortcomings as your own.[150]

This is not a description of the conditions of the church in Corinth at the time the letter was written. At that time the community lived with sedition and schism. But these conditions could not be accepted by the other communities. The idea of the responsibility of the entire "brotherhood," that is, the entire community of Corinth, for one another—a point that is stressed frequently—is not the only noteworthy aspect of the letter. It is also important that the church of *Rome* feels responsible for the church of *Corinth* and, despite the tribulations with which it had to cope itself (cf. *1 Clement* 1.1), charged it through the letter to return to its former state. Thus *1 Clement* begins with these words:

> The Church of God which sojourns in Rome to the Church of God which sojourns in Corinth . . .[151]

We will be able to examine the responsibility of communities for one another in connection with Christian charitable activity. At any event, this responsibility has its foundation in the fraternity of

the entire church. Even believers found it extraordinary that all
Christians were brothers and sisters of one another. The Apologists
frequently emphasize the use of "brother" as form of address as a
specifically Christian characteristic, in contrast to pagan practice.
In Minucius Felix's dialogue *Octavius* (9.2), Caecilius observes:
"They call one another promiscuously brothers and sisters."[152]
Caecilius, who represents paganism in the dialogue, says this in the
midst of a long list of rumors and prejudices which circulated
against Christians at that time. Aristides of Athens (*Apology* 15.7)
and Tertullian (*Apology* 38.8–9) says the same. Tertullian (*Apology*
38.8–9) also includes a magnificent theological justification for the
Christian use of "brother" as a form of address:

> But we are your brothers, too, by right of descent from the one
> mother, Nature . . . But how much more fittingly are those both
> called brothers and treated as brothers who have come to know one
> Father God, who have drunk of one Spirit of holiness, who from one
> womb of common ignorance have come with wonder to the one
> light of Truth![153]

The type of care—revolutionary in comparison with pagan
society—extended in principle to all members of the community
in need of help shows that the use of "brother" and "sister" in
Christian communities was not a mere affectation. Care was
extended above all to widows, orphans, the elderly and sick, those
incapable of working and the unemployed, prisoners and exiles,
Christians on a journey and all other members of the church who
had fallen into special need. Care was also taken that the poor
received a decent burial.[154]

The care of the Christian communities for their unemployed
and for those unable to work is worth particular attention. They
insisted that all who were able to work did so; they even arranged
jobs for them, as much as they were able to. But anyone no longer
able to work could be sure of receiving support from the community. They had a system of aiding employment and a network of
social security which was unique in the ancient world.[155] It rested
both on mutual help and on voluntary contributions gathered
primarily at the Sunday Eucharist. Justin (*Apology* 1.67) describes
this collection in his well-known depiction of Christian liturgy:

The wealthy, if they wish, contribute whatever they desire, and the collection is placed in the custody of the president. [With it] he helps the orphans and widows, those who are needy because of sickness or any other reason, and the captives and strangers in our midst.[156]

This well-organized welfare system was not limited to each local church. We have a whole list of sources which indicate that aid was also extended to neighboring Christian communities in particular need. The church of Rome was particularly known for its assistance of churches in other cities. As Eusebius (*Ecclesiastical History* IV.23.10) relates, Bishop Dionysius of Corinth wrote as follows, about the year 170, to the Roman church:

This has been your custom from the beginning, to do good in manifold ways to all Christians, and to send contributions to the many churches in every city, in some places relieving the poverty of the needy, and ministering to the Christians in the mines, by the contribution which you have sent from the beginning, preserving the ancestral custom of the Romans, true Romans as you are. Your blessed bishop Soter has not only carried on this habit but has even increased it.[157]

Fraternity was thus not an empty word either in individual communities or in the church as a whole. "While Christian doctrine appeared utopian and unrealistic in the eyes of their foes, its practical application showed it to be a solid concept for keeping the economic and social needs of at least the members of the community under control."[158]

All this also makes clear what the ancient church understood as love (*agapē*). Love was not a noble feeling, but very concrete assistance—especially for fellow believers. In the tradition of Matt. 5:43–48 *agapē* can occasionally include people outside the church.[159] But the mainstream of New Testament language reserves *agapē* for *conduct within the communities*. Thus Aristides says of Christians in his *Apology* (15.5, 7), in exact correspondence to the terminology of the New Testament letters:

They do good to their enemies; and they love one another.[160]

Ignatius speaks in his letter to the church of Smyrna (6–7) of heretics who are not concerned with *agapē*; he concretizes this by saying that they pay no attention to widows and orphans, prisoners and released slaves, the hungry and thirsty. They die in their conflicts, though it would be so important for them *to love*. When the same Ignatius says, in the prescript of his letter to Rome, that the church at Rome presides in *agapē*, he evidently refers to the same conduct that Dionysius of Corinth described some decades later in the letter we have just cited—their support of foreign churches. Ignatius wished to say that the church of Rome is the normative authority in the reality which constitutes the essence of the church, fraternal love. The church of Rome presides in love.[161]

Though the ancient church may often have failed in *agapē*, the following citations show that Christians and to some extent even pagans saw fraternal love as something specifically Christian. Tertullian (*Apology* 39.8) states simply:

Look . . . how they love one another.[162]

Minucius Felix (*Octavius* 9.2) notes the comment:

They fall in love almost before they are acquainted.[163]

He later (*Octavius* 31.8) explains in more detail:

Our bond, which you resent, consists in mutual love, for we know not how to hate; we call ourselves "brethren" to which you object, as members of one family in God, as partners in one faith, as joint heirs in hope. You do not acknowledge one another, amid outbursts of mutual hate; you recognize no tie of brotherhood, except indeed for fratricidal murder.[164]

4
GOD'S CONTRAST-SOCIETY

The last citation brings us to the main theme of this unit (IV). The ancient church also understood itself as a *contrast-society*. The categories of "Once and Now," and "Darkness and Light" are opposed to each other in this period just as they were in the New Testament.[165] A passage from Justin's *Apology* (1.14) offers a case in point:

We who once reveled in impurities now cling to purity; we who devoted ourselves to the arts of magic now consecrate ourselves to the good and unbegotten God; we who loved above all else the ways of acquiring riches and possessions now hand over to a community fund what we possess, and share it with every needy person; we who hated and killed one another and would not share our hearth with those of a different tribe because of their [different] customs, now, after the coming of Christ, live together with them.[166]

Justin's final comment is especially important, as it makes clear that all national barriers had collapsed as far as the ancient church's consciousness was concerned. There are no longer Greeks, barbarians, or Scythians (Col. 3:11); the Christian community gathers all peoples at the one Eucharistic table. What counts is no longer the differences among nations, but the fundamental opposition between pagan society and the new society of God. As Ignatius wrote to the Ephesians (10.1–2):

Now for other men "pray unceasingly," for there is in them a hope of repentance, that they may find God. Suffer them therefore to become your disciples, at least through your deeds. Be yourselves gentle in answer to their wrath; be humble minded in answer to their proud speaking; offer prayer for their blasphemy; be steadfast in faith for their error; be gentle for their cruelty, and do not seek to retaliate.[167]

An instructive text from Ignatius's letter to the church at Magnesia (5.2) shows that he is not speaking merely of poor individual examples among the pagans, but of *pagan society as a whole*. In this letter, he compares paganism and Christianity with two different coins. Each carries a special stamp:

The unbelievers bear the stamp of this world, and the believers the stamp of God the Father in love.[168]

To be mentioned here above all are of course the Christian Apologists. Development of the contrast between church and paganism is always a decisive aspect of their writings. It is not unusual for this contrast to be formulated with extraordinary severity, as it is by Minucius Felix (*Octavius* 35.6):

You forbid adultery, yet practise it; we are born husbands for our wives alone; you punish crimes committed, with us the thought of crime is sin; you fear the voice of witnesses, we the sole voice of conscience which is ever at our side; and finally, the prisons are crowded to overflowing with your following and not a single Christian is there, except on charge of his religion, or as a renegade.[169]

This text, like many others, shows the extraordinary consciousness the church had at that time of its difference from pagan society. Who among us could dare to say today that there are no Christians in prison except those persecuted for their faith? Evidently Minucius Felix could say this without appearing ridiculous. But let us leave the question of fact to one side; the gap between this and the church today is not only a matter of facts. The entire mode of thought which the cited passage reflects disagrees with us. We simply no longer view the church as a society opposed to the rest of society. For this reason Minucius Felix's text will nowadays appear unacceptably arrogant even to the majority of *Christian* readers. Unfortunately we must say that at the time it was written the majority of pagans reacted to Christianity in precisely the same way. The greatest opposition was to the idea that a numerically very tiny group of people placed themselves in opposition to the entire rest of society *in their faith and in their manner of life.* Christians were accused of "hatred of the human race" (*odium generis humani*).[170] The self-consciousness reflected in the *Octavius* was by no means an exception. When a plague afflicted Alexandria about the year 260, that city's bishop, Dionysius, wrote as follows in a letter reported by Eusebius (*Ecclesiastical History* 7.22):

> The most, at all events, of our brethen in their exceeding love and affection for the brotherhood were unsparing of themselves and clave to one another, visiting the sick without a thought as to the danger, assiduously ministering to them, tending them in Christ, and so most gladly departed his life along with them; being infected with the disease from others, drawing upon themselves the sickness from their neighbours, and willingly taking over their pains . . . In this manner the best at any rate of our brethren departed this life, certain presbyters and deacons and some of the laity . . . . So, too, the bodies of the saints they would take up in their open hands to their bosom, closing their eyes and shutting their mouths, carrying them on their shoulders and laying them out; they would cling to them, embrace them, bathe and adorn them with their burial clothes, and after a little receive the same services themselves, for those that were left behind were ever following those that went before. But the con-

duct of the heathen was the exact opposite. Even those who were in the first stages of the disease they thrust away, and fled from their dearest. They would even cast them in the roads half-dead, and treat the unburied corpses as vile refuse.[171]

Confronted with such texts, a modern Christian is likely to say that such generalizations are inadmissible. This is the black-and-white picture typical of legends. There were always Christians who failed and there was always exemplary conduct on the part of non-Christians. It is not even unusual for non-Christians to be better than Christians. This is the general line of a stereotyped contemporary Christian argument which has almost advanced to the rank of a form of sermon. It reveals more than clearly the widespread *Christian inferiority complex.* The Christians of the first three centuries would surely have been perplexed enough to shake their heads at us. They were in a position to argue in a completely different fashion. Even as intelligent and reflective a man as Origen (*Contra Celsum* 3.29) could dare to write as follows:

> God . . . caused churches to exist in opposition to the assemblies of superstitious, licentious, and unrighteous men. For such is the character of the crowds who constitute the assemblies of the cities. And the Churches of God which have been taught by Christ, when compared with the assemblies of the people where they live, are as 'lights in the world.' Who would not admit that even the less satisfactory members of the Church and those who are far inferior when compared with the better members are far superior to the assemblies of the people?[172]

But Origen is not content with such general statements. In the passage which follows he compares the *Christian* churches in Athens, Corinth and Alexandria with the *civil* assemblies of these three cities, in order to show that the text he has cited from Phil. 2.15 ("like the stars in the sky") also applies to his own day (3.30).

The contrast to pagan society stands more than clearly in the background even when the Christian Apologists do not argue directly in the form of contrast, but develop in a positive fashion the beauty of the Christian way of life. An example of this may be found in a magnificent section of Aristides' *Apology* (15—16), which can serve to summarize what has been said so far:

> But the Christians, O King, while they went about and made search, have found the truth; and as we learned from their writings,

they have come nearer to truth and genuine knowledge than the rest of the nations. For they know and trust in God, the Creator of heaven and of earth . . . from whom they received commandments which they engraved upon their minds and observe . . . Wherefore they do not commit adultery nor fornication, nor bear false witness, nor embezzle what is held in pledge, nor covet what is not theirs. They honour father and mother and show kindness to those near to them; and whenever they are judges, they judge uprightly. They do not worship idols (made) in the image of man; and whatsoever they would not that others should do unto them, they do not to others; and of the food which is consecrated to idols they do not eat, for they are pure. And their oppressors they . . . comfort and make them their friends; they do good to their enemies . . . Further, if one or other of them have bondmen or bondwomen . . . through love toward them they persuade them to become Christians, and when they have done so, they call them brethren without distinction . . . They go their way in all modesty and cheerfulness. Falsehood is not found among them; and they love one another, and from widows they do not turn away their esteem; and they deliver the orphan from him who treats him harshly. And he, who has, gives to him who has not, without boasting. And when they see a stranger, they take him in to their homes and rejoice over him as a very brother; for they do not call them brethren after the flesh, but brethren after the spirit and in God. And whenever one of their poor passes from the world, each one of them according to his ability gives heed to him and carefully sees to his burial. And if they hear that one of their number is imprisoned or afflicted on account of the name of their Messiah, all of them anxiously minister to his necessity, and if it is possible to redeem him, they set him free. And if there is among them any that is poor and needy, and they have no spare food, they fast two or three days in order to supply to the needy their lack of food. They observe the precepts of their Messiah with much care, living justly and soberly as the Lord their God commanded them . . . And if any righteous man among them passes from the world, they rejoice and offer thanks to God; and they escort his body as if he were setting out from one place to another . . . Such, O King, is the commandment of the law of the Christians, and such is their manner of life.[173]

If we are to assess a text like this correctly, its form and purpose must not be overlooked. This is a *public relations* text, we might even say a piece of *propaganda*, which paints an ideal picture. This is how the Christians wish to be seen, how they would like to be. The same is true of many of the other patristic texts cited here, and also even for many of the citations drawn earlier from the New Testament. Even when they speak in the indicative they have hortatory character. "We are like this," always means "This is the way we should be, the way we would like to be." For this reason it is impossible to draw conclusions from texts of this sort about the concrete reality of the Christian communities in a direct and unreflected way. Yet such texts do at least show the self-understanding of such communities in that period, their extraordinary self-consciousness, their claim to be the divine contrast-society to a corrupt pagan society and the necessity of their being such by virtue of their charge from God. This claim alone makes these texts exciting; this claim alone should be sufficient to disturb us.

But in reality these texts show more than Christian self-understanding and self-consciousness. They surely reflect a portion of the reality of the communities themselves. *It would be a miserable hermeneutic to tone down ancient Christian texts merely because we moderns, in our skeptical resignation, no longer consider it possible for communities to take the gospel seriously.* The few but important voices of the ancient *opponents* of Christianity should preserve us from a hermeneutic born of a bad conscience, desirous of preparing a historical alibi for our own conditions. In his satire on *The Passing of Peregrinus* (12–13), Lucian of Samosata tells how this deceiver feigned becoming a Christian, let himself be celebrated by the churches and was then one day imprisoned in Syria as a Christian:

> Well, when he had been imprisoned, the Christians, regarding the incident as a calamity, left nothing undone in the effort to rescue him. Then, as this was impossible, every other form of attention was shown him, not in any casual way but with assiduity; and from the very break of day aged widows and orphan children could be seen waiting near the prison, while their officials even slept inside with him after bribing the guards. Then elaborate meals were brought in, and sacred books of theirs were read aloud . . . Indeed, people came even from the cities in Asia, sent by the Christians at their common expense, to succour and defend and encourage the hero. They show incredible speed whenever any such public action in taken; for in no time they lavish their all. So it was then in the case of Peregrinus; much money came to him from them by reason of his imprisonment, and he procured not a little revenue from it.[174]

Despite its bitter ridicule, Lucian's mockery of naive Christians graphically shows the profound fraternity of the Christian communities, which supported their confessors in prisons and mines without regard for the cost (cf. the exact parallels in Aristides, *Apology* 15). Even more important than Lucian's comments is a letter of the Roman Emperor Julian, a man above any suspicion of favoring Christianity. In his *Letter to Arsarcius, High-priest of Galatia*, Christian solidarity receives high grades from an enemy of Christianity:

> Why do we not observe that it is their (the Christians') benevolence to strangers, their care for the graves of the dead and the pretended holiness of their lives that have done the most to increase atheism (Christianity)? . . . When . . . the impious Galilaeans support not only their own poor but ours as well, all men see that our people lack aid from us.[175]

The Apologists' remarks about the inner solidarity of the Christian communities are evidently accurate. The social system of the church functioned so well that even non-Christians could be supported. This solidarity must have made a profound impression on outsiders; it was one of the reasons for the rapid expansion of Christianity. Moreover, Julian sought to "imitate" the churches' program of support in an "artificial creation, in order to deprive Christians of this weapon."[176] His attempt failed. The strength and inimitability of the ecclesial support program lay precisely in the fact that it was neither centrally controlled nor decreed from above, but rather had its base in the individual local churches where it was constantly reborn of the inner conviction and free consent of the communities. Its ultimate source was fraternal love, its ultimate location the Eucharistic celebration of the communities assembled on the Lord's day.

5
THE CHRISTIAN REFUSAL

It is impossible to write about the ancient church as a contrast-society without treating the topic of its *social refusal*. Up to a certain point Christians were indeed loyal to the state. They paid their taxes, recognized civil authority in principle, and prayed for the emperor. All that was undisputed by Christians; they even stressed it frequently to allay the mistrust of the pagans. Nonetheless there was a clear distance between the Christian communities and the rest of society — especially in the first two centuries. This distance was concretized in constant refusals. In Minucius Felix's *Octavius* (12.5–6), Caecilius expressed, no doubt quite accurately, the objection of many pagans:

> Have not the Romans without your God empire and rule, do they not enjoy the whole world, and lord it over you? Meanwhile in anxious doubt you deny yourselves wholesome pleasures; you do not attend the shows; you take no part in the processions; fight shy of public banquets; abhor the sacred games, meats from the victims, drinks poured in libation on the altars. So frightened are you of the gods whom you deny! You twine no blossoms for the head, grace the body with no perfumes; you reserve your unguents for funerals; refuse garlands even to the graves, pale, trembling creatures, objects for pity — but the pity of our gods! Poor wretches, for whom there is no life hereafter, yet who live not for to-day.[177]

This long list of pagan charges reveals some of the Christian refusals with regard to society. Christians refrained from attending matches of gladiators and animal fights,[178] from participating in processions and parades,[179] and from eating at public meals and banquets, such as those on imperial holidays.[180] The citation from the *Octavius* also shows clearly that the distance of Christians from pagan society extended to points of detail; they did not adorn themselves with flowers, and they wore no wreaths.

It would be a mistake to presume that Christian refusal took place only when veneration of the gods or the imperial cult came into play. Both of these areas did have an extraordinary significance in the ancient Roman world, but they are not sufficient to explain everything. Christians refusal occurred also in very different areas. It affected the practice of cremation, the exposure of new-born children, and especially pagan marriage morality.[181] The final and most profound reason for the Christian distance from pagan society must have been the preserved knowledge that Jesus wanted to gather the people of God as a divine counter-society. How else was Tertullian's monstrous statement (*Apology* 38.3) conceivable:

Nothing is more foreign to us than the State.[182]

It is certain that not all Christians in Tertullian's day would have agreed with this provocative assertion. But the statement was possible. It ultimately had its basis in the awareness that the Christian communities formed a distinct *people*. When Origen stressed against Celsus that something new had come into the world with the death of Jesus, he meant "the sudden birth of the race of Christians which was, so to speak, born in an instant" (*Contra Celsum* 8.43).[183]

It was not only in a *religious* or *spiritual* sense, but also in a social sense that Origen and many other theologians of the first few centuries referred to Christians as a "people." This is obvious simply from the way he describes the Jews (*Contra Celsum* 5.43):

> Would that they had not sinned and broken the law, both earlier when they killed the prophets and also later when they conspired against Jesus! Otherwise we might have an example of a heavenly city such as even Plato attempted to describe, although I doubt whether he was as successful as Moses and his successors when they trained an 'elect nation' and a 'holy people', devoted to God.[184]

According to Origen, everything true of the Old Testament people of God is all the more true of the Christian people, who "came to exist as a society in an amazing way" (*Contra Celsum* 8.47).[185] They form "in each city" of the Roman Empire "another sort of country, created by the Logos of God." In this way "God's country (I mean the church)" is formed (*Contra Celsum* 8.75).[186]

The theologians of that day sought in ever new terms to find an exact expression of the *social dimension of the church*. The church is a *people*, a *race*,[187] a *city*.[188] In his *Commentary on Daniel* (4.9), Hippolytus, who characterized the Roman state as a demonic imitation of the true state, that is the Christian people, goes further than anyone else:

> For as our Lord was born in the forty-second year of the emperor Augustus, whence the Roman empire developed, and as the Lord also called all nations and tongues by means of the apostles and fashioned believing Christians into a *people*, the people of the Lord, and the people which consists of those who bear a new name—so was all this imitated to the letter by the empire of that day, ruling

'according to the working of Satan'; for it also collected to itself the noblest of every nation, and, dubbing them Romans, got ready for the fray.[189]

A favorite apologetic structure of the ancient church stands behind this strange argumentation. Everything great and good in paganism is considered an imitation of the Judeo-Christian heritage (sometimes even a demonic copy). We need not be concerned here with the naiveté of this scheme and with the dubious nature of Hippolytus's picture of history. The decisive point in our context is Hippolytus's presupposition that the church is a people, created by Christ from all peoples, which stands opposed to the Roman Empire as a *counter-society*.

Hippolytus was not alone with the astonishing self-consciousness. While far from all theologians of the ancient church were as hostile to the Roman state as he was, the idea of the social composition of the church and its contrast function to the rest of society were self-evident. Let us look again at Origen in this context. The Platonist Celsus, against whom Origen is defending Christianity, had attacked the church for (among other things) its deliberate distance from society; for him this was concretized in the Christian refusal to swear by the *tychē* (the genius) of the emperor (*Contra Celsum* 8.67). Celsus (*Contra Celsum* 8.68) can see in this refusal nothing but profound irresponsibility with regard to the state:

> If everyone were to do the same as you, there would be nothing to prevent him (the Emperor) from being abandoned, alone and deserted, while earthly things would come into the power of the most lawless and savage barbarians, and nothing more would be heard among men either of your worship or of the true wisdom.[190]

Origen has a very different opinion of swearing by the genius of the emperor. According to him there are only two possibilities. Either the *tychē* of the emperor is an empty word, in which case it is not permitted to act as if the nonexistent thing were a god by whom one could swear, or the *tychē* of the emperor is an evil demon, in which case it is better to die than to swear by a demon who misleads the emperor to evil (*Contra Celsum* 8.65). We can only agree with Origen on this issue. Was the *tychē* of the emperor anything other than a personification of an unbounded human lust for power? Demons are released whenever human power is divinized.[191]

Origen cannot accept Celsus' objection, which he has to take very seriously, that Christians abandon the emperor and thus evade their social responsibility. He states (*Contra Celsum* 8.68):

> For if, as Celsus has it, every one were to do the same as I, obviously the barbarians would also be converted to the word of God and would be most law-abiding and mild. And all other worship would be done away and only that of the Christians would prevail. One day it will be the only one to prevail, since the word is continually gaining possession of more souls.[192]

So Origen is convinced that there is no way to transform society for the better other than through the continual spreading of the church, God's counter-society, in the world. To live in the church according to God's word in no sense means to evade the social responsibility which every person has; on the contrary, it causes Christians to assume their social responsibility in the most radical way possible. For this reason, Origen (*Contra Celsum* 8.75) is also able to reply to Celsus' advice that Christians should accept public office in their own cities:

> But we know of the existence in each city of another sort of country, created by the Logos of God. And we call upon those who are competent to take office, who are sound in doctrine and life, to rule over the churches. We do not accept those who love power. But we put pressure on those who on account of their great humility are reluctant hastily to take upon themselves the common responsibility of the church of God . . . And if those who are chosen as rulers in the church rule well over God's country (I mean the church), or if they rule in accordance with the commands of God, they do not on this account defile any of the appointed civic laws.[193]

In Origen's opinion, Christians fulfill their responsibility to the state by being active in the church, the society which corresponds to the will of God. Decisive in this is the exclusion of all *desire for power*. Domination of some over others is simply not permitted in God's new society. It is by far the best possible service to the state that a new society, one free of domination, should emerge in the midst of a pagan society marked by the demons of power; it can thus make clear what God really wants society to be. As Origen continues (*Contra Celsum* 8.75):

> If Christians do avoid these responsibilities, it is not with the motive of shirking the public services of life. But they keep themselves for a more divine and necessary service in the church of God for the sake of the salvation of men.[194]

What a magnificent passage! It would merit much more attention since it draws out, in precisely the sense of the New Testament, the *authentic function* of the church. The church serves the world best when it takes with radical seriousness its task of being a "holy people" in the sense of 1 Pet. 2:9–10. The church is the *salt of society* precisely by living symbolically God's societal and social order. It is extremely questionable that not a few engaged Christians today act as if responsibility for the world and transformation of the world were possible *only beyond and outside the church*. Obviously a Christian today does have a responsibility to assume in given cases immediate civil responsibility.[195] On this particular point Origen's position can no longer be normative for us. But one thing which Origen saw with notable clarity, more clearly than many contemporary theologians, must remain normative. *The most important and most irreplaceable service Christians can render society is quite simply that they truly be church.*

6
THE CHURCH AND WAR

The problem of renouncing violence and domination has already been touched upon (IV: 5). Not only the early church but also the church of the immediately following centuries addressed this problem again and again. Simply the question whether, and under what circumstances, a Christian could perform *military service* disturbed the Christian churches into the fourth century.

> In the West and in the border provinces threatened by attack there was more willingness to compromise on this issue than in the pacified Greek-speaking provinces . . . Still, according to the church order of Hippolytus of Rome, a baptized soldier had to promise not to perform executions or swear military oaths, and a catechumen or

a Christian who voluntarily enlisted in the military was excommunicated.[196]

But there were also more radical voices which considered Christianity and military service *absolutely incompatible*. In his Montanist period, for example, the rigorous Tertullian (*On Idolatry* 19) wrote as follows:

> There is no agreement between the divine and human sacrament, the standard of Christ and the standard of the Devil, the camp of light and the camp of darkness. One soul cannot be bound to two masters, to God and to Caesar.[197]

Evidently there were Christians who appealed to the Bible for support of their military service, for example to such passages as John the Baptist's address to soldiers (Luke 3:14) or the baptism of the centurion Cornelius (Acts 10). Tertullian's answer (*On Idolatry* 19) leaves nothing to the imagination:

> But how will they make war, yea how will they be soldiers in peace, without the sword, which the Lord hath taken away? For even though soldiers came to John and received their rule of duty, even though a centurion was a believer, the Lord, in disarming Peter, thenceforth disarmed every soldier.[198]

Reality was of course more complex than this rigorous statement; Tertullian himself had spoken quite differently in his *Apology* (cf. 42.3). Still it was extremely important for Christian theology that such statements were expressed. They kept alive a consciousness of the problem. Tertullian recognized with sure instinct that something had happened in Jesus and in his praxis of absolute nonviolence, something which the church could not evade.

Origen too was able to express opposition in principle to any Christian military service. For him the *holiness of the communities* could not be reconciled with violence. In response to Celsus's urgent admonition to "be fellow-soldiers" with the emperor, he answered as follows (*Contra Celsum* 8.73):

> It is also your opinion that the priests of certain images and wardens of the temples of the gods, as you think them to be, should keep their right hand undefiled for the sake of the sacrifices, that they may offer the customary sacrifices to those who you say are gods with

hands unstained by blood and pure from murders. And in fact when war comes you do not enlist the priests. If, then, this is reasonable, how much more reasonable is it that, while others fight, Christians also should be fighting as priests and worshippers of God, keeping their right hands pure and by their prayers to God striving for those who fight in a righteous cause and for the emperor who reigns righteously.[199]

Two elements of this argumentation are particularly noteworthy. First, Origen does not say that we pray "for the victory of the emperor," but "for those who fight in a righteous cause." The two things are not the same. Unfortunately, Christianity very quickly forgot this painstaking differentiation and all too frequently placed its prayer and its influence in the service of interests of power and domination. This was precisely what Origen sought to prevent. According to him, the task of the church consisted in creating an atmosphere in which the demons of war which corrupted men would have to yield. Only in this way would peace become possible. According to Origen (*Contra Celsum* 8.73):

We who by our prayers destroy all daemons which stir up wars, violate oaths, and disturb the peace, are of more help to the emperors than those who seem to be doing the fighting.[200]

Second, Origen's argumentation is noteworthy because he does not defend the church's refusal of military service by arguing that a Christian soldier could become ensnared in the imperial cult. His argument is rather that the church is a *holy, priestly people* and that its members must not be smeared with blood. If we translate the cultic language which Origen used into our contemporary language, this means nothing other than that the church is a divine contrast-society (it is holy), and that it therefore must not use violence (shed blood) like the rest of society. It can perform its specific service to the world (its priesthood) only in absolute nonviolence.

7
THE FULFILLMENT OF ISAIAH 2

Tertullian and Origen recognized clearly that the question of the compatibility of Christianity and military service was not a peripheral issue. At stake is *the church's nonviolence*; and since Christ, the Lord of the church, renounced all force and died impotently on the cross, this concerns the most central part of the church's existence.

The theme of the *nonviolent* church moved all the Fathers, not only Tertullian and Origen. This theme cannot be sought merely in connection with the question of Christian military service; it is also discussed in quite different contexts. One such context is the patristic exegesis of Isaiah 2.

We have already seen that Isa. 2:2–5 (cf. Mic. 4:1–5) is one of the most important Old Testament texts for the concept of the pilgrimage of the nations (cf. I: 5). In the last days, Isaiah says, Mount Zion with the house of the Lord will rise above all other peaks. In other words, in the eschatological age of salvation Israel will begin to shine as God's model society. Then, according to Isa. 2:3*, nations from all over the world will stream toward Jerusalem, in order to learn there the only social order which is worth living and which makes life possible:

> For from Zion a social order will be proclaimed, as the word of the Lord from Jerusalem.

The decisive element in this social order is that it will not remain pure theory, but will be lived in Israel. Otherwise it would hardly fascinate the nations of the world, much less attract them. But it is also decisive that this new order of living recognizes and overcomes the basic problem of all human society: the desire to dominate, the inclination to violence, the eternal rivalries. It is precisely nonviolence, evidently the most important characteristic of the new social order, which makes it so fascinating. As Isa. 2:4 describes it:

> And they shall beat their swords into plowshares,
>   and their spears into pruning hooks;
> nation shall not lift up sword against nation,
>   neither shall they learn war any more.

This text of Isaiah on the eschatological pilgrimage of the nations to Zion and the beginning of God's new society played an extraordinary role in patristic exegesis. The early church Fathers were convinced that the prophecy of Isaiah had been fulfilled. The salvific age of which Isaiah spoke had begun. The Word of the Lord had gone forth. God's new social order had been proclaimed. The house of the Lord was already visible over all hills, and the nations were already streaming into the house of God.

The most magnificent expression of this comes from Origen (*Contra Celsum* 5.33). Like all the Fathers, he interprets the "house of the Lord" as the church, and the peoples who come to the "mountain of the Lord" as Gentile Christians. The law which goes forth from Zion is the "spiritual law," that is the teaching of Jesus.

> Each one of us *has come* 'in the last days,' when our Jesus came, 'to the visible mountain of the Lord,' to the Word far above every word, and to the house of God which is 'the church of the living God, a pillar and ground of the truth.' And we see how he built on 'the tops of the mountains' which are all the sayings of the prophets who are his foundation. This house is exalted 'above the hills' which are those men who seem to profess some exceptional ability in wisdom and truth. And 'all nations' are coming to it, and 'many nations' go, and we exhort one another to the worship of God through Jesus Christ which has shone out in the last days, saying: 'Come, and let us go up to the mountain of the Lord and to the house of the God of Jacob, and he will proclaim to us his way and we will walk in it.' For from those in Sion a spiritual law has come forth and changed from them to us.[201]

Justin, Irenaeus, and Tertullian also interpreted this passage in similar fashion. They were all convinced that *Isaiah 2 had already been fulfilled*. What brought them to this position? First of all, the statement that the Word of the Lord goes out from Jerusalem. The early church probably interpreted its missionary experiences with the Gentiles from the beginning in the light of the prophetic message of the pilgrimage of the nations (cf. III: 8). The Fathers in any case certainly did so. For them it was beyond question that the pilgrimage of the nations to Zion had taken place. Isaiah 2 had been fulfilled inasmuch as the Word of the Lord had reached all nations through the preaching of the apostles who had gone forth from Jerusalem (cf. Acts 1:8) and the nations had become a "people from among the Gentiles" (Acts 15:14*) through their acceptance of the gospel. According to Origen, we, the Gentile Christians, are those who have come "as all nations" to the radiant mountain of the Lord. The Fathers had absolutely no difficulty in identifying the *emergence of the Gentile church* with the *pilgrimage of the nations to Zion*, because to them the "house of the Lord" on Mount Zion was nothing other than the church.

But there was also a second reason leading many Fathers to consider the prophecy of Isaiah 2 as fulfilled. It was not only that the Word of the Lord had gone forth from Jerusalem and reached all nations, but also that *the eschatological state of nonviolence and peace, prophesied by Isaiah, had already become reality in the church*. This notion is so breathtaking and yet so typical of the ecclesiology of the first three centuries that it is worth letting a number of texts speak for themselves. As Justin wrote in his *Apology* (1.39):

> But when the Prophetic Spirit speaks, as foretelling what is going to happen, His words are the following: 'For the law shall come forth from Sion, and the word of the Lord from Jerusalem. And He shall judge the Gentiles, and rebuke many people; and they shall turn their swords into ploughshares, and their spears into sickles; nation shall not lift up sword against nation, neither shall they be exercised any more in war.' That this prophecy, too, was verified you can readily believe, for twelve illiterate men, unskilled in the art of speaking, went out from Jerusalem into the world, and by the power of God they announced to the men of every nation that they were sent by Christ to teach everyone the word of God; and we, who once killed one another, [now] not only do not wage war against our enemies, but, in order to avoid lying or deceiving our examiners, we even meet death cheerfully, confessing Christ.[202]

The reference to martyrs makes crystal clear that Justin is not speaking of a moral education of the entire human race, but of the nonviolence of Christians. The "Once and Now" terminology signals the contrast between the church and pagan society. Equally straightforward is a passage from Justin's *Dialogue with Trypho* (110.2–3):

> For, we Christians, who have gained a knowledge of the true worship of God from the Law and from the word which went forth from Jerusalem by way of the Apostles of Jesus, have run for protection to the God of Jacob and the God of Israel. And we who

delighted in war, in the slaughter of one another, and in every other kind of iniquity have in every part of the world converted our weapons of war into implements of peace — our swords into ploughshares, our spears into farmers' tools — and we cultivate piety, justice, brotherly charity, faith, and hope, which we derive from the Father through the Crucified Savior.[203]

This passage from Justin's *Dialogue* shows more clearly than the *Apology* the original function of the ancient Christian "fulfillment exegesis" of Isaiah 2 (and Micah 4). In controversies with Judaism, an effort was made to show clearly that in Jesus of Nazareth the Messiah had already come. Shortly before the cited passage (110.1–2) Justin had said to his Jewish dialogue partner:

I am aware that your teachers admit that this whole passage refers to Christ; I also know that they affirm that Christ has not yet come. But they say that even if He has come, it is not known who He is, until He shall become manifest and glorious; then, they say, He shall be known. Then, they state, everything foretold in the above-quoted prophecy will be verified, as if not a word of the prophecy had yet been fulfilled.[204]

Isaiah 2 (and Micah 4) have already borne fruit; they had already seen fulfillment. The Messiah has already come; the messianic turn has already occurred. Irenaeus (*Adversus Haereses* IV.34.4) interprets the passage in exactly the same sense:

But if the law of liberty, that is, the word of God, preached by the apostles (who went forth from Jerusalem) throughout all the earth, caused such a change in the state of things, that these [nations] did form the swords and war-lances into ploughshares, and . . . pruning-hooks . . . [that is] into instruments used for peaceful purposes, and that they are now unaccustomed to fighting, but when smitten, offer also the other cheek, then the prophets have not spoken these things of any other person, but of Him who effected them. This person is our Lord.[205]

As in the other cited passages, there is no reference here to transformation of the whole of society, but rather to the people of the Messiah, which lives according to Matt. 5:39, thus beginning the transformation of the world and demonstrating the messianic character of Jesus. The same is true of Tertullian (*Against the Jews* 3.9–10):

"And they shall join to beat their (swords) into ploughs, and their lances into sickles; and nations shall not take up (sword) against nation, and they shall no more learn to fight." Who else, therefore, are understood but *we*, who, fully taught by the new law, observe these practices?[206]

Origen (*Contra Celsum* 5.33) thinks the same way:

No longer do we take the sword against any nation, nor do we learn war any more, since we have become sons of peace through Jesus.[207]

The context of these passages must not be overlooked if their meaning is to be grasped correctly. The "fulfillment exegesis" of Isaiah 2 is originally set in disputes with Judaism; this is evident is Justin, Irenaeus and Tertullian. The Jews argue quite correctly that if nothing in the world has been changed, the Messiah cannot have come. If the Messiah had come, then at least the prophecy of peace in Isa. 2:4 would have become reality. Yet, they say, there is no indication that this has occurred. The world is still full of war; men still fight their battles. So Jesus of Nazareth cannot have been the Messiah.

This Jewish objection must be taken very seriously. It is the strongest objection there is against Christianity. It strikes the innermost nerve of Christian faith. As we have seen, the Fathers evidently took the objection quite seriously. It is above all important that they did not dispute its premises. They agreed completely with Judaism that the world must really be changed when the Messiah comes.

The reply of the early church Fathers to the central Jewish objection to Christianity is not that the world need not be changed, since redemption takes place *invisibly*; nor is it that redemption will not occur until *the end of the world.* Their answer is rather that the Messiah has come and that the world has in fact changed. It has been transformed *in the Messiah's people*, which lives in accord with the law of Christ. There is no longer any violence in the messianic people, the church. There all have become "sons of peace" (Luke 10:6*). There people prefer to be struck on the other cheek than to retaliate (Matt. 5:39). There the making of war has been unlearned. Isaiah 2 has already been fulfilled in the church.

It must be obvious that this answer is quite risky. It endangers the whole of Christology if one day the reality of the church contradicts it. The early church Fathers' willingness to risk such an argument is all the more moving because they had already elaborated a hermeneutical principle which would have offered a more harmless and much less dangerous solution.

Justin (*Dialogue* 110.2) summarizes this hermeneutical principle as follows. As far as Christ is concerned, two parousias are to be distinguished: his first coming in weakness and his second coming in power from heaven. A portion of the Old Testament prophecies relates to his first coming in lowliness, but a second part pertains exclusively to his appearance in power and glory.

How easy it would have been, with this hermeneutical principle, to relate Isa. 2:4 solely to that "eternal peace" which will exist only after Christ's return, in the perfected reign of God. But the early church Fathers did not follow this harmless, safe path (cf. Justin, *Dialogue* 110.5). They insisted that the new worship of God, the new manner of life, the new creation already had visible and tangible effects in the church. They insisted that Isa. 2:4 must have been fulfilled already and that it had been fulfilled already, in the age of the church.

8
THE CONFIRMATION OF TRUTH
THROUGH PRAXIS

In the preceding section we encountered the central objection of Judaism to Christian claims: *How can the Messiah have come if nothing in the world has changed?* Examined more closely, this is not only the basic question of Jews. Every non-Christian raises a similar question. *How can you speak of redemption if nothing in the world has changed since the coming of your redeemer?* For this reason, the truth of Christian faith can shine only when it is intelligible through the praxis of Christians. The ancient church, filled in this respect as in others with biblical sobriety, recognized this connection clearly. It knew that it had to be a *sign* of the truth of the gospel in its entire existence. The astonishing growth which it experienced in a relatively brief period can only be explained through the radiance of that sign.

Norbert Brox has recently pointed out that the ancient church had no structures and strategies for systematic missionary activity. According to Brox, if it is possible at all to speak of the ancient church's missionary theory the most that can be said is this. The twelve apostles preached the gospel in the whole world and established a sufficient number of local churches. This marked the conclusion of mission in the strict sense. The communities established by the apostles existed from then on as signs of the truth. Pagan society was then in a position to choose.[208]

This was in principle the whole missionary theory of the ancient church. A strict distinction was made between the specific and unique missionary charge of the apostles and the task of symbolic presence incumbent upon all churches. Obviously this did not exclude missionary activity in the period which followed the apostles. But it is evident "that Christianity in the pre-Constantinian age achieved its astonishing growth simply through its presence and notability, not through organized missionary efforts."[209]

A great and unshakable confidence that Christian praxis will of itself convince others permeates the writings of all the Apologists. Again and again they tell their pagan readers that Christians have true praxis as well as true teaching, and that the two are profoundly bound together. As Athenagoras (*Supplication for the Christians* 11) wrote:

> But among us you will find uneducated persons, and artisans, and old women, who, if they are unable in words to prove the benefit of our doctrine, yet by their deeds exhibit the benefit arising from their persuasion of its truth: they do not rehearse speeches, but exhibit good works; when struck, they do not strike again; when robbed, they do not go to law; they give to those that ask of them, and love their neighbors as themselves.[210]

Anyone who grasps the need to convince through correct praxis also knows that failure diminishes the symbolic force of the church. Thus Ignatius writes to the church of Tralles (8.2):

> Let none of you have a grudge against his neighbor. Give no occasion to the heathen, in order that the congregation of God may not

be blasphemed for a few foolish persons. For "Woe unto him through whom my name is vainly blasphemed among any."[211]

Polycarp of Smyrna writes in a very similar fashion. The following citation from a letter of his to Philippi (10.2) shows that a fixed parenetic structure is beginning to develop on the basis of Old Testament precedents. The structure will find frequent application in the period which follows.

> "Be ye all subject one to the other, having your conversation blameless among the Gentiles," that you may receive praise "for your good works" and that the Lord be not blasphemed in you.[212]

One of the best and most moving applications of this parenetic scheme may be found in the so-called second letter of Clement, a wide-ranging early Christian homily which cannot be dated precisely. The author first establishes (4.1–3) that true worship of God consists in the right praxis, not in beautiful words:

> Let us, then, not merely call him Lord, for this will not save us. For he says, "Not everyone that saith to me Lord, Lord, shall be saved, but he that doeth righteousness." So then, brethren, let us confess him in our deeds, by loving one another, by not committing adultery, nor speaking one against another, nor being jealous, but by being self-controlled, merciful, good.[213]

Later (13.2–3) the author speaks of denying God through evil deeds. False Christian praxis will inevitably lead pagans to assume that Christian doctrine is merely deception and human invention:

> For the Lord says, "Every way is my name blasphemed among all the heathen," and again, "Woe unto him on whose account my name is blasphemed." Wherein is it blasphemed? In that you do not do what I desire. For when the heathen hear from our mouth the oracles of God, they wonder at their beauty and greatness; afterwards, when they find out that our deeds are unworthy of the words which we speak, they turn from their wonder to blasphemy, saying that it is a myth and delusion.[214]

In all these texts the biblical relation between the church and the honor of God is immediately tangible. When the church is criticized among the nations because of its bad example, the holy name of God itself is dishonored. This presupposes that the church is the sign, the presence, the honor of God in the world. When the church obscures this sign, it impedes the work of salvation and disfigures the true nature of God. If, on the contrary, the church lives the truth of the gospel, then the name of God is glorified among the nations, and God's plan for the world progresses. Against this background, there is much reason to believe that *1 Clement* 59.4 establishes a relationship of knowledge among church, Christ and God. This passage reads as follows:

> Let all "nations know thee, that thou art God alone," and that Jesus Christ is thy child, and that "we are thy people and the sheep of thy pasture."[215]

This is probably a prayer that the church become recognizable as the people of God. In any case, Origen (*Contra Celsum* 3.33) did not hesitate to say:

> The evidences of Jesus' divinity are the Churches of people who have been helped.[216]

Evidently the ancient church saw a much stronger connection between the symbolic character of the church and Christology than we do today. The true nature of Christ can shine forth only when the church makes visible the messianic alternative and the eschatological new creation which have taken their place in the world since Christ.

Such an ecclesiology again raises the question (cf. III: 8) whether Christians do not impose on themselves a horrible compulsion to succeed and a merciless pressure to achieve results. Do they not transform the church into a religious achievement society, the most repulsive sort which exists? How can such an ecclesiology come to terms with the lukewarm and the weak, with those who have sinned and failed, with borderline figures in the church?

These objections, which must be taken with absolute seriousness, show that *church as contrast-society* cannot be achieved simply by investing a greater amount of moral energy than other movements of moral rearmament have mustered over the course of human history. It is not by accident that two units of this book refer to "Discipleship" in their titles (III and IV). Discipleship of Jesus in no way begins by being asked to live more heroically than others do or have done in the past. It rather begins with a superabundant gift. Jesus points with his entire existence to the miracle occurring in history, the arrival of the reign of God. This miracle could not be brought about by human strength; it was uncontrollable and completely gratuitous. Discipleship means to sense the miracle of the reign of God and to pursue radically the path of Jesus, fascinated by the gift of a new possibility of human community.

This path is not a broad and comfortable street on which the mass of people travel. It is narrow and exposed. In the case of Jesus it led to a violent death, and it has also had mortal repercussions for many who followed Jesus. Yet it is the path to life. At its beginning stands the miracle of the reign of God, and this miracle supports all that ensues.

The ancient church knew that its messianic existence, its existence as contrast-society, was possible only on the basis of the miracle which God performed in history (cf. IV: 2). It knew that for the church fully to become church is pure grace. It knew finally that the church lives from the side of the Crucified, that its life stems from death, and that it can save its life only when it is constantly prepared to lose it.

It could not be the task of this book to write about the congregation as the *location of grace* and the church as the *fruit of the cross of Christ*. To do this would have required another book. But precisely because this further area has been bracketed, it is necessary to emphasize once again that the idea of church as contrast-society would be fundamentally misunderstood if the church were not seen as creation of the grace of God and fruit of the cross of Christ. Its contrast to pagan society does not stem from "efficiency and moralism,"[217] but from the miracle of the inbreaking reign of God. It is for this reason that the guilty and the unsuccessful have a place in the church, for grace comes to perfection in human impotence. And it is for this reason that the miracle of new creation shines most beautifully in the church when it emerges as love and reconciliation in situations which—seen from a human perspective—seem lost and hopeless.

Postscript
The Heritage of
Augustine

In units III and IV of this book I have attempted to sketch at least
an outline of the reception of Jesus' praxis of the reign of God in
the age of the New Testament communities and the early church
Fathers. It would have been a mistake from the start to conduct
this attempt with reference to the concept of the reign of God; we
need only realize that the *presence of the reign of God*, which
plays such an important role for Jesus, was transformed into different terminology as early as Paul. Paul hardly speaks of the presence of the kingdom, but refers frequently instead to the *presence
of the Spirit*.

Our extended lingering over the history of the reception of what
Jesus initiated has been obviously worthwhile. We have seen to a
completely unexpected degree how the apostolic and postapostolic
communities continued the praxis of Jesus with fidelity and sensitivity. There would be little point in summarizing the results of our
study once again. It is meaningful, however, to consider another
question, one which imposes itself on us at this point. When did
the highly *continuous* history of reception, which we have seen at
least fragmentarily, actually come to an end?

The question has its pitfalls, for every history of reception continues steadily in some transformations and metamorphoses. We
must therefore ask more precise questions. When did the church
no longer venture to say that it was the messianic location of absolute renunciation of violence? When did the church no longer understand itself as God's contrast-society? When did the idea of

being God's sign among the nations recede in its awareness? When we ask questions with this precision, it is clear that the so-called "Constantinian Turn" marks a profound break. And if we seek a literary indication of this break, Augustine's *City of God* must in any case be mentioned. This last great apology, the climax of all Christian apologies, reflects some very clear shifts which made it impossible to consider the *City of God* in unit IV of this book to an extent corresponding to its importance.

It is true that in this monumental work the contrast-scheme which was so important to the Apologists of the second and third centuries continues to play a decisive role. The city of God (*civitas Dei*) and the earthly city (*civitas terrena*) are frequently contrasted.

The earthly city creates its own gods arbitrarily, while the city of God is created by the true God (18.54). In the earthly city self-love dominates — in the city of God true love, which goes beyond oneself, reigns (14.13, 28). The earthly city is marked by conflict and war; peace is possible only temporarily, and even that is a highly fragile peace brought about by war (15.4, 17); but in the city of God there is a true, eternal peace. The earthly city lusts after domination (1; 4.6; 14.28); in the city of God there are only humility, concern and obedience (14.28).

This list could easily be lengthened. It is an impressive one. If Augustine had simply identified the city of God with the pilgrim church and the earthly city with non-Christian society then the Augustinian conception could be judged the absolute climax of what the early church Fathers developed. Then church and pagan society would stand opposed to one another in stark contrast.

But there is no possibility of saying this. Things are much more complicated in Augustine. While his contrast-scheme is clearly dependent on the older theology, Augustine shifted the emphases quite significantly. The city of God and the earthly city form on earth an irresolvable mixture (*corpus mixtum*), which no longer permits at all a true contrasting of pilgrim church and non-Christian society. Where Augustine does contrast sharply he is in principle always comparing the heavenly and eschatological city of God to the earthly city. The contrast does then function in his work; but this contrast-scheme is of course no longer that of the early church Fathers which was described above.

Augustine conceives and defines the city of God completely on the basis of its protological origin and its eschatological future. We could easily say that he thinks about it on the basis of its transcendent nature. Many citations reflecting this perspective could be adduced. We begin with a single example (*City of God* 15.1):

> The city of the saints is above, though it brings forth citizens here below, in whose persons it sojourns as an alien until the time of its kingdom shall come. On that day it will assemble them all as they rise again in their bodies, and they will receive their promised kingdom, where with their Prince, who is king of the ages, they will reign for all eternity.[218]

This text shows that the city of God has its genuine location "above," in a transcendent realm; its citizens pilgrimaging on earth live in exile. This is obviously nothing new; to see this we need only look at Phil. 3:20–21. But the consistency with which a whole "cosmology" of history is developed along these lines is new. In this passage, and generally throughout the *City of God* (20.9 is an exception), the *kingdom of God* is conceived as purely future and purely transcendent. The *gathering* mentioned here does not refer to anything like the gathering of the people of God on earth in such a way that this people could step forward as a divine sign for the rest of society. Augustine thinks instead of the resurrection of the dead. Even the following passage (*City of God* 2.18) scarcely thinks of the earthly gathering of the people of God, but rather of the transcendent gathering of those rescued from the world, those who one after another leave the world:

> Christ . . . slowly withdraws his family from a world everywhere infected with . . . evils and going to ruin, in order with that family to establish a city everlasting.[219]

It is highly unlikely that Augustine here refers to the earthly gathering of the pilgrim church, for according to him the pilgrim church is not glorious. The age of the pilgrim church is an obscure time in which there is little joy; as the following text (*City of God* 18.49) indicates, where joy does exist, its origin is hope:

In this evil world, therefore, in these evil days, when amid present humiliation the church is preparing for her future high estate, and is schooled by the goads of fear, the tortures of sorrow, the vexations of toil and the dangers of temptation, rejoicing only in hope, in so far as her joy is wholesome, many reprobates are mingled with the good, and both kinds are gathered together as it were into the drag-net of the gospel. And in this world, as it were in a sea, both swim indiscriminately enclosed in nets until shore is reached, where the evil are to be separated from the good, and "God is to be all in all" among the good, as it were in his temple.[220]

The tone of a text of this sort is new; it is scarcely possible to find a comparable tone in the first three centuries. It is not pessimism, but it is *tristesse*. It is the hoping sorrow of Gregorian Chant. It is hard to see how this church could become God's contrast-society in the world; the church is hardly recognizable in its already experienced salvation. Evil and good are mixed in it "without distinction" from a human point of view; "gathering" occasions on earth no division, but on the contrary insoluble confusion. Is it then coincidental that *temple of God*, which in Paul refers to the church *on earth* can now stand only for those who have finally arrived in heaven?

It is time to conclude. The *City of God* is a monumental, grandiose work in which one can almost always find passages which support the opposite of what has just been asserted. Nonetheless, it is surely clear how much has changed since the first three centuries! One thing seems to me certain. In the *City of God* there is hardly any trace of the irruption of something new in history or of the symbolic presence of the reign of God powerfully presenting itself and quite tangible — a presence so characteristic of Jesus.[221] It is true that the early church Fathers rarely spoke of the presence of the reign of God; but they did express verbally in their own language games the new and forceful dimension of God's reign. For Augustine, on the contrary, the city of God has been present since creation; the appearance of Christ hardly changes anything (cf. 12.28; 15.1; 17.1)!

The individualization of history is almost necessarily implied in making the reign of God so radically transcendent. In any case it was Augustine who first coined the famous formula which Adolf von Harnack later used as a refrain in his *What is Christianity?*[222] It was the young Augustine of the *Soliloquies*, who still stood under the spell of Neoplatonism. (But did Augustine ever become completely free of this Platonism?) After one of the most beautiful prayers of Christian antiquity, in which he has prayed for true knowledge, he says the following in the course of a dialogue with his own reason (*Soliloquies* 2.7):

> *Augustine.* Lo, I have prayed to God.
> *Reason.* Now what do you want to know?
> *A.* All those things which I prayed for.
> *R.* Sum them up briefly.
> *A.* I desire to know God and the soul.
> *R.* Nothing more?
> *A.* Absolutely nothing.[223]

Abbreviations

AB	Analecta Biblica
ANF	The Ante-Nicene Fathers, 10 vols. Edited by A. Roberts and J. Donaldson (Grand Rapids: Wm. B. Eerdmans)
EKK	Evangelisch-Katholischer Kommentar zum Neuen Testament
ET	English translation
FC	The Fathers of the Church, 71 vols. (Washington: The Catholic Univ. of America Press)
FRLANT	Forschungen zur Religion und Literatur des Alten und Neuen Testaments
FzB	Forschung zur Bibel
GNT	Grundrisse zum Neuen Testament
HTKNT	Herders Theologischer Kommentar zum Neuen Testament
ITS	Innsbrucker Theologische Studien
LCL	Loeb Classical Library (Cambridge: Harvard Univ. Press; London: William Heinemann)
LF	Library of the Fathers, 48 vols. (Oxford: Parker)
NTA	Neutestamentliche Abhandlungen
NTD	Neues Testament Deutsch
QD	Quaestiones Disputatae
SANT	Studien zum Alten und Neuen Testament
SBS	Stuttgarter Bibelstudien
SUNT	Studien zur Umwelt des Neuen Testaments
TTS	Tübinger Theologische Studien

WMANT   Wissenschaftliche Monographien zum Alten und Neuen Testament

WUNT   Wissenschaftliche Untersuchungen zum Neuen Testament

Notes

1. A. von Harnack, *Das Wesen des Christentums*. All references are to the recent German paperback edition.

2. Ibid., 31.

3. Ibid., 43.

4. Ibid., 90.

5. Ibid., 45.

6. Ibid., 76.

7. Ibid., 31, 43, 90, 155.

8. Ibid., 111.

9. Ibid., 114–15.

10. Ibid., 103.

11. This point is developed especially by K. H. Neufeld, *Adolf Harnacks Konflikt mit der Kirche*.

12. Cf. *Das Wesen des Christentums*, 51–53, 73, 75.

13. Ibid., 73.

14. E. Grässer, "Jesus und das Heil Gottes: Bemerkungen sur sog. 'Individualisierung des Heils,'" 182–83.

15. Gisbert Greshake, "Einige Überlegungen zu den Ursachen des mangelnden Priesternachwuchses," 8–9.

16. Cf. the still unsurpassed study of H. de Lubac, *Catholicism*.

17. For more detailed demonstration of this cf. J. Becker, *Johannes der Täufer und Jesus von Nazareth*.

18. Ibid., 30.

19. Cf. also the applications of the Exodus tradition to later issues in Isa. 40:3–4; 41:17–20; 43:19–20; 48:20–21; 49:9–13; Jer. 2:1–6; Hos. 12:10.

20. Cf. Exod. 15:17; 2 Sam. 7:10; Isa. 60:21; 61:3; Jer. 32:41; 42:10; Matt. 15:13.

21. Cf. especially the *Book of Jubilees* 36:6 and *Psalms of Solomon* 14:3–4.

22. Cf. H. Geist, "Jesus vor Israel – Der Ruf zur Sammlung," 31:44; G. Theissen, *Soziologie der Jesusbewegung*, 33–90, especially 77, 88.

23. The term "gathering" is used increasingly in scholarly literature to describe Jesus' specific activity with regard to Israel. Cf. especially R. Pesch, "Der Anspruch Jesu."

24. Cf. J. Jeremias, *Neutestamentliche Theologie*, 225.

25. For proof of this cf. M. Trautmann, *Zeichenhafte Handlungen Jesu*, 167–233.

26. Ibid., 220–25.

27. It is astonishing that Leopold Ettmeyer does not so much as mention the constitution of the Twelve in his unpublished 155-page dissertation, *Der theologische Ort Israels in der Botschaft Jesu* (Innsbruck, 1979). Under these circumstances, the work's conclusion that Israel is surpassed as a "principle of salvation" is not surprising. This dissertation ignores essential elements of Jesus' praxis of the reign of God, works with unclarified concepts (such as "principle of salvation"), and turns the objective facts upside down.

28. Cf. R. Pesch, "Der Anspruch Jesu," 68.

29. On the difference between the meaning of the parable in Mark and its original meaning cf. R. Pesch, *Das Markusevangelium* 2:305–13.

30. Cf. the slightly different reconstruction of S. Schulz, *Q*, 323–24.

31. D. Zeller ("Das Logion Mt 8,11f/Lk 13,28f und das Motiv der Völkerwallfahrt") has rightly pointed out that Jesus made use of the concept of the pilgrimage of the nations precisely in order to provoke Israel. But this includes rather than excludes Jesus' acceptance of this concept. He was only convinced that no radiance which could attract the nations went forth from Israel as it then existed.

32. Cf. the exegesis of Isa. 2:1–5 in N. Lohfink, *Die messianische Alternative*, 12–13.

33. On Jesus' concept of the pilgrimage of the nations cf. especially J. Jeremias, *Jesu Verheissung für die Völker*.

34. Cf. Isa. 2:1–4; 60:1–22; Jer. 3:17; Zeph. 3:8–11; Hag. 2:6–9; Zech. 2:10–13; 8:20–23.

35. Cf. R. Pesch, "Der Anspruch Jesu," 56.

36. Especially since the judging function already plays a certain role in the mission of the Twelve; cf. Mark 6:11.

37. That Jesus' death is interpreted as a death for Israel in Heb. 13:12 is not unimportant. One must on the whole ask if a universal interpretation, on Jesus' part, of his own death would not have led immediately to the start of the Gentile mission. Cf. R. Pesch, "Voraussetzungen und Anfänge der urchristlichen Mission," 41.

38. R. Schnackenburg, *Gottes Herrschaft und Reich*, 150.

39. J. Jeremias, *Neutestamentliche Theologie*, 167.

40. On this cf. G. Lohfink, "Universalismus und Exklusivität des Heils im Neuen Testament," 63–82.

41. Well noted by J. R. W. Stott, "Reiche Gottes und Gemeinschaft," and G. E. Ladd, *Jesus and the Kingdom.*

42. K. Müller, "Jesu Naherwartung und die Anfänge der Kirche," 20.

43. J. Jeremias, *Neutestamentliche Theologie*, 164.

44. On the notion of disciple cf. above all M. Hengel, *Nachfolge und Charisma* and H. Merklein, "Der Jüngerkreis Jesu."

45. Cf. the important essay of H. Schürmann, "Der Jüngerkreis Jesu als Zeichen für Israel."

46. On Jesus' avoidance of the notion of "remnant" cf. J. Jeremias, *Neutestamentliche Theologie*, 167–74.

47. Cf. A. Polag's reconstruction of the Sermon on the Mount in Q (*Fragmenta Q*, 32–38).

48. Cf. N. Lohfink, *Das Hauptgebot*, 59.

49. J. Jeremias, *Neutestamentliche Theologie*, 216.

50. Cf. the beautiful remarks of R. Riesner, *Formen gemeinsamen Lebens im Neuen Testament und heute*, 21–22.

51. N. Lohfink, *Kirchenträume*, 40.

52. *Keth* 96a. For further statements on the service of a rabbi by his students cf. H. L. Strack and P. Billerbeck, *Kommentar zum Neuen Testament aus Talmud und Midrasch*, 1:920.

53. Thus for example E. Schweizer, *Das Evangelium nach Matthäus*, 281–82.

54. On the reconstruction cf. H. Merklein, *Die Gottesherrschaft als Handlungsprinzip*, 269–75. It is uncertain (and also disputed) whether the third saying (Matt. 5:41) belongs to Q.

55. It is not acceptable to reject in principle a dispatch of the disciples by Jesus. Even the striking phenomenon that the mission tradition contains no Christology tells against this.

56. On the dimension of "signs" in the context of the missionary discourse cf. I. Bosold, *Pazifismus und prophetische Provokation*, 81–92.

57. For more detailed treatment of this problem cf. G. Lohfink, "Der ekklesiale Sitz im Leben der Aufforderung Jesu zum Gewaltverzicht (Mt 5, 39b–42/Lk 6, 29f)," 236–53.

58. Cf. the parable of Elischa ben Abuja, Aboth RN 24.

59. On this cf. the important work of H. Merklein, *Die Gottesherrschaft als Handlungsprinzip.*

60. Cf. Strack and Billerbeck, *Kommentar*, 1:608–09.

61. *Gotteslob: Katholisches Gebet- und Gesangbuch*, No. 639.

62. Cf. N. Lohfink, *Die messianische Alternative*, 12–26.

63. L. Schottroff, "Die enge Pforte," 122.

64. Cf. E. Schweizer, *Evangelium nach Matthäus*, 61.

65. The thesis "that Jesus never depicted the reign of God as efficacious at present in the circle of his disciples or followers" was defended above

all by Werner Georg Kümmel. On the development of Kümmel's position, which had and still has great influence, cf. G. Heinz, *Das Problem der Kirchenentstehung in der deutschen protestantischen Theologie des 20. Jahrhunderts*, 232–35.

66. R. Schnackenburg, *Gottes Herrschaft*, 154.

67. So for example ibid., 247–48, and J. R. W. Stott, *Reich Gottes*. But Stott (13–14) also refers emphatically to the profound relationship between reign of God and people of God.

68. For more detailed treatment cf. G. Lohfink, "Der Ablauf der Ostereignisse und die Anfänge der Urgemeinde," 162–76.

69. For more detail cf. G. Lohfink, "Der Ursprung der christlichen Taufe," 35–54.

70. Cf. G. Lohfink, "Der Ablauf," 170–71.

71. Good insight into the recent discussions of *ekklēsia* is afforded by H. Merklein, "Die Ekklesia Gottes"; and W. Klaiber, *Rechtfertigung und Gemeinde*, 11–21.

72. Cf. ibid., 22.

73. On the following cf. ibid., 11–50, 167–70; and Niels A. Dahl, *Das Volk Gottes*.

74. Cf. W. Trilling, *Das wahre Israel*, and G. Lohfink, *Die Sammlung Israels*.

75. This is developed well by B. Klappert, "Traktat für Israel (Röm. 9–11)," esp. 111–13.

76. Cf. the excellent case studies of C. Ernst, *Teufelsaustreibungen*.

77. J. Jervell, "Die Zeichen des Apostels," 68.

78. Ibid., 54–75, and J. Jervell, "Der unbekannte Paulus," 29–49.

79. On this cf. G. Lohfink, "Der Ablauf," 164–74.

80. H. W. Wolff, *Dodekapropheton 2*, 79.

81. Cf. G. Lohfink, "Jesus hat Gemeinschaft hergestellt," 129–32.

82. This is the argument of the declaration on the question of admitting women to the ministerial priesthood issued on October 15, 1976, by the Sacred Congregation for the Doctrine of the Faith ("Inter Insigniores," *Acta Apostolicae Sedis* 67 [1977] 98–116). The document argues that Jesus called no women to membership in the Twelve, although his conduct with regard to women was in other respects uniquely distinct from that of his environment, and concludes from this that Jesus excluded women in principle from the priesthood.

83. Cf. Strack and Billerbeck, *Kommentar*, 4/1:44–46.

84. E. S. Gerstenberger and W. Schrage, *Frau und Mann*, 123.

85. H. Gülzow, *Christentum und Sklaverei in den ersten drei Jahrhunderten*, 40.

86. Cf. P. Stuhlmacher, *Der Brief an Philemon*, 42.

87. There are several texts—1 Cor. 7:17–24; Col. 3:22–4:1; Eph. 6:5–9; 1 Tim. 6:1–2; Titus 2:9–10; 1 Pet. 2:18–25—which are largely parenesis for

slaves. Nonetheless, apart from 1 Tim. 6:2, they yield hardly any information about our particular question.

88. Cf. A. von Harnack, *Die Mission und Ausbreitung des Christentums in den ersten drei Jahrhunderten*, 1:174–78, and Joachim Gnilka's extended and valuable excursus on "Slaves in the Ancient World and in Early Christianity" (*Der Philemonbrief*, 78–80).

89. This objection has been raised especially by S. Schulz, *Gott ist kein Sklavenhalter*.

90. For a New Testament perspective on women deacons cf. G. Lohfink, "Weibliche Diakone im Neuen Testament."

91. On Aquila and Prisca cf. W. H. Ollrog, *Paulus und seiner Mitarbeiter*, 24–27.

92. H. J. Klauck, *Hausgemeinde und Hauskirche im frühen Christentum*, 26.

93. On the following, cf. B. Brooten, "'Junia . . . hervorragend unter den Aposteln' (Röm 16,7)," and G. Lohfink, "Weibliche Diakone," 391–95.

94. Cf. W. H. Ollrog, *Paulus*, 75.

95. P. Stuhlmacher, *Der Brief an Philemon*, 74.

96. Cf. Acts 2:42; Rom. 15:26; 2 Cor. 8:4; 9:13; Gal. 2:9; Phil. 2:1; Heb. 13:16; 1 John 1:3, 7.

97. In the New Testament the place of the reciprocal pronoun *allēlōn* can occasionally be taken by *heautos* (Eph. 4:32; Col. 3:13, 16; 1 Thess. 5:13; Heb. 3:13; 1 Pet. 4:8, 10) or *heis ton hena* (1 Thess. 5:11).

98. The other texts are Rom. 1:12; 12:5, 10; 13:8; 14:19; 15:5; 1 Cor. 16:20; 2 Cor. 13:12; Eph. 4:25, 32; Phil. 2:3; Col. 3:13; 1 Thess. 3:12; 4:9, 18; 2 Thess. 1:3; Heb. 10:24; 5:14; 1 John 3:11, 23; 4:7, 11, 12; 2 John 5.

99. For the following material I have drawn gratefully on P. Vielhauer "OIKODOME."

100. Ibid., 108.

101. Cf. also the reflections of Pauline praxis in 2 Thess. 3:15 and 1 Tim. 5:20.

102. Cf. N. Brox, "Frühkirchliche und heutige Nöte mit der christlichen Gemeinde," 369–70.

103. Cf. E. Gerstenberger and W. Schrage, *Frau und Mann*, 124.

104. Cf. G. Theissen, "Wanderradikalismus: Literatursoziologische Aspekte der Überlieferung von Worten Jesu im Urchristentum," *Studien zur Soziologie des Urchristentums*, 79–105. Theissen, however, portrays too deep a gap between itinerant charismatics and local communities. The boundaries were less clearly defined and the mutual sympathy was greater than he suggests.

105. Cf. Rom. 12:13; 16:1–2; Heb. 13:2; 1 Pet. 4:9. On this theme cf. F. J. Ortkemper, *Leben aus dem Glauben*, 208–10, 247.

106. J. Gnilka, *Philemonbrief*, 90.

107. A. Texts in which *agapē* certainly means "fraternal love": John

13:35; Rom. 14:15; 1 Cor. 4:21; 8:1; 13:1, 2, 3, 4, 8, 13; 14:1; 16:24; 2 Cor. 2:4, 8; 8:7, 8, 24; Gal. 5:13; Eph. 1:15; 4:2, 15, 16; Phil. 2:1, 2; Col. 1:4; 3:14; 1 Thess. 3:12; 5:13; 2 Thess. 1:3; Philem. 5, 7, 9; 1 Pet. 4:8; 5:14; 2 Pet. 1:7; 1 John 4:7; 3 John 6.

B. Texts in which a final decision about the meaning of *agapē* is not possible, though the meaning of "fraternal love" is more likely: Matt. 24:12; Rom. 12:9; 13:10; 1 Cor. 16:14; 2 Cor. 6:6; Gal. 5:6; Eph. 1:4; 3:17; 5:2; Phil. 1:16; Col. 1:8; 2:2; 1 Thess. 1:3; 3:6; 5:8; 1 Tim. 1:5; 2:15; 4:12; 6:11; 2 Tim. 1:7, 13; 2:22; 3:10; Titus 2:2; Heb. 10:24; 2 John 6; Rev. 2:4, 19.

C. Texts in which the verb *agapan* is certainly used in the sense of "fraternal love": Mark 12:31, 33; Matt. 5:43; 19:19; 22:39; Luke 6:32; John 13:34; 15:12, 17; 2 Cor. 11:11; 12:15; Gal. 5:14; Eph. 5:25, 33; Col. 3:19; 1 Thess. 4:9; James 2:8; 1 Pet. 1:22; 2:17; 1 John 2:10; 3:10, 11, 14, 18, 23; 4:7, 8, 11, 12, 19, 20, 21; 5:2; 2 John 1, 5; 3 John 1; Jude 1.

108. The actual terminology of the New Testament is well illuminated by C. Spicq, *Agapè dans le Nouveau Testament* and H. Montefiore, "Thou Shalt Love Thy Neighbor as Thyself."

109. Rom. 15:2 is decisive; cf. Eph. 4:25, a postpauline text.

110. H. Weinel, *Die Anfänge des Christentums, der Kirche und des Dogmas*, 188; H. Preisker, *Das Ethos des Urchristentums*, 184.

111. For a comparison of Jesus' command of love of enemies with the treatment of enemies in the Old Testament cf. N. Lohfink, *Unsere grossen Wörter*, 232–38.

112. This is recognized by H. Montefiore, "Thou Shalt Love Thy Neighbor as Thyself," 161. Such exegetes as Hans Lietzmann, Otto Michel, Ernst Käsemann and Heinrich Schlier also saw the problem and sought to resolve it in their own ways in their commentaries on Romans.

113. Cf. N. Lohfink, *Unsere grossen Wörter*, 236–37.

114. Correctly maintained by F. J. Ortkemper, *Leben aus dem Glauben*, 183.

115. On the following cf. G. Lohfink, "Paulinische Theologie in der Rezeption der Pastoralbriefe," 109–14.

116. Cf. K. Wegenast, *Das Verständnis der Tradition bei Paulus und in den Deuteropaulinen*, 141.

117. W. Schrage, *Die konkreten Einzelgebote in der paulinischen Paränese*, 107.

118. Cf. G. Lohfink, "Paulinische Theologie," 111–13.

119. The paradoxical tension between *exousia* and *diakonia* in Paul is well expounded by W. Thüsing, "Dienstfunktion und Vollmacht kirchlicher Ämter."

120. Cf. A. Grabner-Haider, *Paraklese und Eschatologie bei Paulus*, 7–11.

121. Cf. Rom. 16:3, 9, 21; 1 Cor. 3:9; 2 Cor. 1:24; 8:23; Phil. 2:25; 4:3; 1 Thess. 3:2; Philem. 1, 24.

122. W. H. Ollrog, *Paulus*, 111–61.

123. Ibid., 63–72.

124. E. Käsemann, *Der Ruf der Freiheit*, 128.

125. On the theme of unanimity in the church cf. Acts 1:14; 2:46; 4:24; 5:12; 15:25; Rom. 12:16; 15:5–6.

126. Reflections on the church as the *basic miracle* worked by God may be found in N. Lohfink, *Die messianische Alternative*, 49–71, and *Kirchenträume*, 152–55.

127. Cf. Rom. 5:8–11; 6:15–23; 11:30–32; 1 Cor. 6:9–11; Gal. 1:13–17, 23; 4:3–7, 8–10; Eph. 2:1–22; 5:8; Col. 1:21–22; 2:13; 3:7–11; 1 Tim. 1:13; Titus 3:3–7; Philem. 11; 1 Pet. 2:10; 2:25; *2 Clement* 1.6–8.

128. For an extended treatment cf. P. Tachau, *"Einst" und "Jetzt" im Neuen Testament.*

129. W. Klaiber, *Rechtfertigung*, 60.

130. A. von Harnack, *Mission*, 388–89.

131. Cf. J. N. D. Kelly, *Early Christian Creeds*, 388–97. The testimony of Niceta of Remesiana is important.

132. R. Riesner, *Apostolischer Gemeindebau*, 86.

133. Cf. H. Braun, *Qumran und das Neue Testament*. 1:201–04.

134. G. Jeremias, *Der Lehrer der Gerechtigkeit*, 350.

135. E.g., in Ephesians. Cf. J. Gnilka, *Der Epheserbrief*, 27–29.

136. J. Munck, *Paulus und die Heilsgeschichte*, 266.

137. Cf. the excellent reflection of R. J. Sider, *Jesus und die Gewalt*, 53, 66–74. There have been attempts for some time now to bring about a synthesis of liberation theology and church renewal, not only in Latin America, but also in a number of North American churches. These efforts have hardly been noted in Germany.

138. On this cf. the important essay of R. Pesch, "Voraussetzungen," 45–54.

139. For details cf. G. Lohfink, *Die Sammlung Israels*, 17–32.

140. Paul literally says, "until the full number of Gentiles enter in" (11:25). The "full number" means the eschatological measure determined by God, not numerical totality.

141. Ulrich Wilckens, *Der Brief an die Römer*, 254–55.

142. M. Kämpchen, "Indisches Christentum zwischen Ideal und Wirklichkeit," 91.

143. ET: Kirsopp Lake, *The Apostolic Fathers*, vol. 1 of two volumes (LCL, 1914), 325.

144. Ibid., 57, 59.

145. Ibid., 113.

146. A. von Harnack, *Mission*, 115–35.

147. H. J. Vogt, "Das sichtbare Reiche Gottes in abendländisch-patristischer Deutung," 80, 89–90.

148. ET: W. M. Green, *The City of God*, vol. 7 of seven volumes (LCL, 1972), 211.

149. ET: FC 36:9–10.

150. ET: *Apostolic Fathers* (LCL) 1:11, 13.

151. Ibid., 9.

152. ET: G. H. Rendall, *Minucius Felix*, (LCL, 1931) 337. [The translation has been modified to reflect Lohfink's literal German rendering of the text.]

153. ET: T. R. Glover, *Tertullian* (LCL, 1931), 177.

154. Cf. *1 Clement* 1.2; Polycarp, *Epistle to the Philippians* 6.1; Justin, *Apology* 1.14, 67; Aristides, *Apology* 15.7–9; Tertullian, *Apology* 39; Cyprian, *Epistle* 62.4; Eusebius *The Ecclesiastical History* IV 23.10.

155. Cf. H. J. Drexhage, "Wirtschaft und Handel in den frühchristlichen Gemeinden," 35–40.

156. ET: T. B. Falls, FC 6:107.

157. ET: Kirsopp Lake, *The Ecclesiastical History*. Vol. 1 of two volumes. (LCL, 1926), 381, 383.

158. H. J. Drexhage, "Wirtschaft," 40.

159. Cf. for example *The Epistle to Diognetus* 5–6, and Theophilus, *To Autolycus* 3.14.

160. ET: D. M. Kay, ANF 10:276–77.

161. Cf. J. A. Fischer, *Die Apostolischen Väter*, 129–30.

162. ET: T. R. Glover, *Tertullian* (LCL), 177.

163. ET: G. H. Rendall, *Minucius Felix* (LCL), 337.

164. Ibid., 413.

165. Cf. for example Origen, *Contra Celsum*, 1.9, 26; *1 Clement* 59.2.

166. ET: T. B. Falls, FC 6:47.

167. ET: *Apostolic Fathers* (LCL), 1:185.

168. Ibid., 201.

169. ET: G. H. Rendall, *Minucius Felix* (LCL), 423.

170. Cf. Tacitus, *The Annals* 15.44. That the accusation of hatred (*odium*) is intended to characterize the conduct of Christians with regard to the community is shown very well by the parallels in *The Histories* (V 5.1), though this passage is concerned with similar phenomena on the part of the Jews: "(They) are extremely loyal toward one another, and always ready to show compassion, but toward every other people they feel only hate and enmity" (ET: C. H. Moore. Vol. 2 of four volumes [LCL, 1931], 181, 183).

171. ET: J. E. L. Oulton, *The Ecclesiastical History*, vol. 2 (LCL, 1932), 185, 187.

172. ET: Henry Chadwick, *Origen: Contra Celsum* (Cambridge: Cambridge University Press, 1953), 147.

173. ET: D. M. Kay, ANF 10:276–78.

174. ET: A. M. Harmon, *Lucian*, vol. 5 of eight volumes. (LCL, 1936), 13, 15.

175. ET: W. C. Wright, *The Works of the Emperor Julian*, vol. 3 of three volumes (LCL, 1923), 69, 71.

176. A. von Harnack, *Mission*, 169.

177. ET: G. H. Rendall, *Minucius Felix* (LCL), 345, 347.

178. Cf. Athenagoras, *The Supplication for the Christians* 35; Theophilus, *To Autolycus* 3.15; Tertullian, *Apology* 38.4–5; 42.7; Minucius Felix, *Octavius* 12.5; 37.11–12.

179. Cf. Minucius Felix, *Octavius* 12.5; 37.11; Origen, *Contra Celsum* 8.21.

180. Cf. Tertullian, *Apology* 35.1; 42.4; Minucius Felix, *Octavius* 12.5.

181. Cf. Origen, *Contra Celsum* 8.55; *The Epistle to Diognetus* 5; Tertullian, *Apology* 9.8; Minucius Felix, *Octavius* 12.5.

182. ET: T. R. Glover, *Tertullian* (LCL), 173. The Latin text reads "*nec ulla magis res aliena quam publica*" (ibid., 172).

183. ET: Chadwick, *Origen: Contra Celsum*, 483.

184. Ibid., 298.

185. Ibid., 486.

186. Ibid., 510.

187. This would be the place to consider the notion of Christians as the "third race." Cf. A. von Harnack, *Mission*, 238–67.

188. Cf. especially *The City of God*, passim. Cf. also Tertullian, *Against Marcion* 3.23.

189. A. von Harnack, *Mission*, 257.

190. ET: Chadwick, *Origen: Contra Celsum*, 504.

191. So, correctly, M. Hengel, *Christus und die Macht*, 12.

192. ET: Chadwick, *Origen: Contra Celsum*, 505.

193. Ibid., 510.

194. Ibid.

195. On the conflicts to which this can lead cf. G. Lohfink, "Der ekklesiale Sitz," 250–53.

196. M. Hengel, *Christus und die Macht*, 48–49.

197. ET: C. Dodgson, LF 10:248.

198. Ibid.

199. ET: Chadwick, *Origen: Contra Celsum*, 509.

200. Ibid.

201. Ibid., 289–90.

202. ET: T. B. Falls, FC 6:75–76.

203. Ibid., 317–18.

204. Ibid., 317.

205. ET: ANF 1:512.

206. ET: S. Thelwall, ANF 3:154.

207. ET: Chadwick, *Origen: Contra Celsum*, 290.

208. Cf. N. Brox, "Zur christlichen Mission in der Spätantike," 192–207.

209. Ibid., 226.

210. ET: B. P. Pratten, ANF 2:134.

211. ET: *Apostolic Fathers*, 219, 221.

212. Ibid., 295.

213. Ibid., 133.

214. Ibid., 149.

215. Ibid., 113.

216. ET: Chadwick, *Origen: Contra Celsum*, 150.

217. Cf. N. Lohfink, *Die messianische Alternative*, 49–71.

218. ET: P. Levine, *City of God*, vol. 4 of seven volumes (LCL, 1966), 415.

219. ET: G. E. McCracken, *City of God*, vol. 1 of seven volumes (LCL, 1957), 207.

220. ET: W. C. Green, *City of God*, vol. 6 of seven volumes (LCL, 1960), 61.

221. Thus also H. J. Vogt, *Reich Gottes*, 86.

222. Cf. the Introduction to this book, "The Heritage of Individualism."

223. ET: T. F. Gilligan, FC 5:350.

Bibliography

Becker, Jürgen. *Johannes der Täufer und Jesus von Nazareth.* Neukirchen and Vluyn: Neukirchener, 1972.

Billerbeck, Paul. *Kommentar zum Neuen Testament aus Talmud und Midrasch.* 3d. ed. Munich: Beck, 1963.

Bosold, Iris. *Pazifismus und prophetische Provokation: Das Grussverbot Lk 10, 4b und sein historischer Kontext.* SBS 90. Stuttgart: Katholisches Bibelwerk, 1978.

Braun, Herbert. *Qumran und das Neue Testament.* Vol. 1. Tübingen, 1966.

Brooten, B. "'Junia . . . hervorragend unter den Aposteln' (Röm 16,7)." In *Frauenbefreiung: Biblische und theologische Argumente,* ed. Elisabeth Moltmann-Wendel, 148–51. 2d. ed. Munich and Mainz, 1978.

Brox, Norbert. "Frühchristliche und heutige Nöte mit der christlichen Gemeinde." *Diakonia* 11 (1980): 364–84.

———. "Zur christlichen Mission in der Spätantike." In *Mission im Neuen Testament,* ed. Karl Kertelge, 190–237. QD 93. Freiburg: Herder, 1982.

Dahl, Nils A. *Das Volk Gottes: Eine Untersuchung zum Kirchenbewusstsein des Urchristentums.* Darmstadt, 1963.

Drexhage, H. J. "Wirtschaft und Handel in den frühchristlichen Gemeinden (1.–3. Jh. n. Chr.)." *Römische Quartalschrift* 76 (1981): 1–72.

Ernst, Cécile. *Teufelsaustreibungen: Die Praxis der katholischen Kirche im 16. und 17. Jahrhundert.* Bern: Huber, 1972.

Ettmeyer, Leopold. "Der theologische Ort Israels in der Botschaft Jesu." Dissertation. Innsbruck, 1979.

Fischer, J. A. *Die Apostolischen Väter.* Munich, 1956.

Geist, Heinz. "Jesus vor Israel – Der Ruf zur Sammlung." In *Die Aktion Jesu und die Re-Aktion der Kirche: Jesus von Nazareth und die Anfänge der Kirche,* ed. Karlheinz Müller, 31–64. Würzburg: Echter, 1972.

Gerstenberger, Erhard S., and Wolfgang Schrage. *Frau und Mann.* Stuttgart: Kohlhammer, 1980. ET: *Woman and Man.* Nashville: Abingdon Press, 1982.

199

Gnilka, Joachim. *Der Epheserbrief.* HTKNT 10,2. Freiburg: Herder, 1971.

———. *Der Philemonbrief.* HTKNT 10,4. Freiburg: Herder, 1982.

Gotteslob: Katholisches Gebet- und Gesangbuch. Stuttgart: Katholische Bibelanstalt, 1975.

Grabner-Haider, Anton. *Paraklese und Eschatologie bei Paulus: Mensch und Welt im Anspruch der Zukunft Gottes.* NTA 4. Münster: Aschendorff, 1968.

Grässer, E. "Jesus und das Heil Gottes: Bemerkungen zur sog. 'Individualisierung des Heils.'" In *Jesus Christus in Historie und Theologie,* (Festschrift für Hans Conzelmann) ed. Georg Strecker, 167–84. Tübingen: J. C. B. Mohr (Paul Siebeck), 1975.

Greshake, Gisbert. "Einige Überlegungen zu den Ursachen des mangelnden Priesternachwuchses." *Priesterliche Existenz heute – Sorge um geistliche Berufe,* 5–19. Vienna, 1980.

Gülzow, H. *Christentum und Sklaverei in den ersten drei Jahrhunderten.* Bonn, 1969.

von Harnack, Adolf. *Die Mission und Ausbreitung des Christentums in den ersten drei Jahrhunderten.* Vol. 1. 3d ed. Leipzig: Hinrichs, 1915. ET: *The Mission and Expansion of Christianity in the First Three Centuries.* 1st ed. New York: Putnam, 1904–1905. 2d ed. London: Williams & Norton, 1908; New York: Harper & Row, Torchbooks, 1962.

———. *Das Wesen des Christentums.* Gütersloh: Siebenstern, 1977. ET: *What Is Christianity?* New York: Harper & Row, Torchbooks, 1957.

Heinz, Gerhard. *Das Problem der Kirchenentstehung in der deutschen protestantischen Theologie des 20. Jahrhunderts.* TTS 4. Mainz: Grünewald, 1974.

Hengel, Martin. *Christus und die Macht: Zur Problematik einer "politischen Theologie" in der Geschichte der Kirche.* Stuttgart: Calwer, 1974. ET: *Christ and Power.* Philadelphia: Fortress Press, 1977.

———. *Nachfolge und Charisma: Eine exegetisch- religionsgeschichtliche Studie zu Mt 8,21f und Jesu Ruf in die Nachfolge.* Berlin: Töpelmann, 1968. ET: *The Charismatic Leader and His Followers.* New York: Crossroad, 1981.

Jeremias, Gerd. *Der Lehrer der Gerechtigkeit.* SUNT 2. Göttingen: Vandenhoeck & Ruprecht, 1963.

Jeremias, Joachim. *Jesu Verheissung für die Völker.* 2d ed. Stuttgart: Kohlhammer, 1959. ET: *Jesus' Promise to the Nations.* Philadelphia: Fortress Press, 1982.

———. *Neutestamentliche Theologie.* 2d ed. Gütersloh: Gerd Mohn, 1973. ET: *New Testament Theology.* New York: Charles Scribner's Sons, 1971.

Jervell, Jacob. "Der unbekannte Paulus." In *Die paulinische Literatur und Theologie,* ed. Sigfred Pedersen, 29–49. Aarhus: Aros, 1980.

————. "Die Zeichen des Apostels: Die Wunder beim lukanischen und paulinischen Paulus." *Studien zum Neuen Testament und seiner Umwelt* 4 (1979): 54–75.

Kämpchen, Martin. "Indisches Christentum zwischen Ideal und Wirklichkeit." *Orientierung* 46 (1982): 91–94.

Käsemann, Ernst. *Der Ruf der Freiheit*. Tübingen: Mohn, 1968. ET: *Jesus Means Freedom*. Philadelphia: Fortress Press, 1970.

Kelly, J. N. D. *Early Christian Creeds*. 3d ed. London: Longman, 1972.

Klaiber, Walter. *Rechtfertigung und Gemeinde: Eine Untersuchung zum paulinischen Kirchenverständnis*. FRLANT 127. Göttingen: Vandenhoeck & Ruprecht, 1982.

Klappert, Berthold, "Traktat für Israel (Röm 9–11): Die paulinische Verhältnisbestimmung von Israel und Kirche." In *Jüdische Existenz und die Erneuerung der christlichen Theologie*, ed. Martin Stöhr, 58–137. Munich: Chr. Kaiser, 1981.

Klauck, H. J. *Hausgemeinde und Hauskirche im frühen Christentum*. SBS 103. Stuttgart: Katholisches Bibelwerk, 1981.

Ladd, G. E. *Jesus and the Kingdom: The Eschatology of Biblical Realism*. Waco, Tex.: Word Books, 1969.

Lohfink, Gerhard. "Der Ablauf der Ostereignisse und die Anfänge der Urgemeinde." *Theologische Quartalschrift* 160 (1980): 162–76.

————. "Der ekklesiale Sitz im Leben der Aufforderung Jesu zum Gewaltverzicht (Mt 5, 39b–42/Lk 6, 29f)." *Theologische Quartalschrift* 162 (1982): 236–53.

————. "Jesus hat Gemeinschaft hergestellt." In *Glaube braucht Erfahrung*, 129–32. 3d ed. Würzburg: Echter, 1977.

————. "Paulinische Theologie in der Rezeption der Pastoralbriefe." In *Paulus in den neutestamentlichen Spätschriften: Zur Paulusrezeption im Neuen Testament*, edited by Karl Kertelge, 70–121. QD 89. Freiburg: Herder, 1981.

————. *Die Sammlung Israels: Eine Untersuchung zur lukanischen Ekklesiologie*. SANT 39. Munich: Kösel, 1975.

————. "Universalismus und Exklusivität des Heils im Neuen Testament." In *Absolutheit des Christentums*, ed. Walter Kasper, 63–82. QD 79. Freiburg: Herder, 1977.

————. "Der Ursprung der christlichen Taufe." *Theologische Quartalschrift* 156 (1976): 35–54.

————. "Weibliche Diakone im Neuen Testament." *Diakonia* 11 (1980): 385–400.

Lohfink, Norbert. *Das Hauptgebot: Eine Untersuchung literarischer Einleitungsfragen zu Dtn 5–11*. AB 20. Rome: Pontifical Biblical Institute, 1963.

————. *Kirchenträume: Reden gegen den Trend.* Freiburg: Herder, 1982.

————. *Die messianische Alternative: Adventsreden.* 2d ed. Freiburg: Herder, 1981.

————. *Unsere grossen Wörter: Das Alte Testament zu Themen dieser Jahre.* Freiburg: Herder, 1977.

————, and Rudolf Pesch. *Weltgestaltung und Gewaltlosigkeit: Ethische Aspekte des Alten und Neuen Testaments in ihrer Einheit und in ihrem Gegensatz.* Düsseldorf: Patmos, 1978.

Lubac, Henri de. *Catholicism.* New York: Mentor-Omega, 1964.

Merklein, Helmut. "Die Ekklesia Gottes: Der Kirchenbegriff bei Paulus und in Jerusalem." *Biblische Zeitschrift* 23 (1979): 48–70.

————. *Die Gottesherrschaft als Handlungsprinzip: Untersuchung zur Ethik Jesu.* FzB 34. Würzburg: Echter, 1978.

————. "Der Jüngerkreis Jesu." In *Die Aktion Jesu and die Re-Aktion der Kirche: Jesus von Nazareth und die Anfänge der Kirche,* ed. K. Müller, 65–100. Würzburg: Echter, 1972.

Montefiore, H. "Thou Shalt Love Thy Neighbor as Thyself." *Novum Testamentum* 5 (1962): 157–170.

Munck, Johannes. *Paulus und die Heilsgeschichte.* Acta Jutlandica 26, 1. Aarhus: Universitetsforlaget, 1954. ET: *Paul and the Salvation of Mankind.* Atlanta: John Knox Press, 1959.

Neufeld, Karl Heinz. *Adolf Harnacks Konflikt mit der Kirche: Weg-Stationen zum "Wesen des Christentums."* ITS 4. Innsbruck: Tyrolia, 1979.

Ollrog, W. H. *Paulus und seine Mitarbeiter: Untersuchungen zu Theorie und Praxis der paulinischen Mission.* WMANT 50. Neukirchen and Vluyn: Neukirchener, 1979.

Ortkemper, Franz Josef. *Leben aus dem Glauben: Christliche Grundhaltungen nach Röm 12–13.* NTA Münster: Aschendorff, 1980.

Pesch, Rudolf. "Der Anspruch Jesu." *Orientierung* 35 (1971): 53–56, 67–70, 77–81.

————. *Das Markusevangelium.* 2 vols. HTKNT 2. Freiburg: Herder, 1976–77.

————. "Voraussetzungen und Anfänge der urchristlichen Mission." In *Mission im Neuen Testament,* ed. Karl Kertelge, 11–70. QD 93. Freiburg: Herder, 1982.

Polag, Athanasius. *Fragmenta Q: Textheft zur Logienquelle.* Neukirchen and Vluyn: Neukirchener, 1979.

Preisker, Herbert. *Das Ethos des Urchristentums.* 2d ed. Gütersloh, 1949 (first published in 1933).

Riesner, Rainer. *Apostolischer Gemeindebau: Die Herausforderung der paulinischen Gemeinden.* Giessen and Basel: Brunnen, 1980.

————. *Formen gemeinsamen Lebens im Neuen Testament und heute.* Theologie und Dienst. Giessen and Basel: Brunnen, 1977.

Schottroff, Luise. "Die enge Pforte." In *Provokation Bergpredigt*, ed. V. Hochgrube, 117–29. Stuttgart, 1982.

Schnackenburg, Rudolf. *Gottes Herrschaft und Reich: Eine biblisch-theologische Studie*. Freiburg: Herder, 1959. ET: *God's Rule and Kingdom*. New York: Herder & Herder, 1963.

Schrage, Wolfgang. *Ethik des Neuen Testaments*. GNT 4. Göttingen: Vandenhoeck & Ruprecht, 1982.

———. *Die konkreten Einzelgebote in der paulinischen Paränese: Ein Beitrag zur neutestamentlichen Ethik*. Gütersloh: Gerd Mohn, 1961.

Schürmann, Heinz. "Der Jüngerkreis Jesu als Zeichen für Israel." In *Ursprung und Gestalt: Erörterungen und Besinnungen zum Neuen Testament*, 45–60. Düsseldorf: Patmos, 1970.

Schulz, Siegfried. *Gott ist kein Sklavenhalter: Die Geschichte einer verspäteten Revolution*. Zurich and Hamburg, 1972.

———. *Q: Die Spruchquelle der Evangelisten*. Zurich: Theologischer Verlag, 1972.

Schweizer, Edward. *Das Evangelium nach Matthäus*. NTD 2. Göttingen: Vandenhoeck & Ruprecht, 1973.

Sider, R. J. *Jesus und die Gewalt*. Maxdorf, 1982. English original: *Christ and Violence*. Scottdale, Pa.: Herald Press, 1979.

Spicq, Ceslaus. *Agapè dans le Nouveau Testament*. 3 vols. Paris: Gabalda, 1957–59. ET: *Agape in the New Testament*. 3 vols. St. Louis: Herder, 1963–66.

Stott, J. R. W. "Reich Gottes und Gemeinschaft." *Theologische Beiträge* 8 (1977): 1–24.

Stuhlmacher, Peter. *Der Brief an Philemon*. EKK 18. 2d ed. Zurich: Benzinger; Neukirchen and Vluyn: Neukirchener, 1981.

———. "Jesu vollkommenes Gesetz der Freiheit: Zum Verständnis der Bergpredigt." *Zeitschrift für Theologie und Kirche* 79: (1982) 283–322.

Tachau, Peter. *"Einst" und "Jetzt" im Neuen Testament: Beobachtungen zu einem urchristlichen Predigtschema in der neutestamentlichen Briefliteratur und zu seiner Vorgeschichte*. FRLANT 105. Göttingen: Vandenhoeck & Ruprecht, 1972.

Theissen, Gerd. *Soziologie der Jesusbewegung: Ein Beitrag zur Entstehungsgeschichte des Urchristentums*. Munich: Chr. Kaiser, 1977. ET: *Sociology of Early Palestinian Christianity*. Philadelphia: Fortress Press, 1978.

———. *Studien zur Soziologie des Urchristentums*. WUNT 19. Tübingen: J. C. B. Mohr (Paul Siebeck), 1979.

Thüsing, Wilhelm, "Dienstfunktion und Vollmacht kirchlicher Ämter nach dem Neuen Testament." *Bibel und Leben* 14 (1973): 77–88.

Trautmann, M. *Zeichenhafte Handlungen Jesu: Ein Beitrag zur Frage nach dem geschichtlichen Jesus*. FzB 37. Würzburg: Echter, 1980.

Trilling, Wolfgang. *Das wahre Israel: Studien zur Theologie des*

Matthäus-Evangeliums. SANT 10. 3d ed. Munich, 1964.

Vielhauer, Philipp. "OIKODOME: Das Bild vom Bau in der christlichen Literatur vom Neuen Testament bis Clemens Alexandrinus." In *Oikodome: Aufsätze zum Neuen Testament*, 2:1–168. Munich: Chr. Kaiser, 1979.

Vogt, H. J. "Das sichtbare Reich Gottes in abendländisch-patristicher Deutung." In *Reich Gottes — Kirche — Civitas Dei: 16. Forschungsgespräch des Internationalen Forschungszentrums Salzburg*, ed. B. Ludger and T. Michels, 77–102. Salzburg, 1981.

Wegenast, K. *Das Verständnis der Tradition bei Paulus und in den Deuteropaulinen.* WMANT 8. Neukirchen and Vluyn: Neukirchener, 1962.

Weinel, Heinrich. *Die Anfänge des Christentums, der Kirche und des Dogmas.* 2d ed. Tübingen: J. C. B. Mohr, 1915.

Wilckens, Ulrich. *Der Brief an die Römer.* EKK 6,2. Zurich: Benziger; Neukirchen and Vluyn: Neukirchener, 1980.

Wolff, Hans Walter. *Dodekapropheton 2: Joel und Amos.* Neukirchen and Vluyn: Neukirchener, 1969. ET: *Joel and Amos.* Hermeneia. Philadelphia: Fortress Press, 1977.

Zeller, D. "Das Logion Mt 8,11f/Lk 13, 28f und das Motiv der Völkerwallfahrt." *Biblische Zeitschrift* 15 (1971): 222–237; 16 (1972): 84–93.

Index